How to Do *Everything* with

Windows Vista™

Curt Simmons

New York   Chicago   San Francisco   Lisbon
London   Madrid   Mexico City   Milan   New Delhi
San Juan   Seoul   Singapore   Sydney   Toronto

The *McGraw·Hill* Companies

McGraw-Hill books are available at special quantity discounts to use as premiums and sales promotions, or for use in corporate training programs. For more information, please write to the Director of Special Sales, Professional Publishing, McGraw-Hill, Two Penn Plaza, New York, NY 10121-2298. Or contact your local bookstore.

How to Do Everything with Windows Vista™

1234567890 DOC DOC 019876

ISBN-13:   978-0-07-226375-6
ISBN-10:   0-07-226375-X

Sponsoring Editor
Megg Morin

Editorial Supervisor
Patty Mon

Project Manager
Vasundhara Sawhney

Acquisitions Coordinator
Carly Stapleton

Technical Editor
Bill Bruns

Copy Editor
Marcia Baker

Proofreader
Elise Oranges

Indexer
Kevin Broccoli

Production Supervisor
Jean Bodeaux

Composition
International Typesetting
and Composition

Illustration
International Typesetting
and Composition

Art Director, Cover
Jeff Weeks

Cover Designer
Pattie Lee

Cover Illustration
Tom Willis

This book is for Dawn, with love.

About the Author

Curt Simmons is a technology author and trainer, focusing on Windows operating systems, Internet technologies, and digital photography. He is the author of more than 50 computing books, including *How to Do Everything with Windows XP, Third Edition* and *How to Do Everything with Your BlackBerry, Second Edition,* both published by McGraw-Hill/Osborne. When he is not writing or training, Curt spends time with his wife and two daughters. Send Curt an e-mail at curt_simmons@hotmail.com.

About the Technical Reviewer

Bill Bruns is the Webmaster and Information Technology Associate for the Student Center at Southern Illinois University. For ten years, he has also been a technical editor, working on more than 125 books relating to the Internet, web servers, HTML, operating systems, and office applications. Bill, his wife Debbie, his daughter Marlie, his son Will, and his three bearded dragons live on the edge of the Shawnee National Forest in Carbondale, Illinois. You can reach him at billbruns3@yahoo.com.

Contents

Acknowledgments   xiii
Introduction   xiii

PART I   **Get to Know Windows Vista**

CHAPTER 1   **Explore the Vista Desktop** **3**
                Start Your Computer   4
                Get to Know Your Windows Vista Desktop   5
                      Check Out the Recycle Bin   6
                      Manage Your Taskbar   10
                      Explore the Start Menu to Get to All the Programs   10
                Log Off Your Computer   10
                Restart or Turn Off Your Computer   12

CHAPTER 2   **Manage Your Computer with the Control Panel** **13**
                Open the Control Panel   14
                Add Hardware   18
                Administrative Tools   18
                AutoPlay   18
                Backup and Restore Center   18
                BitLocker Drive Encryption   18
                Color Management   19
                Date and Time   19
                Default Programs   20
                Device Manager   21
                Ease of Access   21
                Folder Options   23
                Fonts   23
                Game Controllers   23
                Indexing Options   23
                Internet Options   24
                iSCSI Initiator   24
                Keyboard   24
                      Speed   25
                      Hardware   25

Mail   26
Mouse   26
    Buttons   26
    Pointers   27
    Pointer Options   28
    Wheel   29
    Hardware   29
Network and Sharing Center   29
Offline Files   29
Parental Controls   29
Pen and Input Devices   30
People Near Me   30
Performance Information and Tools   30
Personalization   31
Phone and Modem Options   31
Power Options   31
Printers   31
Problem Reports and Solutions   31
Programs and Features   31
Regional and Language Options   32
Scanners and Cameras   32
Security Center   32
Sound   32
Speech Recognition   32
Sync Center   32
System   33
Tablet PC Settings   34
Taskbar and Start Menu   34
Text to Speech   34
User Accounts   35
Welcome Center   35
Windows CardSpace   35
Windows Defender   35
Windows Firewall   35
Windows Sidebar   35
Windows Sideshow   35
Windows Update   36

CHAPTER 3   **Personalize Your Computer** **37**
Customize Your Start Menu and Taskbar   38
    Use the Start Menu   38
    Customize the Start Menu   41
    Customize the Taskbar   45
Configure Your Display   46
    Display Settings   47
    Window Color and Appearance   49
    Desktop Background   49

Screen Saver 50
Sounds 52
Mouse Pointers 52
Theme 53
Configure Folder Views 54
General 55
View 57
Search 58
Configure Folder Views 58
Windows Sidebar 59
Starting and Configuring the Sidebar 60
Working with Gadgets 63

CHAPTER 4   **Manage Components, Programs, Folders, and Files** **65**
Manage Programs with Windows Vista 66
Install a New Program 67
Uninstall a Program 68
Use Windows Vista's Compatibility Mode 70
Manage Windows Vista Components 72
Turn On a Windows Feature 72
Turn Off a Windows Feature 73
Manage Folders and Files 73
Create, Rename, and Delete Folders 74
Use Folder Menu Options 74
View Menu 76
Use Folder Compression 76
Create a Compressed Folder 76
Add Items to and Remove Them from a Compressed Folder . . . 76
Use Extraction 76
About Files 77

CHAPTER 5   **Use the Accessories that Come with Windows** **79**
Calculator 80
Command Prompt 80
Connect to a Network Projector 81
Notepad 81
Paint 83
Remote Desktop Connection 84
Run 84
Snipping Tool 84
Sound Recorder 85
Sync Center 85
Welcome Center 86
Windows Explorer 87
Windows Sidebar 88
WordPad 89
Ease of Access 89

		System Tools	89
		Tablet PC	89
CHAPTER 6		**Manage Hardware**	**91**
		Understand Hardware	92
		The Golden Rules of Windows XP Hardware	93
		Install a Plug-and-Play Device	94
		Remove a Plug-and-Play Device from Your Computer	95
		Install a Non-Plug-and-Play Device	95
		Use Device Manager	97
		Examine a Device's Properties	97
		Windows Update Driver Settings	103
		Hardware Troubleshooting Tips	104
CHAPTER 7		**Use Printers, Scanners, and Digital Cameras**	**105**
		Check Out the Printers Folder	106
		Install a New Printer	106
		Configure Your Printer	109
		Manage Print Jobs	114
		Troubleshoot Common Printer Problems	116
		Use Fax Support in Windows Vista	117
		Use Scanners and Digital Cameras with Windows Vista	117
		Install Scanners and Cameras	117
		Manage Scanner and Camera Properties	119

PART II   **Get Connected**

CHAPTER 8		**Create Connections to the Internet**	**123**
		Internet Connections 101	124
		Connecting with a Dial-Up Connection	124
		Connecting with a Broadband Connection	125
		Configure Your Modem	126
		Install a Modem	127
		Configure Modem Properties	127
		Create Connections to the Internet	134
CHAPTER 9		**Surf the Internet**	**139**
		Understand Internet Terms and Technology	140
		Understand the Internet Explorer Interface	140
		Favorites	141
		Tabs	142
		Home	144
		Feeds and Print	145
		Page	145
		Tools	145
		Configure Internet Explorer Through Internet Options	146
		General Tab	146
		Security Tab	148
		Privacy Tab	150

Content Tab 151
Connections Tab 153
Programs Tab 154
Advanced Tab 155

CHAPTER 10   **Run Windows Mail** **157**
How E-Mail Works 158
Set Up Windows Mail 159
Check Out the Windows Mail Interface 161
Send and Receive E-Mail 163
Send an E-Mail 163
Attach a File to an E-Mail 164
Receive Messages 165
Receive Attachments 166
Change Windows Mail Views 166
Create Message Rules 167
Create a New Rule 168
Manage Message Rules 168
Block Senders 169
What Happened to Identities? 170
Manage Your Accounts 171
Customize Windows Mail 171

CHAPTER 11   **Create a Home Network** **173**
Windows Networking Basics 174
Plan Your Home Network 175
Understand Internet Connection Sharing 176
Use the Setup a Network Wizard 177
Set Up Your ICS Clients 182
Internet Explorer 183
Set Up a Wireless Network 183
Use Windows Vista on a Large Network 184
Virtual Private Networking 185
Configure Your Windows Vista Computer
for a VPN Connection 186
Network File and Printer Sharing 188

CHAPTER 12   **Manage Users and Groups** **189**
Understand User Accounts 190
Manage User Accounts 191
Create a New Account 192
Change an Account 194
Manage User Accounts with Computer Management 197
Manage Groups 199

CHAPTER 13   **Windows Vista Security and Remote Connections** **201**
Use Windows Firewall 202
Issues with Windows Firewall 203
Checking Windows Firewall 204
Configure Windows Firewall Settings 205

Use Windows Defender 208
    Run a Scan 209
    Use Windows Defender Tools 210
Configure Parental Controls 213
    Setting Up Parental Controls 214
Configure Remote Desktop 219
    Enable Remote Desktop 221
    Configure the Remote Desktop Client Computer 223
    Make a Remote Desktop Connection 224
    Manage Remote Desktop Performance 224
Use Remote Assistance 227
    Turn On Remote Assistance 228
    Request Remote Assistance 229

PART III   Cool Things You Can Do with Windows Vista

CHAPTER 14   Play Games **233**
Manage Game Controllers 234
Play Games with Windows XP 236
    Playing Games Installed with Windows Vista 236
    Playing Games on the Internet 237
Installing and Playing Your Own Games 237
Troubleshooting Game Problems 237
    A Game Controller Doesn't Work 237
    DirectX Problems 238
    Game Lockup 238
    Set Display Mode: DDERR_GENERIC 238
Use Volume Controls and Sound Recorder 238

CHAPTER 15   Use Windows Media Player **243**
Now Playing 244
Library 247
    Adding an Item to the Library 250
    Creating a Playlist 250
Rip 250
Burn 251
Sync 252
Skin Chooser 252
Media Player Configuration Options 254

CHAPTER 16   Create Movies with Windows Movie Maker **257**
Why Use Windows Movie Maker? 258
Opening Windows Movie Maker 259
Importing Digital Data 260
    Importing from a DV Camera 261
    Importing Existing Video or Pictures on Your Computer 261

Make Movies 262
    Splitting Clips 262
    Combining Clips 263
    Getting Familiar with the Workspace 264
    Trimming Clips 265
    Creating Transitions 266
Add Audio to Your Movies 268
    Adding Audio 268
Adding Titles and Credits 269
Save Movies 270
Publishing Your Movie 271

CHAPTER 17   Manage Digital Photos and Use Windows Slideshow **273**
Connect to Your PC 274
View and Manage Your Photos 274
Use the Photo Gallery 278
    File 279
    Fix 279
    Info 280
    Print 280
    E-Mail 280
    Burn 281
    Make a Movie 281
    Open 281
    Control Toolbar 281
Print Your Photos 282
Burn Your Photos to a CD 283
Use Windows Slideshow 283

CHAPTER 18   Take Care of Windows Vista **285**
Hard Disk Basics 286
File System Basics 286
    FAT32 287
    NTFS 287
Set Hard Disk Properties 287
    General Tab 289
    Tools 291
    Hardware 295
    Sharing 295
    Security 296
    Previous Versions 296
    Quota 296
Schedule Tasks 299
    Create a Task 299
Use Windows Update 301

PART IV   Optimize, Troubleshoot, and Fix Windows Vista

CHAPTER 19   **Manage Disks** **305**
    Manage Disks 306
        Understanding Dynamic Disks 306
        Understanding Disk Status 309
        Formatting a Disk 310
        Creating a New Volume 310
        Assigning a Different Drive Letter and Path to a Volume 311
        Extending or Shrinking a Volume 312
        Other Volume Solutions 312
    Use Windows Vista Backup and Restore 313
        Backing Up Data 313
        Restoring Data 315
    BitLocker Drive Encryption 318

CHAPTER 20   **Solve Problems with Windows Vista** **321**
    Performance Information and Tools 322
    Use System Information 323
        System Summary 325
        Hardware Resources 325
        Components 326
        Software Environment 327
    Use the Reliability and Performance Monitor 328
        Reliability and Performance Monitor Interface 328
        Using the Performance Monitor 329
        Reliability Monitor 331
    Use System Properties to Optimize Windows Vista 333
        Performance Options 333
    Troubleshooting Tips 336
        Using CTRL-ALT-DEL 336
        Use Windows Help 337
        Use Safe Mode 339
        Use System Restore 339
        Running System Restore 341

Appendix   **Install Windows Vista** **343**
    Upgrade to Windows Vista 344
        Check the System Requirements 345
        Back Up Your Data 347
        Check Out Your Device Drivers 347
        Check for Viruses and Disable Antivirus Software 348
        Shut Down All Programs 348
        Upgrade to Windows Vista 348
    Install Windows Vista as a New Installation 349
        Prepare for a Clean Installation 350
    Activate Windows Vista 350

    Index **351**

Acknowledgments

I want to thank everyone at McGraw-Hill/Osborne for giving me the opportunity to write *How to Do Everything with Windows Vista*. Thanks to Megg Morin, my acquisitions editor, for getting me started. Also, a big thanks to Agatha Kim, Carly Stapleton, Bill Bruns, and Marcia Baker for their editorial eagle eyes and for keeping things moving in the right direction. Finally, thanks to my agent, Margot Maley, and to my family for being so supportive of my work.

Introduction

Welcome to *How to Do Everything with Windows Vista*! In my opinion, Windows Vista is the best operating system (OS) Microsoft has produced to date, no matter which version you choose to use. How would you like an OS that is friendly and easy to use, that makes the best use of the Internet and digital media, and rarely—if ever—locks up or acts weird? I thought so. Windows Vista is all these things and more. In fact, no matter what you need, Windows Vista can probably do it in a fun and easy way!

You may wonder, "Is Windows Vista the right operating system for me?" The answer: absolutely! Vista provides for a full range of experience with this new OS. Not only is it the easiest OS to learn that Microsoft has ever produced—you'll be a pro quickly—but it is also the most powerful. With stunning graphics, new features, and the easiest interface you've ever seen, you'll fall in love with Vista in no time. If you're just starting out, all you need is Windows Vista and this book. You'll have the OS mastered in no time.

Speaking of this book, *How to Do Everything with Windows Vista* is designed to be your one-stop source for help in using Windows Vista. This book helps you get started in Chapter 1 and takes you through everything you might want to know how to do. You learn what you need to know quickly and easily, often using a step-by-step format.

This book starts you out at the beginning:

In **Part I**, "Get to Know Windows Vista," you learn all about the Windows Vista interface (such as the Start menu). You also learn how to launch the computer and shut it down, manage your computer with the Control Panel, configure system settings and folders, install applications, use accessories, and manage hardware and printers—plus much more!

In **Part II**, "Get Connected," you learn all about getting connected to the Internet with your Windows Vista computer. You find out how to use Internet Explorer and Windows Mail, plus you learn how to create a home network using Windows Vista. This part also covers more advanced networking topics, such as Remote Desktop and Windows Firewall.

In **Part III**, "Cool Things You Can Do with Windows Vista," we check out the fun stuff Vista provides. You learn about playing games on Windows Vista, how to use the Vista Media Player, and how to use the Movie Maker tool for editing and saving your own home movies, as well as DVD burning. You also see how to make the most of digital photos on Windows Vista.

In **Part IV**, "Optimize, Troubleshoot, and Fix Windows Vista," you learn about the tools and utilities Windows Vista provides to make your work much easier. You find out about disk management, System Information, Windows Help and Support, System Restore, and much more!

Within this book, you can also find a special Spotlight section that gives you a look at how to burn a custom DVD with Windows DVD Maker. Be sure to check it out!

Finally, the book wraps up with the Appendix, which covers installing Windows Vista. In fact, if there is something you can do with Windows Vista, this book covers it!

I've written this book in an easy-to-read format. You can read it cover-to-cover, or you can skip around and find specific information you need—the choice is yours. To help you along the way, this book includes

- **How To sidebars** These boxes tell you how to do things, usually in a step-by-step format. Be sure to check them out—they are full of quick and helpful information.

- **Did You Know? sidebars** These boxes contain ancillary information you might find useful (and even entertaining).

- **Notes** These boxes provide you with helpful information. You should always read every Note.

- **Tips** These boxes provide you with a friendly piece of advice or a little extra information that might make your work and play with Windows Vista easier. Be sure to read them!

- **Cautions** These boxes point out a potential problem or pitfall—so beware!

Are you ready to experience Windows Vista? Then it's time to get started. Before you do, though, I would love to hear from you. Send me e-mail at curt_simmons@hotmail.com.

Part I

Get to Know Windows Vista

Chapter 1

Explore the Vista Desktop

How to...

- Start your computer
- Explore your Desktop
- Examine icons
- Manage and configure the Recycle Bin
- Use the Taskbar and Start menu
- Log off, restart, and shut down your computer

Finally! If you're like me, you've been waiting for the new Windows operating system (OS) for years—and it's finally here! Welcome to Windows Vista, which is a real treat for the average home computer user or even computer enthusiasts. Windows Vista not only looks sharp, it also makes many complicated tasks, such as networking, much easier. In addition, Windows Vista is robust, stable, and secure, and it includes a number of bells and whistles you're going to enjoy.

If you are new to Windows, or perhaps to computing in general, this chapter was written especially for you. Windows Vista is a powerful system that can do practically anything you need (except paint your house), and it's the easiest OS to use that Microsoft has ever produced. You can find your way around Vista and get to the things you need much more easily and quickly than in previous versions of Windows. In this chapter, you get to know Windows Vista by learning about the basic system features that enable you to use your computer effectively and efficiently.

Start Your Computer

If you just purchased a new computer with Windows Vista preinstalled, your first task is to unpack it, attach your peripherals (your keyboard, mouse, printer, speakers, and so forth), and then start the computer. Your computer comes with a booklet that explains how to attach peripherals and start the computer. Most computers have a power button on the front of the case that you must switch on. Check out your computer's documentation to find the on button.

Once you flip the switch and your computer has power, you will most likely see a brand-name screen or maybe even a black screen with a bunch of information about your computer's hardware. Next, you see the Windows Vista starting screen as your computer boots up. If your computer is new and has Windows Vista preinstalled, the first time your computer boots up, Windows Vista will ask you some questions to customize your computer and finish the installation. (See the appendix for more information about installation.) At some point, Windows Vista asks you to enter a user name and a password. This is the user name and password you use each time you log on to Windows. Windows Vista can be a secure OS, so you can expect user names and passwords to be important. You can learn all about Windows Vista user management in Chapter 12.

Get to Know Your Windows Vista Desktop

Windows Vista uses a Desktop for the standard user interface, as have previous versions of Windows, such as XP. The *Desktop* is where you access your system components, applications you want to use, the Internet, and basically everything else. Think of the Desktop as, well, a *desktop*. The ideal desktop has everything you need within quick and easy reach. On your computer, the same idea holds true.

As you can see in Figure 1-1, the Desktop contains an open area, the Recycle Bin (usually on the upper-left side), and a Taskbar at the bottom that contains the Start button on the left and a Notification Area on the lower-right side. Windows Vista also contains a new Windows Sidebar to the right of the screen, which we explore later in this book.

FIGURE 1-1   The Windows Vista Desktop

The items you see on your Desktop may vary from those shown in Figure 1-1, especially if you just bought a new computer with Windows Vista preinstalled. The manufacturer of your computer (such as Compaq, HP, or Dell) may have set up a number of preconfigured options and even advertisements to appear on the Desktop. In short, if you have a new computer, you may have a lot of . . . well, *junk* on your Desktop, and Windows Vista itself even includes several advertisements there. You can safely ignore these icons or drag them to the Recycle Bin to get rid of them forever. You can learn more about using the Recycle Bin in the next section.

You may also see a number of shortcuts. *Shortcuts* are simply icons on your Desktop that enable you to access some system component or application quickly and easily without having to wade into the OS and retrieve it. A shortcut icon appears on your Desktop with a little arrow in the corner.

Shortcuts can be helpful, but if you have too many, they can clutter your Desktop and make it confusing. The good news is you do not have to keep any advertisements or shortcuts on your Desktop that you do not want. Simply delete them. When you delete a shortcut, you aren't deleting the program. You are only deleting the little icon on your Desktop that points to the program. This feature lets you decide what should be on your Desktop and what should not.

Check Out the Recycle Bin

By default, Windows Vista provides you with only one primary Desktop icon, which is the Recycle Bin. All the other stuff you need to access is found on the Start menu. So, what is the Recycle Bin? The *Recycle Bin* is a place where you put garbage. You can remove old files and items you no longer need, and add them to the Recycle Bin.

Want to know a secret? When you delete a file from your system (anything at all, a document, picture, shortcut—whatever), it isn't really deleted. It is sent to the Recycle Bin, where it waits to be deleted. Why? The Recycle Bin is an excellent Windows feature that prevents you from losing data that you may want to keep. When you delete an item from your computer, it is removed from its current location and placed in the Recycle Bin. It stays in the Recycle Bin until you choose to empty the Recycle Bin or the Recycle Bin becomes too full. Only then is the item deleted forever.

Now, before you get too happy, remember, this secret applies to files on local hard drives on your computer. It isn't true for network drives or removable storage drives, such CD-RW discs. Once you delete something from one of these locations, it is immediately deleted instead of being stored in the Recycle Bin, so be careful!

I give you an overview of the other Desktop elements because we use them extensively throughout the book. However, the Recycle Bin is covered only in this chapter, so I spend a little more time with it to make sure you know "how to do everything."

Use the Recycle Bin as a Way Station

As mentioned, any time you delete an item, it is sent to the Recycle Bin. You can open the Recycle Bin and see what's inside by double-clicking the Recycle Bin icon on your Desktop (you can also right-click the icon, and then click Explore). You can see the items in the Recycle Bin waiting to be deleted, as Figure 1-2 shows.

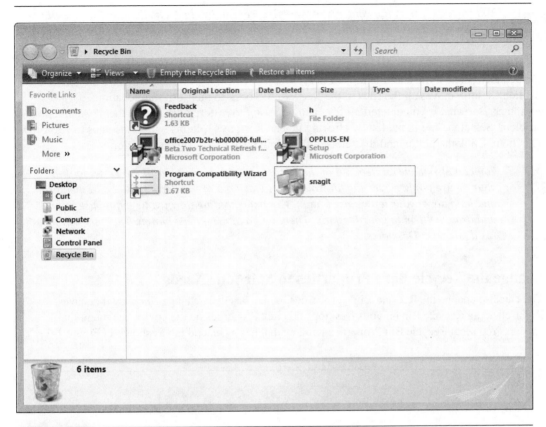

FIGURE 1-2   Items in the Recycle Bin

TIP

In the Views menu, you can choose Extra Large Icons, Large Icons, Medium Icons, Small Icons, Details, or Tiles. By using these choices, you can see large icons, small icons, a list of files, or even a detailed list telling you the item's original location and the date it was moved to the Recycle Bin.

In addition to the Views drop-down menu and the Organize drop-down menu, which enable you to determine how items are displayed in the Recycle Bin folder, two other buttons are available in the Recycle Bin toolbar on the upper part of the Recycle Bin window. You can click the Empty the Recycle Bin button, which permanently deletes the items in the Recycle Bin. You *cannot* recover these items once they have been emptied from the Recycle Bin, unless you use a third-party program, such as Norton SystemWorks.

TIP　*You can also empty the contents of your Recycle Bin by right-clicking the Recycle Bin icon on your Desktop, and then clicking Empty Recycle Bin on the menu that appears.*

You also have a Restore All Items button in the Recycle Bin tasks window. Suppose you accidentally delete a file and it is moved to the Recycle Bin? No problem. Clicking the Restore All Items button moves all the files in the Recycle Bin back to their original locations on your computer. But what if you deleted 30 files and you want to restore only one of them? Again, no problem. Select the file in the list by clicking it. The Restore All Items button changes to Restore This Item. Click the button and the selected file is put back in its original location.

NOTE　*You can also move an item out of the Recycle Bin by dragging it to the Desktop. Put your mouse pointer over the file you want to take out of the Recycle Bin, and then press and hold down your left mouse button. Continue holding down your left mouse button, and drag the item to your Desktop. Then, let go of the mouse button. The item will now reside on your Desktop.*

Change the Recycle Bin's Properties to Suit Your Needs

You can also change the Recycle Bin's properties, which basically changes the way it behaves. Right-click the Recycle Bin on your Desktop and click Properties on the contextual menu that appears. You see a Recycle Bin Properties window that has a General tab as shown in Figure 1-3.

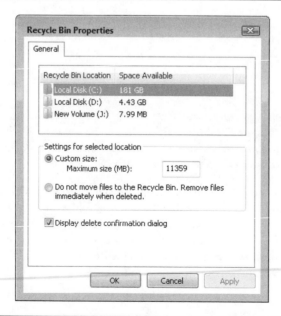

FIGURE 1-3　Recycle Bin Properties

The Recycle Bin Location and Space Available options show you how much data is in the Recycle Bin for you personally, and, if the Public folder is in use, for the Public folder, which other people on your network can access. The two radio buttons in the middle of the dialog box enable you either to configure your drives independently or use the same setting for all drives. This feature applies to you only if you have more than one hard disk in your computer. In most cases, the default setting that configures all your drives the same way is all you need. If you want to configure these global settings, click the Global Settings button toward the bottom of the Recycle Bin Properties window. Let's say your computer has two hard drives. One has 5GB, while the other has only 1GB. You can spare 10 percent of the 5GB drive for the Recycle Bin, but what if your 1GB drive is already crowded? You might not want 10 percent of that drive used for the Recycle Bin, so you can give it a lower percentage, such as 5 percent. Again, under normal circumstances and with most computers, you don't need to worry about any of this, but it's good to know the options exist in case you have some specific hard-drive space issues.

Also, note that the dialog box enables you to determine how big the Recycle Bin can grow before items are automatically deleted. By default, this value is 10 percent of your disk drive's capacity and, in most cases, this default setting is all you need.

Next, you see a radio button that tells your computer to delete items immediately instead of moving them to the Recycle Bin. As you can guess, this feature automatically deletes items when you click Delete. This provides you with absolutely no protection in case you accidentally delete a file you want. Let's say you're writing your life story and you accidentally delete the document. If you selected this check box, the document would immediately be removed from your computer—you would not be able to retrieve it. I strongly recommend that you do *not* select this option. No matter how good your computing skills, you will occasionally make a mistake and accidentally delete something. The Recycle Bin is your safety net, so you can get that document back. By selecting this check box, you have no protection—so don't do it!

NOTE *Remember, you don't have to wait until your Recycle Bin is full to empty it—and, in fact, most people don't. Some people empty it every time they put documents in it, while others empty it on a weekly basis after they have reviewed its contents to make sure nothing was accidentally deleted. There is no right or wrong approach, of course; find what works best for you.*

Finally, you see a Display Delete Confirmation Dialog check box at the bottom of the General tab. This tells Windows to give you that aggravating "Are You Sure?" message every time you delete something. This option is selected by default, and although the configuration message is sometimes a pain, it is a good safety check. I recommend you leave this setting enabled.

You may also see also see a Network tab, which enables you to select shared folders on your network and monitor the files that are deleted from these locations. This feature works well for someone who needs to monitor folders and files on a network, but for most of us with home networks, you can simply ignore this option.

Manage Your Taskbar

The Taskbar is the small bar across the bottom of your Desktop (refer to Figure 1-1). The *Taskbar* contains your Start menu, which is explored in the next section, and a Notification Area, which is the separate box on the right side. Any applications you have open or any windows you have minimized also show up on the Taskbar. If you want to view one of these programs or windows on your Desktop so you can work with it, just click its corresponding icon.

The *Notification Area* contains a clock, probably a volume control icon, and maybe several other icons, depending on what is installed on your computer. The Notification Area is an easy way to access some applications you may use frequently. If you right-click any of the items in the Notification Area, you can usually close or remove the item from the Notification Area, or you can click Properties, so you can configure the item. For example, if you right-click the clock in the Notification Area, you can then choose Adjust Date/Time. This action opens a simple window where you can change the current date and current time. These settings are easy and self-explanatory.

You can customize the Taskbar and Notification Area in a number of different ways. See Chapter 3 for details and step-by-step instructions.

Explore the Start Menu to Get to All the Programs

If you have ever visited a theme park, you know that typically one main entrance leads you to all the attractions the park has to offer. The main entrance to Windows Vista's is the Start menu, which appears on your Taskbar in the lower-left portion of your screen.

The Start menu is your gateway to most Windows components and the applications that you install. If you have used Windows previously, the Start menu is certainly nothing new. However, in Windows Vista, the Start menu has been redesigned, so you can access your programs, documents, and common Windows components more easily. If you click the Start button, a pop-up menu appears, as Figure 1-4 shows.

Because the Start menu has been redesigned for Windows Vista, I devote more time to it in Chapter 3. You can learn all about the available options and how to configure the Start menu, so it is just right for you.

Log Off Your Computer

Windows Vista is designed to be a multiuser computer. This means several different people can use the same computer, but still keep their settings, files, and folders separate. For example, at home, you and some family members may share the computer; or, if your computer is on a network, several different users may access it. In Windows Vista, all your settings and documents are tied to your user account. This way, several people can use the same computer and have different computer settings, documents, and even e-mail accounts. If someone else uses your computer, Windows Vista keeps track of that person's settings, as well as your own settings.

FIGURE 1-4   Start menu

With all this in mind, Windows Vista enables you to log off the computer, so someone else can log on without having to restart the computer. To log off, click the Start menu and point to the arrow next to the lock icon. A submenu appears where you can click Log Off. You are then logged off the computer and taken to the Windows Vista logon screen where you can select your user name and password to log on.

Restart or Turn Off Your Computer

When you finish using Windows Vista, you can choose to shut down the computer or, in the case of problems or if something new is installed, you can restart it. To shut down or restart your computer, click the Start menu, point to the arrow next to the lock icon, and click Shut Down.

To Turn Off or Not to Turn Off, That Is the Question!

I teach several online courses, and as I'm teaching, students frequently want to know if they should leave their computer on when it's unattended or if they should always shut down. Does frequently shutting down damage the computer?

These are common, but important, questions. First things first: You can shut down or restart your computer without damaging your system or hardware—but you shouldn't shut down or restart a bunch of times during the day. For any given day, shut down and/or restart only once or twice. Many people get up in the morning, turn on the computer, and leave it on for the entire day. This is perfectly fine.

Computers today support a number of power-management features that enable the computer to go into standby mode when it isn't being used. I show you how to configure these options in Chapter 3. With power-management features enabled, you don't have to turn off your computer at all! I have five computers in my study, and they all remain on 24 hours a day, seven days a week. The only exception is if I'm traveling and going to be away for several days; only then do I turn off the computers.

Chapter 2

Manage Your Computer with the Control Panel

How to...

- Access the Windows Vista Control Panel
- Discover Vista categories
- Access Control Panel icons
- Use Control Panel icons to configure your computer

Quick—how many of you know how to set the clock on your VCR? I thought so. The proverbial joke about using a VCR and staring at the unsettable, blinking 12:00 certainly has a great element of truth. The reality of electronic devices and computers is simply this: You don't have to know everything about the device or computer to use it. You need to know some basic functions, but for the most part, you can ignore many features and use the product without problems. However, if you know how to set your VCR clock, you can record all kinds of television shows automatically and use a number of other management features of your VCR. True, you don't need to know how to set the clock, but you can use your VCR much more effectively if you do.

Windows Vista, along with other computer operating systems, is much the same. You don't have to know a whole lot of technical stuff to use Vista, but if you know how to configure its features and functions, Vista will do more work for you. While it's true that computer operating systems are becoming more complex with each new release, they are also becoming easier to use because they give users more management tools. One of those tools in Windows Vista is the Control Panel. The *Control Panel* provides a number of tools that enable you to determine how various components of Windows Vista look and act. If you know how to use these tools, you gain greater control over Vista, and—just as with your VCR clock—your Vista system can more effectively meet your needs.

In this chapter, you learn how to manage your Windows Vista computer using the tools provided in the Control Panel. This chapter explores all the Control Panel options; shows you what they do; and then shows you how, when, and why to configure them. Because of their specific nature, some Control Panel tools are best explored in other chapters and, in such cases, I direct you to those chapters.

Open the Control Panel

You can open the Control Panel in three major ways. First, you can click the Start menu, and then click Control Panel. This is probably the most common and easiest way of accessing the Control Panel. Second, you can access the Control Panel from within any other Vista window by simply typing **Control Panel** in the Address bar found on the window. This causes the current window to change to the Control Panel. Finally, many folders give you a link to the Control Panel in the Favorite Links panel on the left side of the folder window. No matter how you get there, when the Control Panel opens, your initial view appears as shown in Figure 2-1.

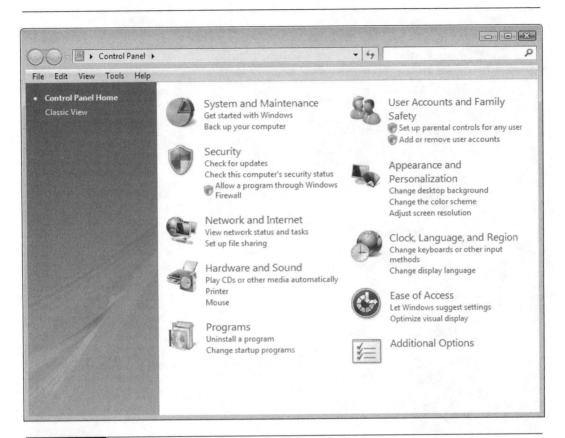

FIGURE 2-1   Control Panel

If you've used any version of Windows, you'll first notice the Control Panel in Windows Vista looks a little different. The Windows Vista Control Panel Home is divided into *categories,* similar to Windows XP. If you click a category, the window that opens presents a list of tasks you may want to perform and related Control Panel icon(s) you may want to choose, as you can see in Figure 2-2.

Before you get too concerned about these differences, let me tell you that the task and icon options are essentially the same. For example, as you can see in Figure 2-2, I have the option to change the computer's firewall settings, update settings, Defender settings, and so forth. However, I can also click each category icon and end up with the same configuration options. There's no difference—it's just that the task option tries to help you locate the tasks you want to perform in case you don't know which Control Panel icon to select.

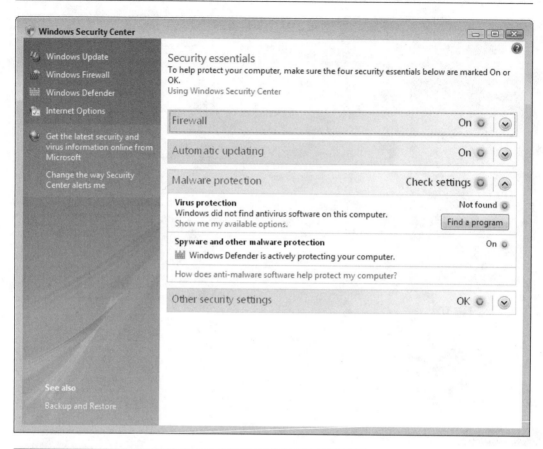

FIGURE 2-2 Click a category to see options

Now, all of this may sound great, and it can be helpful. However, you need to know two important things. The Control Panel Home does not provide you access to every available Control Panel tool—it provides you access only to the more commonly used tools. Even though Microsoft considers the tools found in Control Panel Home the most common, many Control Panel tools are not available from this view. So, to see all your Control Panel options, click the Switch to Classic View link found on the left-hand side of the Control Panel window. This gives you the typical icon list found in previous versions of Windows, as you can see in Figure 2-3.

TIP *You can switch back and forth between Classic view and Control Panel Home view by clicking the link in the Control Panel box on the left-hand side of the window. You can access items in either view as needed—just use whichever view you like best.*

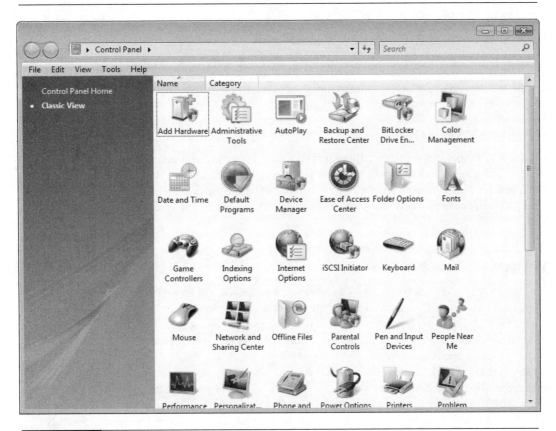

FIGURE 2-3   Control Panel Classic View

Now that you've taken a look at Vista's Control Panel views, turn your attention to the programs the Control Panel offers. In the following sections, we explore all the Control Panel icons, and you learn what you can do with each. To see all the Control Panel icons, you need to use the Classic view. So, if you haven't done so already, click the Classic View link in the Control Panel window to switch to that view.

NOTE   *To avoid repeating information in this book, some Control Panel icons are briefly discussed in this chapter with a reference to another part of the book where the configuration is explored. Some configuration options are much more complicated than others and deserve their own chapters.*

Add Hardware

The good news is installing hardware on Windows Vista is easier than ever before. In fact, most of the time, all you have to do is connect the device to Windows Vista and begin using it. However, if you need help installing hardware, the Add Hardware applet in Control Panel gives you all you need. See Chapter 6 to learn more about hardware and this applet.

Administrative Tools

Windows Vista includes a folder called Administrative Tools. In the *Administrative Tools folder,* you can find several different tools that help you manage the Windows Vista computer, including the Computer Management console and Performance Diagnostic console. Because of the more complex nature of these tools, we explore and use them in a variety of chapters throughout the book.

AutoPlay

The *AutoPlay applet* tells Windows Vista what to do when you use certain media. For example, if you insert a music CD, your AutoPlay settings tell Windows Vista what program should open to play the CD. Do you have programs that open when you double-click photos or insert CDs or DVDs that you don't want to use? Look no further—this applet is the place to go to change what default program opens these items.

If you double-click the AutoPlay applet, you see a basic window listing different kinds of media. Simply click the drop-down menu for the kind of media you're using and choose what you want Windows Vista to do, as Figure 2-4 shows. Notice also that you can choose the Take No Action option if you don't want any program to open on its own. When you're done, simply click Save. You can return to the AutoPlay applet at any time and make further changes as your needs change.

Backup and Restore Center

As a safety precaution, you need to back up data on your computer and even restore it in case of a failure. You can learn more about backing up and restoring data in Chapter 19.

BitLocker Drive Encryption

Windows Vista includes a new feature called *BitLocker Drive Encryption.* This new security feature enables you to encrypt an entire drive, so no one (besides you) can access data on that drive, even if they try to use password-cracking programs. This security feature is a great alternative when you have sensitive data on your computer. Because this feature is a security solution, you can find out more about it in Chapter 19.

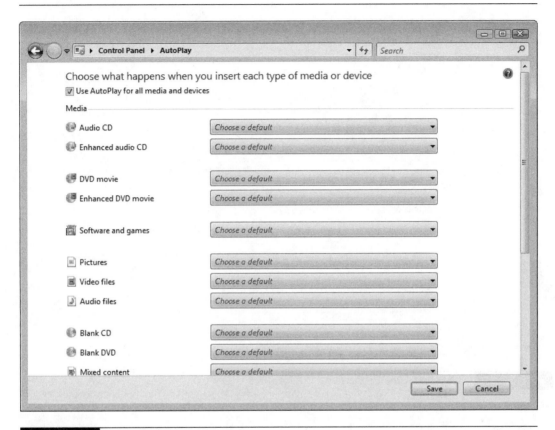

FIGURE 2-4   AutoPlay applet

Color Management

The *Color Management applet* enables you to adjust color settings for your computer's graphics card and even create profiles. In most cases, you never need to use this applet, but if you're having problems with the color on your sound card or monitor, you can check out this applet for additional help.

Date and Time

The *Date and Time icon* in the Control Panel enables you to set the clock in your operating system as you might guess. When you double-click the icon, you see a simple interface containing a clock with a calendar that shows you the date. You can access the tabs here to adjust your date and time settings. As you can see in Figure 2-5, this interface is easy to configure.

FIGURE 2-5 Date and Time Properties

 *If you need to adjust your computer's date and time, you don't have to use the Control Panel icon. Just right-click the time in your Notification Area and choose Adjust Date/ Time.*

The Internet Time tab in Vista Date and Time Properties tool enables you to synchronize your computer with an Internet time server to make sure your computer always has the exact time. This feature, if configured, occurs automatically and without interrupting you, but you must be connected to the Internet for synchronization to occur. Also, if you're using Windows Vista in a corporate network that uses a proxy server or a firewall, the time synchronization feature may not be allowed because it's managed by servers on your local network.

Default Programs

The *Default Programs icon* enables you to set what default actions are taken with programs, different kinds of files, autoplay settings, and what default programs are installed on your computer. The settings you find here are self-explanatory. Just remember, to use this applet, you need to change the default way that Windows Vista handles certain programs or file types.

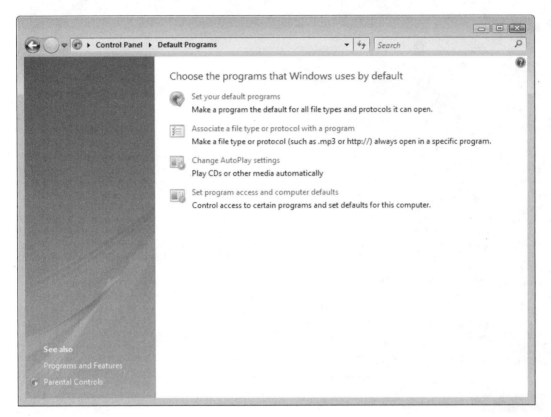

Device Manager

Device Manager is a tool that has been around in Windows for years. It easily enables you to turn on or off devices, troubleshoot devices, and even remove hardware from the system. You can learn how to use Device Manager in Chapter 6.

Ease of Access

Ease of Access, formerly called Accessibility Options, enables you to configure the computer's input and output behavior for people with certain disabilities. These options make computing much easier for these individuals. Windows Vista provides excellent support for accessibility configuration, and you use this icon in the Control Panel to configure most of them.

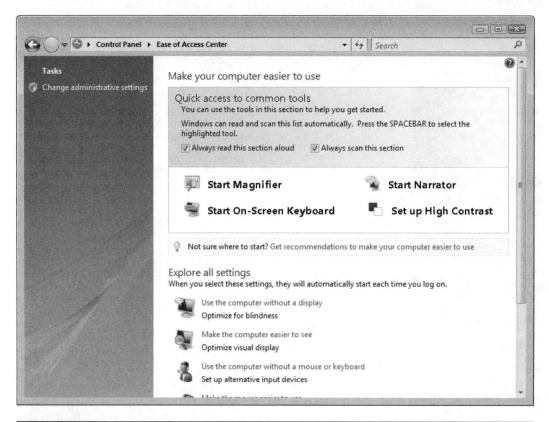

FIGURE 2-6   Ease of Access Center

If you double-click Ease of Access in the Control Panel, a Properties window appears with several different options you can configure for special needs, as Figure 2-6 shows. Simply select items you want to use. The following list reviews the options available.

- **Magnifier**   This option turns on an onscreen magnifier, so objects on the screen can be magnified according to your settings.
- **Narrator**   This option is a feature you can turn on, so open Windows and dialog boxes are read out loud from the computer's speakers.

- **On screen Keyboard**   This option provides you with a small keyboard on the screen that you can use with a mouse. This feature is helpful to persons who cannot type on a physical keyboard.
- **High Contrast**   This option turns on high contrast on your display, which can be helpful to persons who are visually impaired.
- **Other options**   If you scroll toward the bottom of the window, you can see options to use the computer without a display; optimize the visual display; and use alternative input devices, as well as configure mouse options, keyboard options, sounds, and basic reasoning tasks. These items are all self-explanatory if you need to make changes to them.

Folder Options

Folder options enable you to determine how folders look and what actions are taken. You can access folder options from this applet in Control Panel or you can access this same properties dialog box from within any folder in Windows Vista. See Chapter 4 to learn more about folders.

Fonts

The *Fonts folder* in the Control Panel holds all the fonts your computer can use. When you open Fonts, you see a list of all the fonts available. You can't configure anything here, with the exception of removing or adding fonts to the folder. In general, this is not something you need to do, because Windows Vista and your applications handle the needed and used fonts. You can determine which fonts you want Windows Vista and your applications to use by configuring the Display properties or configuring a specific application's properties. You can also double-click any font in the Fonts folder to learn more about the font and to see a sample of how the font looks.

Game Controllers

The *Game Controllers icon* in the Control Panel provides a location to manage any gaming devices attached to your computer, such as joysticks and other playing devices. You can learn all about this icon in Chapter 14.

Indexing Options

Windows Vista indexes the items on your computer, so you can search for documents, photos, and other files more quickly and easily. As a general rule, Windows Vista does a good job of indexing items, but you can configure a few additional indexing options or modify the indexing process using the Indexing Options applet in the Control Panel, as shown in the following illustration. For example, you can choose whether to index encrypted files or certain file types. For typical users, though, you don't need to do anything with the Indexing Options applet.

Internet Options

The *Internet Options applet* in the Control Panel can be used to configure, as you might guess, Internet Explorer (IE) and possibly other Internet applications. You can access this same Properties window from within IE itself. These options are explored in Chapter 9.

iSCSI Initiator

The *iSCSI Initiator Control Panel applet* is used to help you connect to tapes, or to CD, DVD, or disk drives available on your network. If you are using a home network or don't have these devices available on your business network, there is nothing you need to do with this applet. If your network does use these items, you can access the iSCSI Initiator properties to configure connection options.

Keyboard

The *Keyboard icon* in the Control Panel enables you to configure how your keyboard operates. When you double-click this icon, you see two tabs, which are explained in the following sections.

Speed

The *Speed tab* enables you to configure how fast your keyboard responds to keystrokes. The Speed tab gives you a few simple options for adjusting your keyboard's speed.

First, you see two slider bars for character repeat. The first—*Repeat Delay slider bar*—determines how much time passes before a character repeats when you hold down a key. If you are a fast typist, you will probably want this setting moved to Short.

The second—*Repeat Rate slider bar*—determines how fast a character repeats when you hold it down. The Repeat Delay determines how fast the initial repeat begins, while the Repeat Rate determines how fast the characters are repeated. A medium setting (between Slow and Fast) is typically all you need.

At the bottom of the window, you see the Cursor Blink Rate. Use the slider bar to change this rate. You can see the cursor blinking on the tab for test purposes. The best setting is typically toward the Fast end of the slider bar.

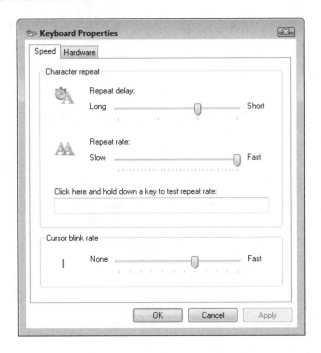

Hardware

The *Hardware tab* lists the type of keyboard attached to your computer. Two buttons are available that enable you to troubleshoot the keyboard if you're having problems. Or, you can click the Properties button to access the device's properties sheets. You can learn more about configuring devices for your system in Chapter 6.

Mail

The *Mail icon* provides you with a simple interface to determine what mail profile should be used by default. You may only need this icon if you have multiple identities or mail accounts. See Chapter 10 to learn more about Windows Mail.

Mouse

The *mouse* is a universal input device that lets you point-and-click your way into Windows oblivion. The mouse itself is a simple device but, surprisingly, you can access a number of configuration options for the mouse by double-clicking the Mouse icon in the Control Panel. You see a few tabs and several different options, and the following sections show you how to configure your mouse so it operates and behaves in the best way for you.

Buttons

The *Buttons tab,* shown in Figure 2-7, provides a place where you can determine how your mouse buttons work.

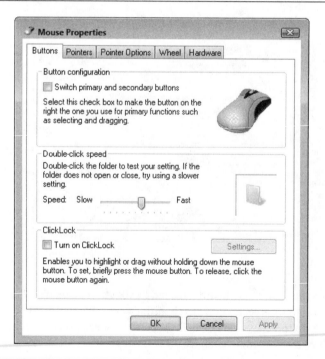

FIGURE 2-7   Buttons tab

First, you can check the box to Switch Primary and Secondary Buttons, so your mouse functions as a left-handed mouse. If you choose the right-handed option, the mouse buttons are as follows:

- **Left button**   Select or drag
- **Right button**   Context menu or special drag

If you choose the left-handed option, the mouse buttons are as follows:

- **Left button**   Context menu or special drag
- **Right button**   Select or drag

As you can see, choosing the left-handed option reverses which button performs which action.

Next, you can use the slider bar to speed or slow your mouse's double-click speed. Most people use a medium setting (where the slider bar is in the middle), but find the setting that works best for you.

Finally, you have an option at the bottom of the window called ClickLock. *ClickLock* enables you to drag items around your Desktop without having to hold down the mouse button continuously (the left mouse button for right-handed users). Select the Turn on ClickLock check box to use it, and then click the Settings button that becomes accessible. The Settings window gives you a slider bar, so you can determine how long you have to hold down the left mouse button before it locks into place, enabling you to drag items without holding it down.

You need to play around with the slider bar setting for ClickLock to find which setting works for you, but keep in mind that short ClickLock settings are usually more aggravating than helpful. This setting causes your left mouse button to lock quickly every time you press it, so don't start out with a short setting when you are configuring ClickLock.

Pointers

The *Pointers tab* provides a place to configure the way your pointer appears on your Windows Vista computer. What you are doing may cause your mouse pointer to change its appearance. For example, a typical pointer is simply an arrow, but if your system is busy, your mouse pointer changes to an hourglass. You can use the Pointers tab to customize the pointers as you want.

At the top of the window, you see a Scheme drop-down menu that enables you to select preconfigured Windows schemes. Scroll down and select some of them. You can see the various pointers change in the Customize window. Select a scheme you want and click Apply to use that scheme.

Aside from using the standard Windows Vista pointer schemes, you can also create your own schemes by modifying the desired pointers. If you click the Browse button, you can choose to use a different cursor file, such as one you downloaded from the Internet or obtained from a CD-ROM. Now, you can select a desired pointer, and then create and save your own custom pointer scheme.

Although animated pointers are fun, they often put a burden on computer processors and may affect the performance of your computer. For this reason, you may want to avoid using them.

Pointer Options

The next tab under Mouse properties tab provides Pointer Options, as shown in Figure 2-8. This simple *Pointer Options tab* gives you a series of check boxes or slider bars, which you can use to configure how your mouse pointer moves around the screen.

You can play around with these settings to determine which (if any) of them you would like to use:

■ **Motion** Use the slider bar to determine how fast your pointer moves when you move your mouse. You can try different adjustments to find the speed you like. If you click the Accelerate button, you can also select how fast your pointer moves when you begin moving your mouse.

FIGURE 2-8 Pointer Options tab

■ **SnapTo**   This option automatically moves your mouse pointer to the default button in any given dialog box. You can try this option to see whether you like it, but many users (myself included) find SnapTo more aggravating than helpful.

■ **Visibility**   The visibility options control how your pointer looks when in motion—you have three check box options. First, you can choose to use a mouse trail, which leaves a disappearing trail when you move your mouse. Some people like this setting, some don't (it gives me a headache), but you can experiment with it. Next, you can choose to hide your mouse pointer when you type. This just makes your mouse pointer disappear when not in use. Finally, you can choose to use the CTRL key to help you locate your mouse pointer if it seems to have disappeared from the screen.

Wheel

For mice that use a control wheel in addition to right and left buttons, use the *Wheel tab* to determine how quickly the wheel moves the mouse. The configuration option here enables you to set how many lines are scrolled when you move the wheel or you can choose to move through an entire page. Select the desired radio button, and then enter a scroll value to experiment with these settings.

Hardware

The *Hardware tab* lists the type of mouse attached to your computer. Two buttons are available that enable you to troubleshoot the mouse if you're having problems or you can click the Properties button to access the device's properties sheets. You can learn more about configuring devices for your system in Chapter 6.

Network and Sharing Center

Windows Vista includes a Network Center for using a home or office network. You'll find this tool makes networking much easier and more enjoyable, and we discuss it in Chapter 11.

Offline Files

Offline Files enable you to store documents on a network server and have your Vista computer synchronize your local work with that server. Because Offline Files are only typically used in a business networking environment and managed by a network administrator, this book doesn't examine the specifics of their use.

Parental Controls

With all the possible dangers on the Internet, Windows Vista includes software that enables parents to place restrictions and controls on their children's user accounts. You can learn how to configure and use parental controls in Chapter 13.

Pen and Input Devices

If you're using electronic pens and other Tablet PC pointer devices, you can configure their behavior using the *Pen and Input Devices applet* in Control Panel. If you open the properties dialog box, you can see a Pen Options tab, Pointer Options tab, and Flicks tab, as shown in the following illustration. The configuration options you see on these tabs are self-explanatory and can help you configure the Pen and Input Device, so it works in a way that is helpful to you.

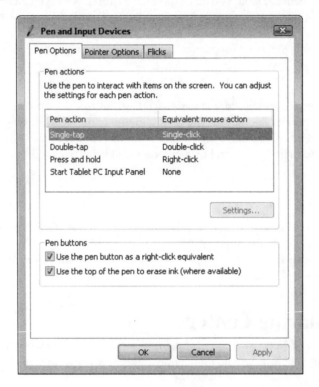

People Near Me

People Near Me enables you to find and be found by other people on a network, so you can collaborate on tasks and possible share programs. If this feature is in use on your business network, you can use the simple sign-in tab and Settings tab here to enable collaboration.

Performance Information and Tools

Windows Vista includes some new performance information and tools options to help you get the most from the OS. See Chapter 20 to learn more about this feature.

Personalization

The *Personalization option* enables you to determine how Windows Vista looks. You can find more about the Personalization tool in Chapter 3.

Phone and Modem Options

The *Phone and Modem icon* in the Control Panel provides a place where you manage phones and modems attached to your computer. In the past, modems were painfully difficult to set up and troubleshoot, but Windows Vista makes modem configuration much easier. As you might guess, modem setup and configuration is a lengthy topic, so you learn how to do it all in Chapter 8.

Power Options

Windows Vista is equipped to save energy by using power schemes you can configure. These options can automatically turn off your monitor or hard drive after a certain period of inactivity. Power options are also available within Display properties, and Chapter 3 explores these power options.

Printers

The *Printers folder* is devoted to any printers or fax machines attached to your computer, and it includes a helpful wizard you can use to set up these devices. As you can imagine, printing and faxing can be a complex topic, so check out Chapter 7 for all the details.

Problem Reports and Solutions

The *Problem Reports and Solutions* option in Control Panel enables you to check for online solutions or to see more information about existing problems in Windows Vista. The interface you see is self explanatory.

Programs and Features

Programs and Features enable you to install new programs, remove programs, add or remove components of installed programs, and install and remove Windows components. These features are explored in Chapter 4. Refer to that chapter for step-by-step information.

Regional and Language Options

Regional and Language Options in the Control Panel provides you a place to configure your computer to use different language symbols, currency, and other specific regional representations. For example, let's say you are using Windows Vista in France, and you want Windows Vista to calculate money in European currency. You can enable this option by using Regional and Language Options. When you open Regional and Language Options, you see a standard Regional Options tab, a Languages tab, and an Administrative tab. Each tab contains drop-down menus, so you can select the desired regional settings.

Scanners and Cameras

Reflecting the popularity of scanners and digital cameras, Windows Vista includes a Control Panel icon to help you manage these hardware devices. You can learn about the installation and management of scanners and cameras in Chapter 7.

Security Center

The *Windows Vista Security Center* helps you manage security settings and configuration on Windows Vista. You can learn more about the options found in the Security Center in Chapter 13.

Sound

The *Sound* applet gives you the option to select playback devices, recording devices, and manage basic Windows sounds. The options you see here are self explanatory.

Speech Recognition

The *Speech Recognition icon* in the Control Panel enables you to configure text-to-speech translation, as Figure 2-9 shows. This means Windows Vista can read aloud any text in Windows that you want read. Simply click the options and follow the steps to set up speech recognition and your microphone. To be able to communicate with your computer, you should also click the Take Speech Tutorial, so you can understand the commands and process for talking to Windows Vista.

Sync Center

The *Sync Center* enables you to synchronize your files with network files used in an Offline Files configuration. See Chapter 5 to learn more about the Sync Center.

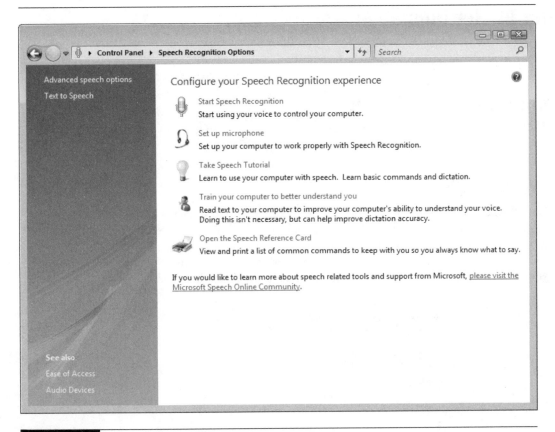

FIGURE 2-9   Speech Recognition

System

The *System icon* in the Control Panel contains some basic information about your computer and provides you quick access to Device Manager, Remote Settings, System Protection, and Advanced System Settings. To see the old-style System Properties dialog box, click the Advanced System Settings button. Many of the options you find here are covered in various places throughout the book.

TIP   *You can also quickly access this same Properties window by right-clicking Computer from the Start menu and choosing Properties.*

Tablet PC Settings

If you're using a Tablet PC, you can access the Tablet PC Settings applet in the Control Panel to configure basic usage options, such as handwriting recognition, display, and other such items.

Taskbar and Start Menu

The *Taskbar* and *Start Menu icon* enables you to configure these items to suit your needs. You can learn about Taskbar and Start menu configuration in Chapter 3.

Text to Speech

Have Windows read to you! Windows Vista can read text on your screen or any documents containing text. This feature is enabled by a default speech profile and, in most cases, you don't have to configure anything else. If you open the properties dialog box, notice you can turn on speech recognition, so it runs each time the computer starts. Also notice on the *Text to Speech tab,* you can choose a desired voice and use the slider bar to configure the speed at which text is read.

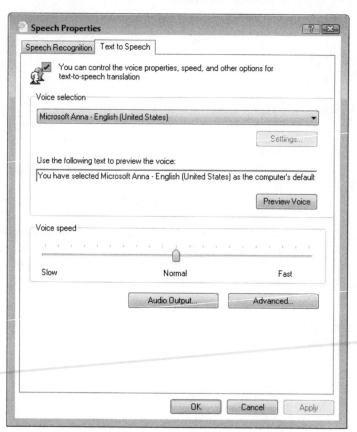

User Accounts

The *User Accounts icon* gives you an interface with which you can create new user accounts and manage existing user accounts, so different people can log on to your Windows Vista computer. Without a valid user name and a password, different users cannot log on, so you use this window to create these accounts. A number of important issues related to user account management are covered in Chapter 12.

Welcome Center

The *Welcome Center* is a new feature in Windows Vista that gives you basic information about your computer and access to some common items. The Control Panel applet simply opens the Welcome Center.

Windows CardSpace

The *Windows CardSpace* is a new feature allowing you to create relationships with websites and online services. It's a consistent way for sites to request information from you, review the identity of a site, manage your information in relation to the site, and review information before sending it to a site. It is essentially a replacement for user names and passwords that you submit to a site.

Windows Defender

Windows Defender is a program that keeps spyware and adware off your computer. By default, it automatically runs, helping to keep your computer safe. You can learn more about Windows Defender in Chapter 13.

Windows Firewall

Windows Firewall was formerly called Internet Connection Firewall in early versions of Windows XP. You can find out more about Windows Firewall in Chapter 13.

Windows Sidebar

The new *Windows Vista Sidebar* is a small utility that runs on your desktop where you can use little applications called gadgets. See Chapter 3 to learn more about using Windows Sidebar.

Windows Sideshow

Windows Slideshow is a tool that uses a secondary display to access information on your computer by using remote devices and peripherals. You use it to do things like check your

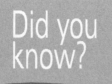

Proxy Servers and Firewalls Protect Computers

Many corporate environments use proxy servers or firewalls. To protect the internal network from the various risks posed by Internet traffic, proxy servers or firewalls examine all traffic flowing into the network from the Internet. The configuration of the proxy server or firewall may cause some Internet traffic to be filtered or not allowed to pass. Proxy servers and firewalls access Internet content for internal network clients, so no client is ever in direct contact with the Internet. This feature ensures the internal network is safe and unauthorized content does not enter the network from the Internet. In fact, your Windows Vista computer contains a personal firewall you can use to help protect it against attacks from the Internet. See Chapter 13 to learn more.

calendar, read e-mail, or scan top news stories even when your computer is turned off. See Chapter 17 to learn more.

Windows Update

Windows Update enables your computer to download and install updates to Windows Vista automatically from Microsoft's web site. The feature is safe and easy, and you can find out more about it in Chapter 19.

Chapter 3

Personalize Your Computer

How to...

- Customize your Start menu and Taskbar
- Customize the appearance and behavior of the Windows Vista Desktop
- Customize the Windows Sidebar
- Customize your folders

If you have used Windows XP, the Vista Start menu and other desktop items won't be a complete mystery to you. Vista builds on the XP Start menu and desktop design to keep the Windows desktop from being a clutter of options and features, so you can find your way around more easily. Yet, once you begin making your way around Windows Vista's interface, you may decide you want to change some things about the way Windows Vista looks and behaves. That's fine, and Windows Vista gives you a number of different options for configuring the interface, including folder view options, so the operating system (OS) is easy to use and helpful to you. In this chapter, you explore how to customize your Start menu, Taskbar, Desktop, folder views, and the new Windows Sidebar.

Customize Your Start Menu and Taskbar

The Windows Vista Start menu is your gateway to everything Windows Vista has to offer. You can access everything the computer provides, as well as any programs you install from the Start menu. The Taskbar continues to be an important feature in this version of Windows because it gives you a handy way to access open documents, programs, folders, and such. In the next few sections, you learn how to use and customize the Start menu, and how to customize the Taskbar.

Use the Start Menu

The Vista Start menu, as Figure 3-1 shows, gives you an easy place to access the most common Windows configuration items, as well as those items you like to use the most.

The Windows Vista Start menu is divided into two portions, as you can see in Figure 3-1. The left-hand side lists programs, and the right side provides access to common Windows folders, in addition to Help and Support, Network, Documents, and so forth. As far as those items you like to use the most, the Start menu lists them for you, which means if you open a program, the Start menu remembers it and places an icon in the Start menu, so you can more easily open the program next time.

Let's consider an example. I recently installed Microsoft Word on my Vista system. To open Word, I have to choose Start | All Programs | Microsoft Office | Microsoft Word. Once I open Word a time or two, the Word icon is added to my Start menu. The next time I want to use Word, all I have to do is choose Start and click the Word icon.

In a nutshell, the Start menu is simply adding shortcuts to itself on your behalf. You can easily manage these icons by right-clicking them. This action gives you typical menu options for

FIGURE 3-1   The Start menu

the shortcut, such as Open, Send To, Copy, Remove from This List, Rename, and Properties. If
you want to remove the shortcut from the Start menu, just choose Remove from This List. This
action removes the shortcut only from the Start menu—it does not remove the program from
your computer, so you don't have to worry about that.

When you right-click an item, you also see an option called Pin to Start Menu. This action
simply moves the item to the top-left portion of the window, where it's always visible. You'll
notice the Internet Explorer (IE) icon is available there by default, but you can remove it if you
like by right-clicking the items and choosing Remove from This List.

Finally, you can also click All Programs to access typical Windows menus and installed
applications. You can click a folder in the list to open it, and just click the Back button to return
to the Start menu options.

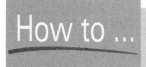

Reduce Clutter in Recent Items

As a writer, I use a lot of documents, as you might imagine. Although the Recent Items folder, which can be accessed from the Start menu, is useful to me, it can get overcrowded, and then it becomes more confusing than helpful. So, what do I do if I need to remove some documents from Recent Items—or even all of them? First, let me clarify an important point. Like all items on the Start menu, Recent Items simply stores *shortcuts* to those documents, not the actual documents themselves. You can remove some items from Recent Items—or all of them—without deleting any of the actual documents from your computer. In fact, you can remove anything from the Start menu without damaging or deleting items on your computer, because all the items on the Start menu are shortcuts.

So, if you want to remove stuff from Recent Items, you can do one of two things. First, you can choose Start | Recent Items and, on the pop-out menu that appears, right-click any item you don't want in the folder and click Delete—doing this deletes the shortcut, not the document itself. Second, if you want to empty every document completely from the menu, access the Advanced tab of the Customize Start Menu window and clear the Store and Display a list of recently opened items check box. This stops Recent Items from keeping track of what has been opened, which you may want for privacy purposes. See the next section for more information about customizing the Start menu.

NOTE *If you want to use IE from the Start menu, you can see easy usage options by right-clicking the icon. For example, you can choose to browse the Internet or even access the Internet Properties window. See Chapter 9 for more information about configuring Internet properties.*

On the right side of the Start menu, you see common Windows items that you will need to access:

- **User name and personal folders**   In the first section, you see your user name, Documents, Pictures, Music, and Games. Each of these items is a folder that contains personal information and files. For example, you can store all your documents, pictures, music, and games in their respective folders and easily access your data from the Start menu. The My Documents folder is the default storage location for files of all kinds, including pictures, music, and movies. My Documents contains default subfolders of My Music, My Pictures, My Videos, and others. Also, notice that a picture appears on the Start menu above your user name. You can change this picture by changing the picture tied to your user account. See Chapter 12 to find out how.

- **Search**   The *Search feature* enables you to find items on your computer, including documents, photos, e-mails, movies, and so on. You can also use the Search dialog box at the bottom of the Start menu to search for anything on your computer or even the Internet.

- **Recent Items**   Point to the *Recent Items option* to see a pop-out menu of recent items you've accessed on your computer.

- **Computer**   The *Computer option* is the default folder that stores information about drives connected to your computer.

- **Network**   The *Network folder* contains information about other computers and shared folders on your network and the Internet. You learn more about networking in Chapter 11.

- **Connect To**   If you have any network connections, such as a local area connection, wireless connection, dial-up connection, DSL connection, and so forth, you'll see a Connect To option on the Start menu. By clicking the *Connect To option,* you can immediately access your connections. If you don't have any network devices configured, you won't see this option.

- **Control Panel**   The *Control Panel option* is the default location for managing all kinds of programs and services on your Vista computer. Chapter 2 is devoted to the Control Panel.

- **Default Programs**   You can use the *Default Programs option* to make basic settings to the way Windows Vista handles programs. For example, you can click this option and determine what program opens all music files, what program opens all photos, and so forth. This option is also available in the Control Panel (see Chapter 2).

- **Help and Support**   Windows Vista includes a *Help and Support feature* that can answer your questions and even locate answers on the Internet. See Chapter 20.

- **Updates and Lock**   You see two buttons at the bottom of the right Start menu pane. One is an *updates button* that enables you to quickly install updates and restart your computer simply by clicking this button. You can also click the *lock button* to lock your computer, so a password must be entered before the computer can be used.

- **Log Off/Shut Down**   The standard *Log Off/Shut Down options* enable you to log off or shut down/restart the computer. Click the arrow next to the lock icon to access them. See Chapter 1 for details.

TIP

If you used Windows XP, you may be wondering where the Run dialog box is. The Run dialog box enables you to start a program or open a folder by just entering the path to it. This option has been moved down into the Accessories folder on the Start menu. However, you can drag it from Accessories to the Start button and it will be pinned to your Start menu, as with any other program in Windows Vista.

Customize the Start Menu

To customize the Start menu, you need to access the Start menu's properties. To do this, open the Control Panel, double-click the Taskbar and Start Menu icon, and then click the Start Menu tab. If you don't see a Taskbar and Start Menu icon, switch the Control Panel to Classic view using the Control Panel link on the left side of the window. You can also more easily right-click the Start button and click Properties. No matter how you've chosen to get there, you arrive at the Taskbar and Start Menu Properties window, as you can see in Figure 3-2.

You have the option on the Start Menu tab to use either the current Vista Start menu or the Classic Start menu, which is simply the Start menu found in previous versions of Windows. Because the two are different, the following sections explore the configuration of each.

Vista Start Menu

To continue using the Vista Start menu, click the Customize button. Doing this takes you to a Customize Start Menu window (see Figure 3-3), which enables you to customize how the Start menu looks.

- **Choose Program Options** You can look through the list of options to determine how links, icons, and menus behave on the Start menu. For example, the first item is Computer. You can choose to display Computer as a link (this is the default), a menu, or not to display the item at all. The options you see here enable you to customize the Start menu items in a way that is helpful to you or not to display items you don't use.

FIGURE 3-2   Taskbar and Start Menu Properties

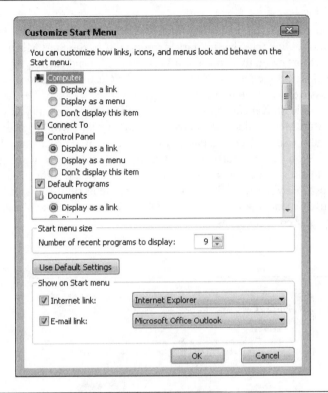

FIGURE 3-3   Choose the Start menu settings you want

■ **Start menu size**   As previously mentioned, Vista displays programs you opened recently on the Start menu in an attempt to help you work faster. You can determine the number of programs displayed on the Start menu here. The default is 6, but you can change this to any number between 0 and 30.

■ **Show on Start Menu**   This option enables you to show Internet and e-mail applications on the Start menu, and then provides a drop-down menu for selecting the application (IE and Windows Mail, by default). If you have other browser or e-mail clients installed on your computer, you can use the drop-down menu and select a different browser and/or e-mail client, or just clear the check boxes if you don't want these items displayed at all.

TIP

Notice the Use Default Settings button. If you make some changes to the Start menu and later can't seem to undo them, just return to the Customize Start Menu dialog box and click the Use Default Settings button. This puts the Start menu back to its original settings.

Classic Start Menu

The Classic Start Menu can be used instead of the new Vista Start Menu. In the Taskbar and Start Menu Properties window, click the Classic Start Menu option on the Start Menu tab. This option enables you to use the Start menu that appears in Windows 2000 and earlier. If you want to use the Classic Start Menu, select the radio button and click the Customize button. This gives you a single Customize Classic Start Menu interface, as Figure 3-4 shows.

You see the same basic Start menu options, just in a different format. If you want to add items to the Classic Start Menu, click the Add button and a wizard will help you select items on your computer to add. Use the Remove button to remove items. The Advanced button opens Windows Explorer, so you can manually add and remove the items you want. You can also resort the items and clear recent documents, programs, web sites, and so on. The Advanced Start Menu Options window that you see enables you to, among other things, display a number of Windows items and use expandable (menu) folders. These items are self-explanatory—feel free to experiment and try new configurations.

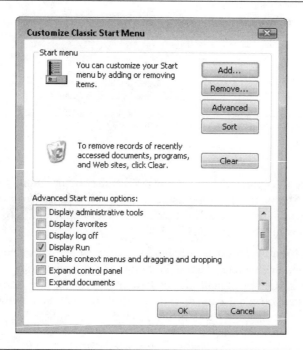

FIGURE 3-4   Customize Classic Start Menu

How to ... **Add More Start Menu Shortcuts**

Always remember, the Start menu contains shortcuts to items you want to access. Therefore, you can add nearly any program to the Start menu. Here's how:

1. Locate a desired program icon you want to add to the Start menu, right-click the item, and then click Add to Quick Launch.

2. Click the Start menu and you can see the item was added to the Start menu.

3. You can remove the item from Quick Launch at any time by right-clicking it on the Start menu and then clicking Remove from this List.

Customize the Taskbar

Along with Start menu properties, you can customize your Taskbar properties as well. You can access the Taskbar and Start Menu Properties window by double-clicking the icon in the Control Panel. Or, right-click on any empty area of the Taskbar, click Properties, and then click the Taskbar tab, as Figure 3-5 shows.

You have two basic customization areas—Taskbar Appearance and also a Notification Area tab. In the Taskbar Appearance area, a few check box options enable certain features:

- **Lock the Taskbar** You can drag the Taskbar to different places on your Desktop. For example, if you want the Taskbar to appear on the top of the screen instead of the bottom, just drag it to the top. If you select the Lock the Taskbar check box, the Taskbar is then locked on the bottom of the screen and you cannot move it or drag to make it larger.

- **Auto-Hide the Taskbar** This feature keeps the Taskbar out of your way. When you aren't using the Taskbar, it disappears below your screen view. When you need it, just point your mouse to the location of the Taskbar and it will reappear. Some people like this setting, so be sure to experiment with it.

- **Keep the Taskbar on Top of Other Windows** As you are using various windows, they may cover up portions of the Taskbar. This setting always keeps the Taskbar on top.

- **Group Similar Taskbar Buttons** This feature keeps similar items together. For example, if you open two web pages, and then minimize them both, they will appear next to each other on the Taskbar. If you have too many, it groups them into one button with a pop-up menu to select the specific item.

- **Show Quick Launch** This option turns on the old-style Quick Launch section of the Taskbar where you can access popular programs by clicking their icons on the Taskbar.

FIGURE 3-5   Taskbar tab

The Notification Area tab, shown in Figure 3-6, has check box options for a number of programs that are working on your computer, and it can notify you of certain application functions. You can choose to hide inactive icons, which is selected by default (and it keeps your Taskbar cleaner) and you can click the Customize button to determine what items are located on the Notification Area. You can choose to show the clock in the Notification Area, along with Volume, Network, and Power (for laptop computers). The main thing to remember here is this: you can click the Customize button to remove items from the Notification Area if it gets too crowded or you simply have too may icons that you don't need access to.

Configure Your Display

One of the primary places you configure the way your Windows Vista system looks is through your Personalize properties. If you remember from Chapter 2, Personalization is an icon in the Control Panel, which you can open to configure various settings that affect the appearance of your Windows Vista display. Click Start, choose Control Panel, and then double-click the

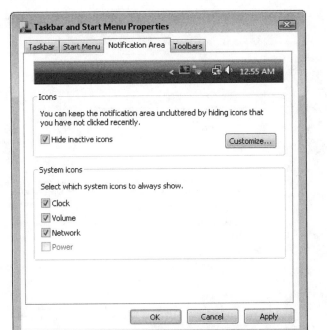

FIGURE 3-6   Notification Area tab

Personalization icon to open it. Once you open Personalization (shown in Figure 3-7), you see several link options, all of which are explored in the following sections.

The Personalization icon officially resides in the Control Panel, but you don't have to open the Control Panel to access the feature. Just find an empty area on your Desktop (a place where there is no folder or icon), right-click the Desktop, and choose Personalize. The same Personalization window appears.

Display Settings

Use the Display Settings tab to manage the actual video-card hardware that resides within your computer. A few basic options are offered, as you see in Figure 3-8.

First, you see a Screen Resolution slider bar. You can adjust the resolution to suit your needs, and, as you adjust it, you can see your Desktop area gets either larger or smaller (including your icons), depending on the location of the slider bar.

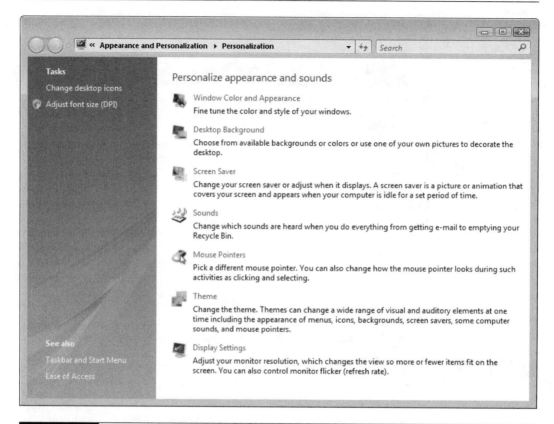

FIGURE 3-7   Personalization options

You also see a Colors drop-down menu that enables you to select the number of colors Windows Vista can use to generate all the graphics and pictures that appear on your monitor. True Color (32 bit) is the highest color scheme you can use and, depending on the quality of your video card, you may have only a few color options available. When you demand more colors from your display adapter, you get lower performance out of it. However, if you demand higher resolution, you may get fewer colors.

You also have an Advanced Settings button. This option opens the properties sheets for your video card. In general, the default settings found on these sheets are all you need, and you shouldn't change any of them unless your video-card documentation tells you to do so.

TIP   *Are you having problems with your screen flickering? No problem. On the Advanced Settings tab of Display Properties, click the Advanced button, and then click the Monitor tab. Change the refresh rate to at least 90. This usually stops the screen flicker aggravation. If you don't see a refresh rate of 90, you may need to lower your resolution to get more refresh choices.*

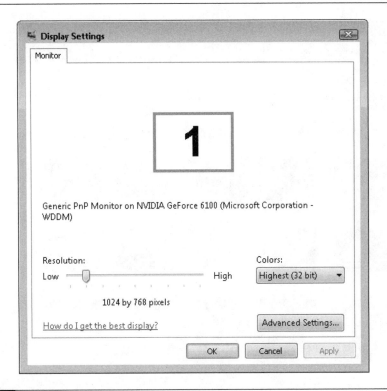

FIGURE 3-8   Display Settings

Window Color and Appearance

The Window Color and Appearance option enables you to choose a different glass style for the interface. The *glass style* is simply a display feature that makes windows have different levels of transparency or related glass-looking effects. Simply click the different icons you see here to apply a desired style. You can also access Appearance Settings, so you can fine-tune how different colors and fonts are used within Windows. As a general rule, you don't need to make any changes here unless you are trying to achieve a specific look.

Desktop Background

The *Desktop Background option* enables you to choose either a picture to display on your desktop or a solid color. The interface is rather simple, as you can see in Figure 3-9. Simply access the drop-down menu and choose a picture category, and then click on a picture thumbnail to select it and click OK. Notice you can also select Browse and choose one of your personal photos. Windows Vista can display essentially any kind of photo file, such as TIFF, JPEG, PNG, and others. Once you choose a photo, you can click a radio button at the bottom of the window to determine how to position it. Your choices are Fit to Screen, Tile, and Center.

FIGURE 3-9   Choose a desktop picture or a solid color

If you don't want to use a photo on your desktop, choose the Solid Colors option from the drop-down menu and choose a color. You can also click the More button to access a standard Color dialog box where you can choose the color you want.

Screen Saver

The *Screen Saver option* provides two functions: It enables you to configure a screen saver for your computer and it enables you to configure power management options. A *screen saver* is a simple program that runs once your computer has been idle for a certain period of time. In the past, the screen saver protected monitors from "burn in." When a monitor was left unattended for too long and one continuous picture or window was displayed, the image could burn itself on to the monitor and always be sort of floating in the background. Monitors today aren't susceptible to this problem, so screen savers are used more for decoration and security. The following two sections explore both screen savers and Windows Vista's power-management features.

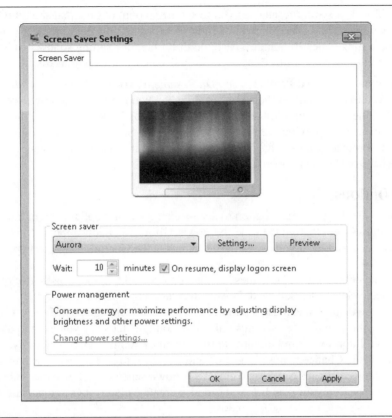

FIGURE 3-10   Screen Saver settings

Use a Screen Saver

The Screen Saver tab is easy to use, as you can see in Figure 3-10. Just use the drop-down menu to select a screen saver, and a sample of it will be displayed in the test window. Once you find one you like, click the Apply button.

Once you select a screen saver you want to use, you have a few other options as well:

■ **Settings**   The *Settings button,* which opens a small window specific to the screen saver, enables you to configure the screen saver. These settings are easy and self-explanatory. You can play around with them to find the settings you want. Also, if you choose the Photos screen saver option from the drop-down menu, click the Settings button, so you can determine what photos on your computer are displayed as the screen saver.

■ **Preview**   If you click *Preview,* your screen first goes blank, and then the screen saver begins, so you can see whether you like it. Just move your mouse to get control of your system again.

■ **Wait** The *Wait scroll box* enables you to set the amount of time that should pass before the screen saver comes on. There is no right or wrong setting, but to protect your screen, keep the setting under 30 minutes. Also, don't set the time setting so low that it comes on after one minute or so of inactivity—you'll find such a setting aggravating.

■ **On Resume, Password Protect** The *On Resume, Password Protect check box option* returns you to the Windows Welcome screen when you move your mouse to regain control of the system. In other words, you'll have to log back in each time the screen saver comes on. In previous versions of Windows, the Screen Saver tab offered a Password Protect option——this is the same thing, but it's enabled with your user account, so you have only one password to remember.

Use Power Options

The Screen Saver tab also provides a button to access energy-saving options through the Change Power Settings link. After clicking the link, the Power Options window appears (this has the same properties sheets you see if you click Power Options in the Control Panel), as Figure 3-11 shows.

You have some default power "schemes" available to you and, in most cases, one of these will probably meet your needs: Balanced, Power saver, and High performance.

Okay, here's the deal. You can use a particular scheme and change any of the settings you want by using the Change plan settings links. For example, let's say you want to use the Balanced plan, but I don't want my monitor to turn off until 30 minutes of inactivity. No problem. Just click the Change plan settings link and change it to 30 minutes. You can also change all the settings and click Save As to create your own scheme. Just give the scheme a name, and it will appear in your plan list. You can also create a plan from scratch using the Create a plan link on the left side of the window.

Sounds

Windows Vista uses sounds when certain actions occur on your computer to alert you. For example, when you log off Windows, a sound is played. You can determine what sounds are played for what events by choosing options on the Windows Sounds dialog box, as Figure 3-12 shows. As with Power Options, you can make any desired changes, and then save your changes as a scheme.

Mouse Pointers

You can also use the Personalize window to choose how your mouse works and behaves. You'll see the Mouse Properties dialog box and you can learn more about configuring your mouse in Chapter 2.

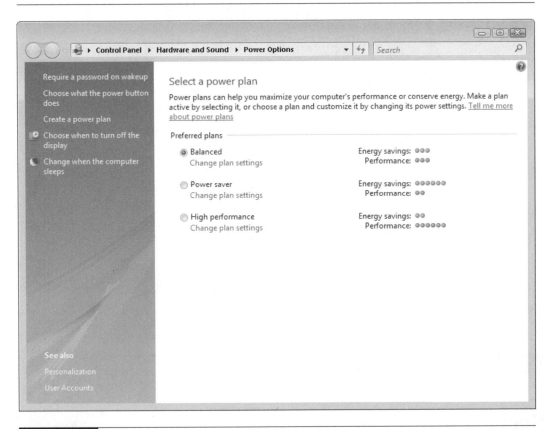

3

FIGURE 3-11 Power Options

Theme

A *theme* is a group of settings applied to Windows Vista under a single name. The settings usually relate to each other, creating a theme of some kind. If you've used Windows before, you're familiar with the concept of themes. The Theme Settings dialog box (see Figure 3-13) enables you either to choose a theme from the drop-down menu or to make changes to a theme on your computer, and then save them as a personal option. Simply make modifications to any other Personalization options, and then click the Save As button on the Theme Settings dialog box to save your changes as a personal theme.

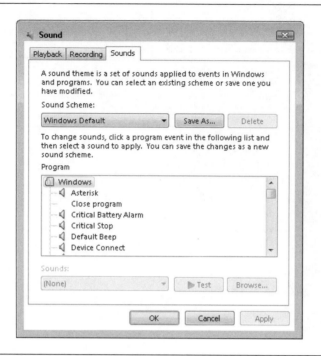

FIGURE 3-12 Windows Sounds

Configure Folder Views

Aside from using an appearance scheme, so your folders appear with a certain color and font, Windows Vista also includes several capabilities that enable you to customize your folders. Remember, a folder is simply a storage location. Windows Vista has several folders it creates and uses, and you can also create your own. See Chapter 4.

Folder options do not affect folder toolbars, but you can change folder toolbars, which you learn about in the section "Toolbars."

You can configure folder options from either one of two places. You can double-click the Folder Options icon in the Control Panel or you can configure folder options from within any Windows folder. For example, you can double-click Computer, and then choose Organize | Folder Options. Doing this opens the same folder options you see when you open the Control Panel icon. You can use the Organize menu to access folder options from any folder in Windows Vista.

FIGURE 3-13 Theme settings

 Important to note is this: If you access folder options within a window and make changes, you are making changes to the appearance of all your folders. In other words, you cannot individually configure folder options for each folder—one setting applies to all folders in Windows. However, you can individually change View options (such as details, icons, and other options).

Once you open Folder Options (regardless of where you open it), you see a simple interface with three tabs.

General

The major appearance changes you can make to your folders are performed on the *General tab,* which presents you with a list of radio buttons, as Figure 3-14 shows.

You can choose radio button options from three different categories:

■ **Tasks** The two radio button options here enable you to see previews and filters, so you can see the actual content in the folders. Or, you can choose to use Windows classic folders. It's best to keep the preview and filters option selected, so you can take advantage of the folder features Windows Vista has to offer.

FIGURE 3-14 General tab

■ **Browse Folders** These options let you choose how your folders are displayed when you are browsing through a folder structure. For example, let's say you open My Computer, and then you open the Control Panel. You can have My Computer open in a window, and then have the Control Panel open in a separate window. Or, you can choose to use the same window, so with My Computer open, when you open the Control Panel, it replaces what you see in My Computer. There is no right or wrong option, but if you work with a number of windows at one time, you may find the Open Each Folder in the Same Window option less cluttering to your Desktop.

TIP *When using the Open Each Folder in the Same Window option, click the Back button on the folder's toolbar to return to a previous window. For example, if you open My Computer, and then open the Control Panel, just click the Back button to return to My Computer—just as you would when surfing the Internet.*

■ **Click Items as Follows**   You can have your mouse clicks act as though your Windows Vista interface were the Internet. On the Internet, you simply click once with your mouse to open any item—all Internet movement is performed through hyperlinks that connect web pages and Internet sites together. You can have your computer act this way as well, so you only have to point to an item to select it, and then click it one time to open it (no more double-clicking). You can enable this option and try it out—it does take some getting used to, however. Just click the Single-Click radio button option to enable it.

View

The *View tab,* shown in Figure 3-15, contains a number of check boxes that enable you to make decisions about files and folders. The options found here concern the display of certain file types, folder views, and other lower-level settings. Windows Vista does a good job of configuring the

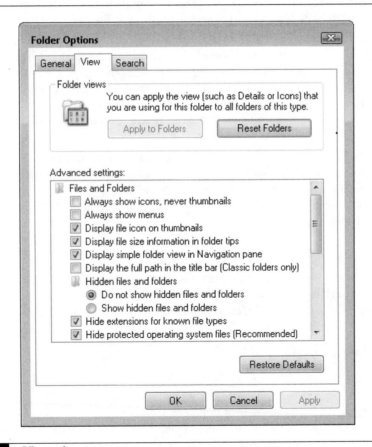

FIGURE 3-15   View tab

common settings and changing them may cause problems—so my recommendation is that you do not make any changes to the options found on this tab unless you have a specific reason to do so. Because you probably don't need to use these options, I only list here some of the more common ones and indicate whether they are enabled by default:

- **Display All Control Panel Options and All Folder Contents**   Do you remember how the Control Panel displays only the most common icons? If you don't like that feature, click this check box to turn it off (this option is not selected by default).

- **Do Not Show Hidden Files and Folders; Hide Protected Operating System Files**   These two separate options, both of which are enabled by default, keep the hidden files and folders in Windows Vista from being shown. Windows Vista hides folders that hold OS files, as well as many of the individual files that make Windows Vista run. Obviously, you don't need to do anything with these files, and Windows Vista hides them to help prevent tampering or accidental deletion. You should leave these settings as they are, so Windows Vista continues to hide system files and folders.

- **Hide Extensions for Known File Types**   This option provides for hiding file extensions. For example, let's say you create a Microsoft Word document called Cat. The document's full name is Cat.doc. The *Hide Extensions option* hides the .doc extension and all other extensions for files that Windows recognizes. This makes your folder files cleaner and easier to read. This option is enabled by default; however, you may want to turn on file extensions, which can help you get more familiar with the kinds of files you are working with.

- **Remember Each Folder's View Settings**   You can use the View menu in a particular folder to determine how the folder appears and what you can view (you learn about these options in the section "Configure Folder Views and Toolbars"). This setting tells Windows to remember each folder's view settings. This option is enabled by default and you should keep it enabled.

Search

Every folder in Windows Vista contains a search function so that you can find items you need more quickly. The Search tab gives you some basic check box options so you can determine how you want searching to work within a folder. The options you see here are self-explanatory.

Configure Folder Views

Once you make some decisions about how you want your folders to appear using the Folder Options window, you can customize your folder views and toolbars. When you open a folder, you see a Views menu, which is shown open in Figure 3-16.

The options you see here enable you to choose from Extra Large Icons, Large Icons, Medium Icons, Small Icons, Details, and Tiles. Simply move the slider bar to select a view option.

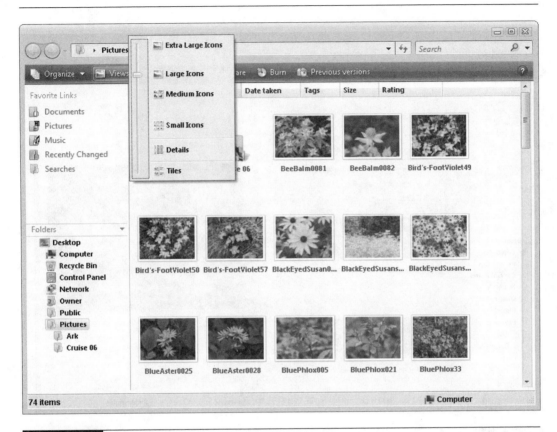

FIGURE 3-16 Views menu

You can also adjust the appearance of folders using the Organize | Layout menu option. Here, you can choose the desired panes you want to see within your folders, such as the Search pane, Preview pane, Reading pane, and Navigation pane. You might try clicking the different options and see which features you are likely to use. One note: The reading pane is helpful if you have a folder of documents because it can display a reading sample of the document within the folder when you select it. This is quick way to see what is in the document without having to open it, as you can see in Figure 3-17.

Windows Sidebar

The *Windows Sidebar,* a new feature in Windows Vista, is designed to hold little programs and games, called *Gadgets,* and, for the most part, the Sidebar simply provides some additional fun and functionality to Windows Vista. If the Sidebar proves popular, you can expect many more

FIGURE 3-17 Folder view using the Reading pane

Gadgets to be available for download from http://gallery.live.com. The good news is the Sidebar is easy to use and the following sections show you how.

Starting and Configuring the Sidebar

The Sidebar is functional and it's on your desktop by default when you install Windows Vista. You also see it on the right side of your screen by default, and it will likely contain some default Gadgets, as you can see in Figure 3-18. Each of the items you see on the Sidebar are Gadgets: They can be changed, removed, and some can be personalized.

You can exit the Sidebar by right-clicking, and then clicking Exit—the Sidebar restarts again when you restart Windows. The Sidebar also has a Notification Area icon when it is active,

3

FIGURE 3-18   Windows Sidebar

Did you know?

Your Folders Can Take You to the Internet

One of the design goals Microsoft has for Windows Vista is to make the OS more integrated with the Internet. Notice the folder's Address bar looks a lot like the IE browser's Address bar. This similarity is by design and, as you might guess, you can jump from a local folder to the Internet without even changing to a different window. In the folder's Address bar, just select what is currently listed, press BACKSPACE or DEL, type the Internet URL you want, and then press ENTER. Your computer will launch an Internet connection and take you to the Internet site—very cool!

which gives you the same menu options. You can right-click the Sidebar and access Properties (or access Windows Sidebar from the Control Panel) and configure a few options, as shown in Figure 3-19. You can make the Sidebar always appear on top of other windows and determine whether the Sidebar should start when Windows starts. You can also make the Sidebar appear on

FIGURE 3-19   Windows Sidebar properties

the left or the right of your desktop. And, if you have a multiple monitor configuration, you can determine on what monitor the Sidebar should appear. You can also view available Gadgets from the Properties dialog box. As you can see, the options are rather simple.

Working with Gadgets

The Sidebar doesn't do anything without Gadgets, so you'll spend your time determining what Gadgets you want to see on the Sidebar and changing them, as necessary. To access Gadgets, click the Gadgets button on the Sidebar (looks like a + sign), or you can right-click the Sidebar, and then click Add Gadgets. In the Gadgets window that appears (see Figure 3-20), review the available Gadgets and simply drag the ones you like to the Sidebar. You can also get more Gadgets by clicking the Get more gadgets online link, which takes you to Microsoft.com.

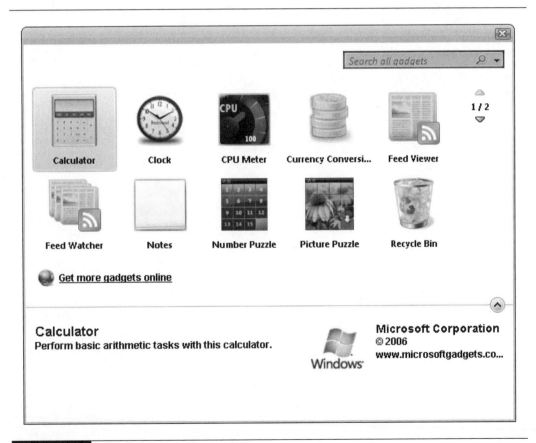

FIGURE 3-20   Available Gadgets

If you right-click a Gadget on the Sidebar, you'll see some different options, depending on the Gadget. For some, you can choose to detach them from the Sidebar, so you can place them anywhere on the desktop you want. Others provide you with a Settings option, so you can adjust the way they work. For example, if you use the Slide Show Gadget, you can right-click it, and then click Settings, so you can determine what photos should display on the Sidebar. As you can see, the options here are rather easy and self-explanatory, so just experiment with them and have fun!

Chapter 4

Manage Components, Programs, Folders, and Files

How to...

- Install and remove Windows Vista components
- Install, manage, and remove programs
- Create and configure folders and files

The Windows Vista operating system (OS) is a rich, robust system, which is full of tools and features that help you make the most of your computing experience. Moreover, you can easily add new programs and even Windows Vista components, so your computer will do exactly what you need it to do. From Microsoft Office to Adobe Photoshop Elements to games and tax programs, you can purchase and install multitudes of programs on Windows Vista, as well as several additional Vista tools not included by default. In this chapter, we look at how to manage programs and components on your Vista system, how to add and remove them, and how to manage folders and files, so you can keep up with the files you create.

Manage Programs with Windows Vista

A *program* is software you install on Windows Vista to perform some task. Programs can come in many forms, such as applications, games, and utilities. The purpose of a program is to give your computer some needed functionality. For example, Windows Vista doesn't ship with advanced photo-editing software. To perform photo editing on Windows Vista, you need a program that provides this functionality, such as Adobe Photoshop Elements. The program is installed on Windows Vista from a CD-ROM. After installation, you can use the application on your Windows Vista computer.

If you purchased your computer with Windows Vista preinstalled, a number of programs are probably already installed on your computer. Choose Start | All Programs to see all the programs currently installed.

In Windows Vista, new programs you have not opened are displayed in yellow when you look at them by choosing Start | All Programs. Once you open a program, this highlight is removed, so you can keep track of which programs you have already explored and which ones you haven't. If you don't like the highlight feature, you can remove it by accessing the Start menu properties. See Chapter 3 for more information about Start menu customization.

Before installing a program, you should make certain it is compatible with Windows Vista. Before you purchase a program, check out the information on the box—it should tell you on the box that the program will work with Windows Vista. The odds are good that applications that functioned well under Windows XP will also work with Windows Vista, although compatibility cannot be guaranteed. Once you are sure your program will work under Windows Vista, you need to install the program.

NOTE

In addition to software considerations, the program you want to install may also require a certain amount of random access memory (RAM), a minimum amount of available hard disk space, possibly a certain graphics card, and perhaps other requirements. Make sure your system can accommodate these needs before you buy it—or be ready to update your system or buy other equipment to support the new program.

Install a New Program

Programs you purchase are placed on a CD-ROM for easy installation. In fact, most programs today include an autostart file to help you get the program installed quickly and easily. For example, when you place the CD-ROM into the CD-ROM drive, the disk spins, and then a dialog box appears on your screen asking whether you want to install the application. This procedure varies from manufacturer to manufacturer, so you need to follow the documentation or onscreen instructions that came with the program you purchased.

If you put the CD-ROM into the CD-ROM drive and nothing happens, you can manually start the setup program by opening My Computer. Right-click the CD-ROM icon, and then choose either Install or AutoPlay. If nothing happens, right-click the CD-ROM icon and choose Explore. You'll probably see some folders and files in the CD-ROM folder. Find an icon called Setup.exe, as shown in Figure 4-1. (You may not see the .exe extension if the Hide Extensions for Known File Types option is enabled. See Chapter 3 for more details.) Double-click the Setup icon and the installation should start. Once you start the installation process, follow the instructions that appear.

FIGURE 4-1   Locate Setup.exe on the installation disc

You should always examine the setup instructions that come with any program. Every program is different, so be sure to follow the particular manufacturer's instructions for installing the program on your computer.

Uninstall a Program

Just as you can install programs on Windows Vista, you can also uninstall them. For example, let's say you use a particular application and, at a future date, you purchase a different application to replace your older one. If the application you purchase is not an upgrade to the old one, you may want to remove the old application from Windows Vista. After all, the application takes up disk space and, because you're not going to use it any longer, you don't need it cluttering up your system.

Once you remove an application from your system, you may not be able to use any of the files generated by that application. For example, if I remove Photoshop Elements from my computer, I may be unable to open any Photoshop Elements files (PSD) unless I have another program that can read them. Make sure you no longer need an application before removing it from your computer.

Use a Program's Uninstall Option

Some programs come with their own uninstall option. You put the CD-ROM into the CD-ROM drive, and a window appears that enables you to install additional components or to remove existing ones—or the entire program. Microsoft Office, for example, offers this feature. Some programs also offer a built-in uninstall routine. You can choose Start | All Programs, point to the program's folder, and a menu pops out with an uninstall option. Not all programs have this feature, so don't worry if you don't see this option.

Use Programs in the Control Panel to Remove a Program

You can also use Programs in the Control Panel to remove a program. In Programs, you see icons for Currently Running Programs, Installed Programs, Startup Programs, and Windows Features. Double-click Installed Programs, and you'll see a list of programs currently installed on your computer, shown in Figure 4-2. To remove one of them, simply select it and click the Change/ Remove button. Follow any additional prompts that appear.

Some programs show a Change button and a Remove button, while some show only a Change/Remove button. If you have programs that can be upgraded or if additional parts of the program can be installed, you'll see both Change and Remove. This arrangement enables you to install additional portions of the program or to remove the program or components from your computer.

Under no circumstances should you delete a program's folder if you can use the CD-ROM or the Programs option. Deleting the folder does not allow Windows Vista to delete and clean up after the application properly, so this should be considered a last-resort option. Also, before using this option, check your program's documentation for specific information about uninstalling the program from Windows Vista.

FIGURE 4-2   Click the Change/Remove button to remove a program

Download Programs from the Internet

The Internet contains a wealth of applications that you can download and use on your computer—and many of them are free. For those that aren't free, you can often download an evaluation version of a program to determine whether you like how it works on your computer before purchasing it. You can also download all kinds of Windows utilities and games.

When you choose to download an application from the Internet, you click a link on the web site that starts the download to your computer. When this happens, a dialog box appears in which you can choose whether to open the application from its current location or save it to disk. If you choose to open the application, the setup files are downloaded to your computer and setup begins. If you choose to save the application instead, the files are all saved to a place you specify in this dialog box (such as your Desktop or My Documents folder). You can then start setup yourself when you are ready. There is no right or wrong here, it's just a matter of preference.

TIP   *If you are given the option to perform a custom install, do it! Sometimes, other programs, and even spyware, are installed with downloaded applications, and a custom installation will help you see and choose exactly what is being installed.*

If you choose to save a program to disk when you start the download, the program is downloaded in a compressed format. *Compressing* a file saves time when downloading. Usually, the application appears as a simple icon. Double-click the icon to uncompress and start the installation. Windows Vista includes compression software, so you can open and use

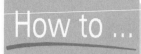 **Forcibly Remove a Program**

If you cannot use Programs or the program's uninstall option, you can forcibly remove a program by following these steps:

1. Open My Computer, and double-click your C drive icon.

2. Locate a folder called Program Files and double-click it. You may need to click the View All Contents link as prompted.

3. Look through the folders and find the one that contains the program you want to uninstall. Typically, the name of the folder will state the program's name or the manufacturer's name.

4. Right-click the folder and click Delete to remove it from your computer. Make sure you are deleting the correct folder before completing the action.

compressed folders (see the section "Use Folder Compression"). For specific installation steps, refer to the web site where you downloaded the program.

Use Windows Vista's Compatibility Mode

Windows Vista includes a feature called *Compatibility Mode,* which allows it to act like a previous version of Windows—specifically, Windows 95, 98, Me, NT, 2000, or XP. Compatibility Mode enables you to use older applications that might not work with Windows Vista. When in Compatibility Mode, Windows Vista acts like the previous version of Windows (which you select), so the application is "tricked" into thinking it is installed on the correct OS.

Important to note is that Compatibility Mode is intended for standard applications and even games. However, Compatibility Mode is not designed for use with programs that run portions of your system configuration. For example, antivirus programs that are incompatible with Windows Vista should not be used, because the program may damage your system in Compatibility Mode. The same is true for disk-management utilities and backup software. In other words, if the application is used to manage the OS or some portion of the OS, it should not be used with Compatibility Mode—you need to upgrade and get the compatible version of the software.

The *Program Compatibility Wizard* helps you use Compatibility Mode:

1. When you try to start a program that is not compatible with Windows Vista natively, the Program Compatibility Wizard will automatically start.

2. Click Next on the Welcome screen that appears.

3. In the next window, choose a radio button option. You can choose to view a list of programs, use the program currently in your CD-ROM drive, or locate the program manually. Then, click Next.

4

Did you know?

About Downloaded Programs, Viruses, and Spyware

Internet programs are a great way to get utilities, applications, and games for your computer—and computer viruses and spyware as well! Computer viruses are made up of malicious code that often hides within other code—such as in a setup program for an application. Spyware consists of programs that hide in your computer and gather personal information about you. To protect your computer from infection, I highly recommend you purchase some antivirus software for your Windows Vista computer. Vista's new Windows Defender can also help protect your computer against spyware and adware. Aside from using antivirus software and Windows Defender, another great way to keep from getting a computer virus resides right in your own head—common sense! Be wary of downloading programs from Internet sites that don't appear to be on the up-and-up. Don't run programs that you receive via unsolicited e-mail, Internet pop-up boxes, or from unknown sources in other ways. Your best bet is to download software from respected Internet sites and companies only. When in doubt—don't download!

4. In the selection window, choose the application you want to run in Compatibility Mode, as shown here. Click Next.

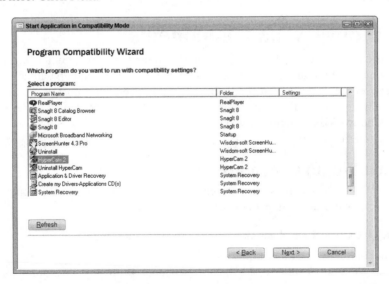

5. Choose the appropriate radio button, so your Vista computer will act like Windows 95, NT 4.0, 98/Me, or Windows 2000 / XP. Click Next.

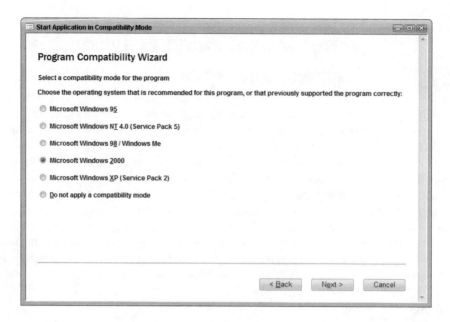

6. The Test window appears. Click Next to open the program and test its functionality.

7. A window appears asking you whether the program worked correctly. Choose the correct radio button, and then click Next and Finish.

Manage Windows Vista Components

Windows Vista provides a way for you to include additional Windows components, now called "features," which are not installed by default. This way, you don't end up with a bunch of OS junk you'll never use. However, unlike previous Windows versions, most of the components you will use are already installed on your computer, so the odds are good you will never need to add or remove Windows Vista features. If you need to, however, this section shows you how to turn Windows Features on or off.

Turn On a Windows Feature

Turning on a Windows Feature is easy. Once again, you use Programs in the Control Panel. To turn on a Windows Feature, follow these steps:

1. Open the Control Panel and double-click the Programs and Features icon.

2. Double-click Windows Features.

3. In the Windows Features dialog box, shown in the following illustration, locate the feature you want to turn on and click to enable the check box.

4. Click OK to close the Windows Features dialog box

Turn Off a Windows Feature

Just as you turn on any Windows Feature you want to use, you can also turn off those you do not want. This action reduces OS clutter. To remove a feature, return to the Windows Features dialog box and simply uncheck the selected check box of the feature you don't want to use. In the following illustration, I have turned off the FreeCell game, so it no longer appears in my Games folder.

Manage Folders and Files

As you may have learned from the first few chapters of this book, Windows Vista manages data by using various folders to store that data. Just as you wouldn't dump a bunch of single papers into a filing cabinet and expect to find what you need, Windows Vista doesn't store information in a haphazard way. Windows Vista uses folders to keep OS files, program files, and even your own files organized. In this section of the chapter, you learn how to manage your files and folders.

Before we begin, I would like to offer a big warning. You can manage your own folders and files, but you should never make changes to any of the folders and files found in C:\Windows. These folders and files are used by the Windows Vista OS to function. Tinkering with them can—and probably will—cause Windows Vista to stop working. So, you should manage your own files and folders, and let Windows Vista manage its files and folders.

Create, Rename, and Delete Folders

You use folders in Windows Vista to store data, such as documents, pictures, spreadsheets, you name it—any type of file or application can be stored in a folder. Depending on your needs, you may not require additional folders. After all, Windows Vista automatically tries to place files in your Documents folder or one of its subfolders, such as Pictures. However, you may need to create your own folders to manage data. For example, each time I begin work on a new book, I create a folder on my computer where I store all the files for the book. Within that folder, I then create additional folders for each chapter. This way, a specific folder exists for each chapter document and the graphics files for that chapter, so I can keep it all organized. You can create folders within folders, and folders within those folders, to as many levels as you want or need.

Although folders are great, don't get too wild with folder creation. Too many folders can be more confusing than helpful, so keep your folder structure in check to make sure it meets your needs.

The good news is you can easily create, rename, and delete folders as needed. To create a new folder, open the folder in which you want to create the new folder, such as Documents, or simply open your C drive. Choose Organize | New Folder. A new folder appears. Press BACKSPACE on your keyboard and type a desired name for the new folder.

If you want to create a new folder directly on your Desktop, right-click on an empty area of your Desktop, and choose New | Folder.

At any given time, you can rename a folder by right-clicking the folder and choosing Rename. Then, type a new name and press ENTER. This feature makes it easy to keep your folders organized.

Finally, you can delete any folder by right-clicking the folder and choosing Delete. This moves the folder, and everything in the folder, to the Recycle Bin. Remember, everything in the folder is deleted as well, including files, applications, and other folders—anything at all.

Use Folder Menu Options

Windows Vista folders contain a few menu options above the folder window: Organize, Views, Share, and Previous Versions. If you're looking for old-style File, Edit, and other menus from previous Windows versions, they are no longer available under the new Vista interface. However, if you want to use the old-style menus, you can access Folder Options in the Control Panel (or on the Organize menu) and choose Use Windows classic folders on the General tab.

Organize Menu

The *Organize menu* enables you to manage files and folders. Aside from using the File menu to create a new folder, you can also select a file or folder, choose File, and then choose any of the following options (which may or may not appear, depending on the file, folder, or application you selected):

- **Cut**   This option removes a selected subfolder or file.
- **Copy**   This option copies a selected subfolder or file.
- **Paste**   This option pastes a previously copied subfolder or file.
- **Undo/Redo**   This action will undo or redo the last action taken.
- **Select All**   This option selects all subfolders and files.
- **Layout**   This pop-out menu enables you to configure the layout of the folder. You can choose to use Classic menus, include a search pane, preview pane, reading pane, and navigation pane.
- **Folder and Search Options**   This action opens the Folder Options dialog box that is also available in the Control Panel. See Chapter 3 for details.
- **Delete**   This action deletes the currently selected subfolder or file.
- **Rename**   This action renames the currently selected subfolder or file.
- **Remove Properties**   This action removes the properties for the selected folder or file.
- **Properties**   This action opens the old-style Properties dialog box.
- **Close**   This action closes the folder.

How to Use a UNC Path

A Universal Naming Convention (UNC) is a method used to connect to network folders or files on Windows networks (and also to Linux and Macintosh servers running Samba). You can use the UNC path in the Run dialog box or in the Address bar of any Explorer window in Windows Vista. The UNC path is represented by two backslashes (\\), then the name of the computer you want to connect to, then the share name, and then the file name. Each portion of the path is connected by a single backslash. So, if I want to connect to a particular file called *bass* in a shared folder called *fishing* on a computer named *Curt123,* the UNC path is \\curt123\fishing\bass.doc.

View Menu

The *View menu* enables you to configure the appearance of your folder. You can learn about this option in Chapter 3.

Use Folder Compression

Windows Vista includes a built-in feature to help you conserve disk space: *folder compression*. Compression shrinks the normal size of a folder and its contents to free up more disk space that you can use for other purposes. Compression in Windows Vista is quick and easy to use.

Create a Compressed Folder

You can create a compressed folder just as you create any other folder. In the folder where you want to create the new compressed folder, choose File | New | Compressed Folder if you have turned on Classic Menus. Or, locate the folder, right-click it, and click Send To | Compressed folder to compress the existing folder. If you want to create a compressed folder on your Desktop, right-click on an empty area of the Desktop, and choose New | Compressed Folder. Either way, a new compressed folder appears. Compressed folder icons have a zipper on them, so you can identify them, like the icon shown here.

Pictures

Add Items to and Remove Them from a Compressed Folder

You can add files and folders to a compressed folder, and then remove them, just as you would in any other folder in Windows Vista. Once you drag a file or folder into a compressed folder, the item is compressed. Once you drag the item out of the folder, it is automatically decompressed—there's no configuration to worry about. Additionally, you can perform all other actions with the file, such as opening, renaming, deleting, and so forth—just as you would if the file were in a regular folder.

Use Extraction

Windows Vista uses the *WinZip* technology to compress folders. A part of that technology is the extraction option. The *extraction option* enables you to pull all items from a compressed folder and place them in a folder that isn't compressed. This action extracts—or decompresses—the items, so they are no longer compressed. If you right-click a shared folder, you see the extraction options. You can extract the folder to a different folder or another location, or even choose to e-mail the compressed folder. No matter what option you choose, the Extract Compressed Folders option opens and helps you with the procedure, as the following illustration shows. So what do you do if you have a compressed folder that you don't want to be compressed any longer? You simply right-click the folder, and then click Extract All, which essentially recreates the folder and all data—just without the encryption.

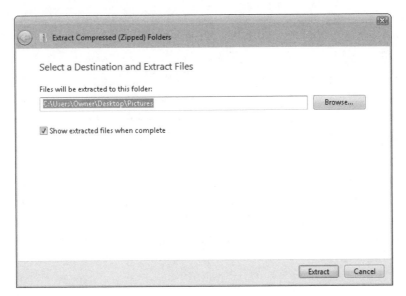

About Files

As you already learned, files are placed in various folders on your computer for safekeeping and organization purposes. Files are created by various programs you installed on your system and they have different file extensions. For example, a Microsoft Word document has the .doc extension, while a document you create with Paint might have the .bmp extension (bitmap). In short, some kind of program is necessary to create a file of any kind. The good news about files is you don't have to manage them individually. You can right-click any file and see the same options you get with a folder, such as Send To, Copy, Cut, and so on. You can also drag and move files around to different locations on your computer without damaging them.

Chapter 5

Use the Accessories that Come with Windows

How to...

- ■ Access Windows accessories
- ■ Use Windows accessories
- ■ Configure Windows accessories

Windows Vista continues the Windows tradition of providing a group of programs on your computer collectively called accessories. *Accessories* are just that—programs that help you do some kind of job or specific function. They are not large applications, like Microsoft Word or Microsoft Excel, but rather are small programs designed to help you in some way. If you've used accessories in earlier versions of Windows, such as Windows XP, you won't find many surprises here. However, if you are new to Windows in general, this chapter shows you a new world of stuff available on your Vista operating system (OS).

As you might guess, a few of the accessories or accessory categories deserve their own chapters or, by their nature, belong in a different chapter. For example, Windows Sidebar is considered an accessory, but it is covered in Chapter 3. As you progress through this chapter, I let you know if more information about an accessory is included elsewhere in the book. You can locate the accessories on your Windows Vista computer by choosing Start | All Programs | Accessories. You see an expanded menu listing the accessory programs.

Calculator

Windows Vista provides you with a quick, onscreen calculator that you can access at any time using Accessories. Your onscreen *Calculator* works just like any other calculator—use it to count your money, pay your bills, or figure out how much you owe the IRS.

A quick note about the Calculator: You can use the View menu to see a standard calculator or a scientific calculator, as shown in Figure 5-1. Then use the Calculator just as you would a desktop version, but with your mouse or keyboard keypad.

Command Prompt

The Command Prompt in Windows Vista is basically the same as it was in Windows XP, as well as previous versions. From the Command Prompt, you can run programs and utilities, try to fix problems, and make use of a number of other command-line functions and features. In most cases, you'll find command-line syntax and options from the Help files of various Windows Vista programs and utilities. If you're interested in using the Command Prompt, check the Help files of the desired application to find out how the Command Prompt might be useful for the task you are currently performing.

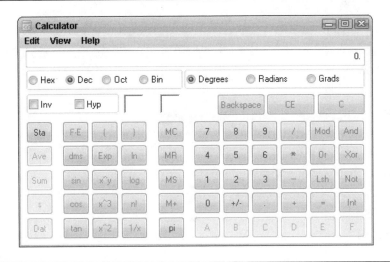

FIGURE 5-1 Scientific calculator

Connect to a Network Projector

Windows Vista includes a new accessory that makes it easy for you to connect to a network projector. This feature, *Connect to a Network Projector,* is helpful for people on business networks that have projectors connected to the network for use in meeting rooms. The idea is to make connecting to these projectors quick and easy. When you click Option in Accessories, as shown in Figure 5-2, you see a connection window that enables you to choose from available projectors on the network or you can enter an HTTP address for an intranet printer. Simply click the desired option and follow the additional steps.

Notepad

Accessories also includes a simple text editor program—*Notepad.* You can open text-only documents in Notepad and make changes to them. Advanced computer users often use Notepad to make text-based changes to their Windows configuration (which is not something you should try on your own!). You can use Notepad for simple tasks, such as typing a message of some kind, sending it via e-mail, or printing it on your printer.

Notepad, shown in Figure 5-3, enables you to open, create, and save text files. You can use the Edit menu to perform cut-and-paste operations, and to choose the font you want to use.

However, Notepad is simply a basic text editor. You cannot format paragraphs or text (making text italic or bold, for example), and you cannot create any tables or use other word processing features. Notepad simply does text—nothing else.

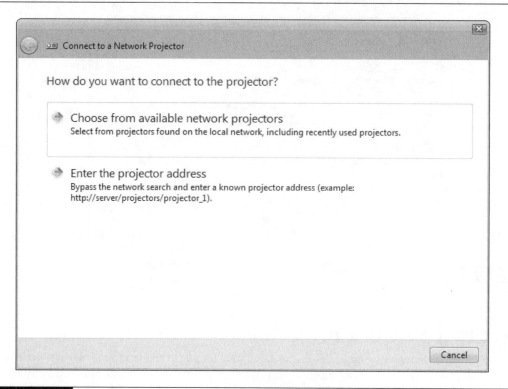

FIGURE 5-2   Choose an option to connect to a network projector

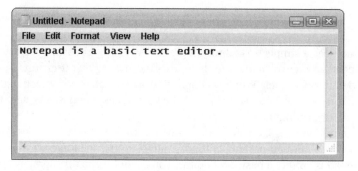

FIGURE 5-3   Notepad is a basic text editor

Paint

Windows Paint is a low-level graphics-creation program that enables you to generate or open various graphics files and save a created graphics file as a bitmap (BMP), JPEG, TIFF, GIF, or other standard file format type. You are limited in what you can do with Paint, but you may find its moderate functionality useful in a variety of ways.

The best way to learn to use Paint is to open it and play around with the toolbar and menu options. You can spend about half an hour playing with Paint and you'll discover most all there is to know.

You can use Paint to open any standard graphics file, such as a BMP, TIF, JPEG, GIF, PNG, or ICO. An example of a JPEG file is shown in Figure 5-4. Once you have the graphics file open,

FIGURE 5-4   Paint provides basic graphics functions

you can click on any of the toolbar buttons to make changes to the graphic. Your toolbar options include a paintbrush, a pencil, a spray can, text, and various line shapes.

Remote Desktop Connection

Windows Vista includes a quick connection dialog box in Accessories for accessing remote desktop connections. *Remote Desktop* enables to you to connect a remote computer for which you have access permissions and use the computer as if you are sitting in front of it. You can learn more about Remote Desktop in Chapter 13.

Run

The Run dialog box, which was previously found on the Start menu in Windows XP, has been moved to the Accessories menu to make the Start menu a bit cleaner. With the *Run dialog box,* you can use UNC path names or old-style Windows navigation to access folders and files on your computer or a network. See Figure 5-5. You can also issue commands as if you were at the Command Prompt here.

Snipping Tool

The *Snipping Tool,* shown in Figure 5-6, is a new utility in Windows Vista that enables you to capture portions of your desktop interface and save them as a picture file. This feature is helpful to people who write instructions or other documentation. The Snipping Tool gives you a quick way to capture any area of the screen and determine how you want the selection captured.

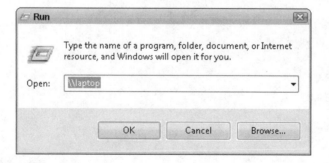

FIGURE 5-5 Run dialog box

FIGURE 5-6   Snipping Tool

Sound Recorder

The *Sound Recorder* is a simple tool that enables you to record sound coming to your computer from the microphone or any input to your computer. To start recording a sound file, simply click the Start Recording button, as shown in Figure 5-7, and then click Stop Recording when you're done. You'll see a dialog box that enables you to save your sound file.

Sync Center

The *Sync Center* is the new and improved Synchronize tool that has been available for the last several versions of Windows. It enables you to synchronize data on your computer with data on a network. For example, let's say you have a collection of Word documents. You regularly edit those documents, but they are centrally located on a server on your network. You want to keep a copy of those documents on your laptop computer, so you can work on them during your bus ride home. If you work on those documents offline, they will have to be synchronized with the network server, so they will be up-to-date. Sure, you can manually copy those documents to the server, but for files you use regularly, Vista can simply do it for you.

Click on the Setup New Sync Partnerships link to see available folders that you can work with. Then, you can simply use the Organize, Views, Sync All, or Stop All buttons to synchronize offline files with other computers or servers on your network, as Figure 5-8 shows. Naturally, in an office environment, you may need additional help from your network administrator to use offline files or the Sync Center.

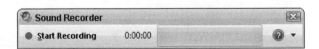

FIGURE 5-7   Sound Recorder

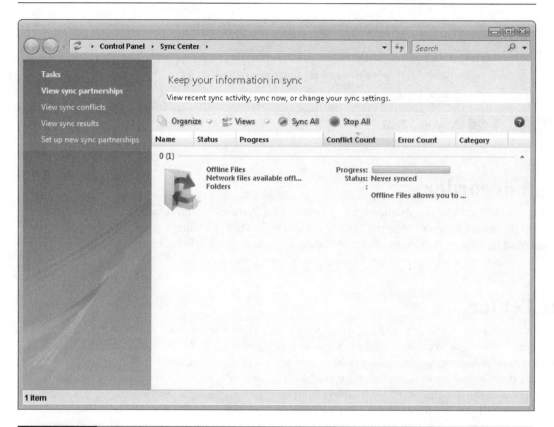

FIGURE 5-8   Sync Center

Welcome Center

By default, the *Welcome Center* appears each time you start Windows, but you can also access it in Accessories. Here, you can gain some basic hardware information about your computer and access some common tasks, such as adding printers and new users, accessing the Control Panel, and so forth. You can also access most of the features you see here directly in the Control Panel, so whether or not you use the Welcome Center is up to you.

Notice in Figure 5-9 that the Welcome Center has a Run at Startup check box option at the bottom of the screen. If you don't want the Welcome Center to appear each time you start Windows, just clear this check box. Aside from Accessories, you can also access the Welcome Center from the Control Panel.

FIGURE 5-9   Welcome Center

Windows Explorer

Another accessory you find in the Accessories menu is *Windows Explorer.* In previous versions of Windows, Explorer was considered the main tool you use to browse and manage files and folders. In Windows Vista, as well as Windows 2000 and Windows XP, Explorer is considered an accessory because the Folder View features of these operating systems make Explorer not so indispensable. However, Explorer is still available if you like working with it.

Windows Explorer provides a single interface to view all the folders on your computer and to make additions to or deletions from them. As you can see in Figure 5-10, Windows Explorer

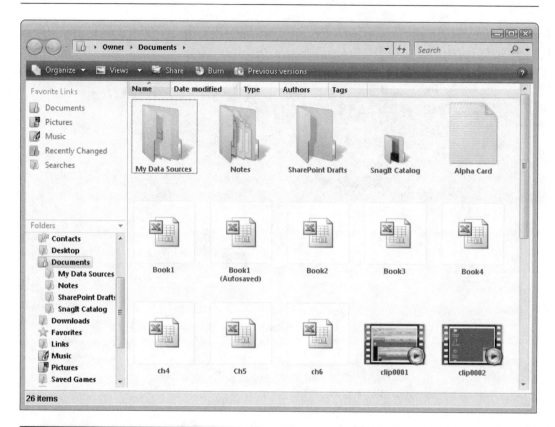

FIGURE 5-10   Windows Explorer

presents all of your folders in a hierarchy. You click the toggle arrows next to what you want to expand, and then continue to click the toggle arrows until you reach the folder you want. Once you reach that folder, select it to see all its contents in the right pane.

TIP   *If you don't like the Tile/Icon view, open the Views menu and choose a desired option.*

Windows Sidebar

You can turn on the Windows Sidebar directly from the Accessories menu (if it is not in use already). You can learn more about using and configuring Windows Sidebar in Chapter 3.

WordPad

WordPad is a text editor similar to Notepad, but it functions more like a word processing application. Remember, however, that WordPad doesn't contain the functionality of most major word processing applications, such as Microsoft Word, but it does contain enough functions to be useful. With WordPad, you can edit and create text just as with Notepad, but WordPad supports major formatting features, such as the use of various fonts and text styles. When you save a WordPad document, the formatting is also maintained as long as you save the file in the rich text format. You can use WordPad to create all kinds of text documents, and while you can use tabs and different paragraph schemes, you cannot create tables or spreadsheets within the documents. However, for a free text editor, this one is certainly not bad at all.

You can easily format text in WordPad. Just type the text you want, and then highlight the text using your mouse. Then, you can use the WordPad toolbar to select a format button, such as bold, italic, font changes, and so on. You can also open the Format menu to see a list of other options.

Ease of Access

Ease of Access is a collection of tools that help people with impairments use Windows Vista. The tools you see here are the same tools found in Windows XP. The folder in Accessories enables you to access some different tools, such as the Ease of Access Center, Magnifier, Narrator, On-Screen Keyboard, and Speech Recognition. You can access the latter tools individually or configure them all using the Access Center. The Ease of Access Center is also available in the Control Panel. You can learn more about it in Chapter 2.

System Tools

The *System Tools menu* gives you several tools that can help your Windows Vista computer run better and solve problems. As with the other major menu sections, these tools deserve their own chapters. You can learn about them in Part IV of this book.

Tablet PC

Windows Vista includes three basic tools that mimic tools found on *Tablet PCs*. You can use an Input Panel to hand write data using your mouse (or a touch screen if you have one), Sticky Notes, and the Windows Journal. These features exist primarily so you can share information with users of Tablet PCs.

Chapter 6

Manage Hardware

How to...

- Install new hardware
- Manage hardware with Device Manager
- Install new hardware drivers
- Use multiple hardware profiles
- Troubleshoot hardware problems

The term "hardware" refers to physical devices that your operating system (OS) uses to accomplish some task. Your keyboard, mouse, CD-ROM drive, floppy drive, modem, and sound card, plus the multitude of other devices attached to your computer, are all collectively called *hardware*. In the past, installing new hardware devices was difficult, but since the early days of Windows, installing and configuring hardware has become much easier. Windows Vista continues this advancement—in fact, Windows Vista can often automatically install and configure new hardware without any help from you.

Nevertheless, you may experience hardware problems if you have upgraded from previous consumer versions of Windows, such as Windows XP. Simply put, Windows Vista is a powerful system, and it must have powerful and compatible hardware on which to run. If you purchased a new computer with Windows Vista preinstalled, you have nothing to worry about unless you want to add hardware. Still, hardware doesn't have to be a computing monster, and this chapter shows you how to install, configure, and troubleshoot hardware problems in Windows Vista.

Understand Hardware

If you are like me, it's usually helpful to understand a potential problem before you try to solve it, so this section tells you a bit about hardware—why it has been a problem in the past and what Windows Vista does to reduce hardware problems. In the past, computer operating systems were "dumb," in the sense that you had to tell them what hardware devices were installed or connected to the computer. You had to specify what sound card, video card, printer, modem, and other hardware devices were installed on your computer. You then had to provide a driver for those hardware devices. A *driver* is a piece of software an OS uses to communicate with a particular device. For example, for your OS to communicate with your modem, a driver must be present, so the OS can manage and use the modem. Each hardware device has its own driver—usually provided by the hardware device manufacturer. To make the hardware work, you had to install it, provide a driver, and then (usually) configure the OS to work with the device, and vice versa (as well as keep the device from interfering with other devices). As you can imagine, this process sometimes became maddening for even the experienced user.

All of this began to change with Windows 95, which introduced a technology called Plug and Play (often referred to as "Plug and Pray"). The idea was to create an OS that was "aware" of its environment. The OS could automatically detect when new hardware was added and attempt to install it. You might have to provide a driver for the hardware via a disk or CD-ROM, but Windows 95 also had its own database of generic drivers that could be used for typical pieces of hardware. All of this sounded wonderful—but if you have used Windows 95, you know that Plug and Play was not perfect. It didn't work well with some hardware, and some hardware didn't work well with Plug and Play.

Windows 98, Windows 2000, Windows Me, Windows XP, and now Windows Vista all use a more grown-up version of Plug and Play. Windows Vista has an extensive driver database, so it can automatically detect and install most devices. This is a great feature, because most of us would rather do something else than tinker with hardware installation. Windows Vista can take care of the entire process—most of the time without any intervention from you.

Plug and Play in Windows Vista is designed to install and remove devices from your computer. How does it work? Here's the chain of events that occurs when you install or connect a new device to Windows Vista:

1. Windows Vista detects that a new hardware device has been added to the system. You usually see a bubble message appear in your Notification Area telling you so.

2. Windows Vista installs the new device and finds a generic driver for the device in its database.

3. Windows Vista allocates resources to the device, so the device can work with your computer.

That's it—in most cases, you don't even have to reboot the computer. When you remove a device from your computer, Windows Vista

1. Detects that a hardware device has been removed.

2. Removes the device from the system and uninstalls the device's driver.

The Golden Rules of Windows XP Hardware

In the introduction to this chapter, I mentioned that Windows Vista demands hardware that can handle the power of Windows Vista. To avoid hardware problems, you should follow some simple Vista hardware rules.

If you purchased a new computer with Windows Vista preinstalled, the hardware that was also installed on the computer will work fine with Windows Vista. The computer manufacturer works with Microsoft to ensure that your computer's hardware is compatible, so you have no worries if you fall into this category.

However, what happens if you later want to upgrade to a different device or upgrade an older computer to Windows Vista? What if you want one of those new, awesome video cards or a new modem? No problem. You can purchase a new device and add it to your computer, and you can often upgrade an older computer to Windows Vista. If you follow some basic rules, you are likely to have few or no problems with hardware. Here they are—the golden rules of Windows Vista hardware:

- If you want to upgrade a computer to Windows Vista from Windows XP, you must check out the computer's hardware carefully and compare it to the hardware requirements of Windows Vista (see the Appendix). Vista may not run on older hardware, and the older computer may not have enough RAM to power the Vista OS. Windows Vista is a powerful system that requires a lot of resources to work correctly. Do your homework first!

- Buy only Plug-and-Play-compliant hardware. How do you know? Because the new hardware device will say Plug-and-Play right on the box. Little hardware is out there these days that is not Plug-and-Play, but if a device doesn't say Plug and Play on the box, keep moving—don't buy it!

- Look for a Microsoft seal of approval or a compatible with Windows Vista statement on the box as well. A lack of these doesn't mean the device won't work, but it should be a warning sign to you. Approved, well-tested hardware tells you on the box that it's compatible with Windows Vista.

- Check out the Windows XP web site at www.microsoft.com/windowsvista for up-to-date information about hardware compatibility.

- Stick to recognizable brand names. Remember, as with most things in life, you get what you pay for. If you choose to purchase FlyByNight's Jiffy Modem on the Internet for $9.95 (with a set of steak knives), don't be surprised if it doesn't work well.

Install a Plug-and-Play Device

Now that you know about the rules for purchasing a new hardware device, installing it is rather anticlimactic. First, always check the device manufacturer's documentation that came with the hardware device for instructions. Most hardware manufacturers include specific step-by-step instructions that tell you exactly what to do to install or attach the device to your computer. If the device is Plug and Play and supported by Windows Vista, installing the device should be easy. Just follow these steps:

1. Attach the new device to the correct port or slot on the back of your computer. If the device is an internal device, first check the installation instructions to see what you need to install first: the hardware or the software. If you need to install the hardware first, shut down and unplug your computer from the power outlet and follow the manufacturer's instructions for removing the computer's case and installing the device in the correct slot.

You absolutely *must unplug your computer from the power outlet before removing the case. Just because your computer is turned off doesn't mean power isn't flowing to some of its components. Play it safe and always unplug the computer!*

2. If the device is an internal device, replace the computer cover and plug the computer back in. If the device is external, make sure it's attached to your computer correctly, and then turn on the device.

NOTE   *In some cases, you should* not *turn on the external device before booting Windows XP. Check the device documentation to make sure.*

3. Turn on your computer and boot Windows Vista. Windows Vista automatically detects the device and installs it on your computer. With some types of devices, some instructions may appear. Follow them as directed. In most cases, installation is handled automatically, and you receive a bubble message from the Notification Area telling you the device has been installed.

TIP   *If you're installing a USB device, parallel printer, or PC card, you probably won't need to reboot the computer. These devices can be automatically detected and installed, so make sure you read the device's installation instructions.*

6

Remove a Plug-and-Play Device from Your Computer

If you want to remove a Plug-and-Play device from your computer, Windows Vista will automatically detect the change and remove the internal software and driver. Shut down Windows Vista and remove the device. If you're removing an internal device, remember to unplug the computer from the power source. Once you finish, reboot Windows Vista. Windows Vista detects that the device is missing and uninstalls the driver from the device.

NOTE   *You can also manually remove a device from Windows Vista without physically removing it from your computer. See the section "Use Device Manager." Also, for USB devices, parallel printers, and PC cards, you can simply remove the device without having to shut down your computer.*

Install a Non-Plug-and-Play Device

As mentioned, virtually all hardware devices sold today are Plug-and-Play-compliant. However, it is possible for a hardware device to work under Windows, but not support Plug and Play. Also, you may have an older device you want to use that does not support Plug and Play. To accommodate these needs, Windows Vista includes an Add Hardware Wizard in the Control Panel. This wizard (which has been around since Windows 98) is designed to help you install non-Plug-and-Play devices, known as "legacy" devices, as well as troublesome Plug-and-Play devices.

Before I show you how to use the wizard, I want to note that, if at all possible, you should use Plug-and-Play hardware. You'll see the best performance and experience the fewest problems if you use Plug-and-Play hardware that is compatible with Windows Vista. In most circumstances, you should never have to use the Add Hardware Wizard. With that said, however, you can try to use devices that are not Plug and Play with the Add Hardware Wizard.

To use the Add Hardware Wizard, follow these steps:

1. Choose Start | Control Panel.

2. Double-click the Add Hardware icon.

3. Click Next on the Welcome screen. The wizard tells you Windows Vista will now search for any Plug-and-Play devices on your computer, shown in the following illustration. Click Next.

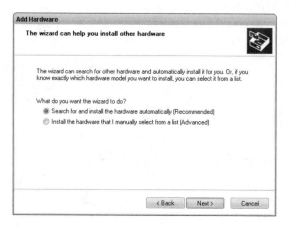

4. You can also choose the Advanced option, so you can install the hardware you want by manually selecting it from a list. If you choose this option, click Next, choose the hardware category, and then click Next, as the following illustration shows. If you have an installation disk for the device, use the Have Disk button to install the drivers from the CD.

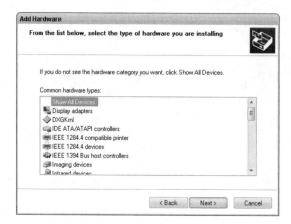

5. Make your selection and click Next.

6. Click Next to install the device.

7. Follow any additional screens that may appear and click Finish.

Use Device Manager

Once you install devices on your computer, you can manage them in a few different places. First, for certain devices—such as printers, scanners, cameras, and modems—an icon appears in the Control Panel. These devices require more management than others do, so Windows Vista helps you by giving them a specific Control Panel option (these are also explored in later chapters). Next, all devices installed or attached to your computer can be managed from a tool called *Device Manager*.

You can access Device Manager in one of two ways. The easiest way is simply to open Control Panel and double-click the Device Manager applet. Also, you can right-click Computer and choose Properties. Click Advanced System Settings, and then click the Hardware tab. Notice you can also access the Add Hardware Wizard and Device Manager from this tab. Click the Device Manager button to open it. Either way, the Device Manager interface is the same, as Figure 6-1 shows.

As you can see, the Device Manager provides an interface similar to Windows Explorer. You see different categories of hardware devices, each with a plus (+) sign next to it. Click the + sign to expand the category to see the actual devices. Notice at the top of the window, you can open the View menu to choose to view devices either by type or by connection. These options show you how different hardware devices are connected and how they are using resources on your computer. This View option can be helpful when troubleshooting.

Examine a Device's Properties

As noted, you can use Device Manager to examine specific properties for a device. First, expand the desired category by clicking the + sign next to it. Second, select the device in Device Manager,

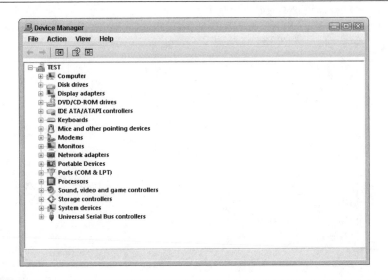

FIGURE 6-1   Device Manager

right-click the device icon, and then click Properties. Once you access the Properties window, you see several tabs for the device. What you see may vary according to the device, but you typically see three basic tabs—General, Driver, and Resources. The following sections explore each of these.

General

The *General tab* gives you information about the device, but one piece of information can be particularly helpful. Along with information on the type of device, manufacturer, version number, and so on is a message about the status of the device, as Figure 6-2 shows.

As you can see in Figure 6-2, the device is working properly. If it were not working properly, you would see a message here telling you what might be wrong (such as a bad driver).

At the bottom of the window, you will see a button that will open the Windows Troubleshooter to help you solve any existing problems with the device. You also see a drop-down menu that enables you to disable the device. This feature allows your system to stop using a device even though it is still installed, which can be helpful when troubleshooting problems.

FIGURE 6-2   General tab

Driver

As you might expect, the *Driver tab,* shown in Figure 6-3, gives you information about the device's driver. You can use this tab to see the publisher of the driver and its date, and whether or not the driver is digitally signed. A *digitally signed driver* means the publisher has included a digital signature to ensure the driver is authentic. Microsoft recommends you use only signed drivers to ensure compatibility with Windows Vista. You also see four buttons that enable you to manage the driver—Driver Details, Update Driver, Roll Back Driver, and Uninstall.

If you click the *Driver Details button,* a window appears that gives you more information about the driver. Typically, this is not information you will need, but it may be useful to support personnel if you ever need to get telephone or web support from Microsoft.

If you click the *Update Driver button,* you can install a new driver for your device. Occasionally, hardware manufacturers publish new device drivers. You can download these new drivers from the manufacturer's web site, and then install them on your computer, and you can also download driver updates automatically through Windows Update. These new drivers often resolve conflicts or problems and ensure compatibility with your OS. When you want to install a new driver, simply access the Driver tab for the device, and then click the Update Driver button. This action opens a Hardware Update Wizard; the upcoming How To box shows you how to use it.

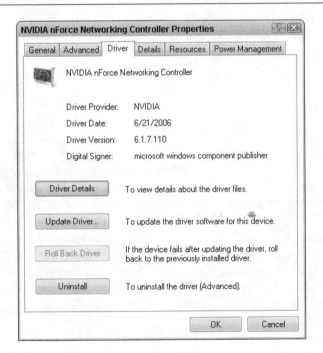

FIGURE 6-3   Driver tab

 **Install a New Driver**

To install a new driver, follow these steps:

1. On the Driver tab, click the Update Driver button, and the Update Driver Wizard appears. You see two selection options: You can install the software automatically or select the driver you want to install by browsing your computer for it.

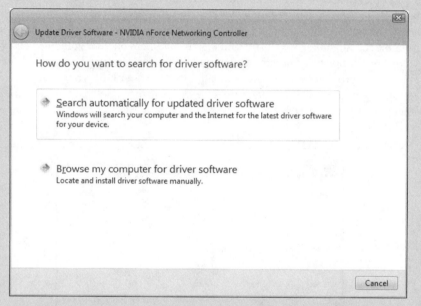

2. If you choose the automatic option, Windows searches its driver database for the best driver and installs it (after this choice, skip to Step 5). However, if you have obtained a new driver from the device manufacturer, you should choose the Install from a List or Specific Location radio button, click Next, and then follow the next steps.

3. In the selection window that appears, choose the location Windows should search for the new driver, or you can choose the Let Me Pick option, so you can manually choose the location of the new driver. For example, if you have the driver on floppy disk, you can make that selection, or if you downloaded the driver, you may want to select it manually.

However, Windows doesn't guarantee you are making a good selection, so be sure you have the correct and most current driver for your device before using this option.

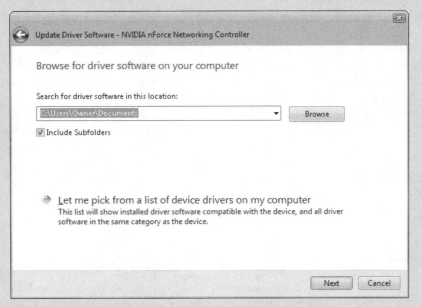

4. In the Update window, select the driver file you want to install, or click the Have Disk button to select the driver from a disk. Make your selection, click Next, and Windows installs the new driver.

5. Click Finish to complete the wizard.

The next button on the Driver tab is the *Roll Back Driver option*. Let's say you download a new driver for a hardware device. You use the Update Driver option to install the new driver, but now your device is not working. You want to return to using the old device driver, but how? In the past, that process could be difficult, but Windows Vista includes this helpful roll-back feature. When you install a new driver, a backup file is created, and the old driver is saved on your computer's hard disk. In case you want to roll back to the old driver, simply click the Roll Back Driver button, and the new driver will be removed and the old one reinstalled. If you like to install new hardware and are constantly on the prowl for better drivers, this feature can be a real lifesaver. Additionally, this feature is often used in Safe mode to update a critical driver that has gone bad and is stopping Windows from booting.

The final option is the Uninstall button. The *Uninstall button* simply removes the driver from your computer, which essentially uninstalls the device from the OS. If you click this option, a warning message appears asking whether you are sure you want to continue.

Did you
know?

What Is an IRQ?

Devices installed on your computer use *interrupt request lines (IRQs)* to gain access to the processor. Your computer's processor is the brain of the computer; it performs all computations and calculations. Most system components use the processor to accomplish tasks. The IRQ enables the device to get to the processor. Because processors in Windows Vista can handle only one processor task, or thread, at a time, the IRQ enables the device to get access to the processor in an organized way. The IRQ prevents two different devices from trying to access the processor at the same time (although certain devices can share an IRQ). IRQ conflicts were common device problems in the past, but Windows Vista automatically handles these settings for you. With Windows Vista using newer hardware, IRQ conflicts are now quite rare.

NOTE
Remember, if you simply remove a device from your computer, Windows Vista will detect the removal and automatically uninstall the driver. Under most circumstances, you don't need to use the Uninstall option on the Driver tab, but the option is made available to you if you want to uninstall the driver without physically removing the device from your computer. However, the next time you reboot, Windows will redetect and reinstall the device unless you physically remove it from the computer.

Resources

The *Resources tab,* shown in Figure 6-4, tells what computer resources the device is using. For some devices, you can use this tab to manually change the resource allocation Windows XP has established for the device. As you can imagine, you have to know what you're doing before you tinker with these settings. I do *not* advise you to make changes here without qualified assistance.

TIP
Making incorrect changes on the Resources tab can cause the device to stop functioning and may also cause other devices to stop functioning. I repeat, I do not *advise you to make changes here without qualified assistance.*

The best thing about the Resources tab is it tells you if any conflicts have occurred with other devices. As you can see in Figure 6-4, no conflicts exist. If conflicts did exist, however, this tab would indicate the kind of conflict and the other device that was conflicting with it. Again, this information is helpful when you're troubleshooting a device that isn't working properly. Note, not all devices give you a Resources tab, so don't worry if you don't see one for the particular device you're inspecting.

FIGURE 6-4   Resources tab

Windows Update Driver Settings

Windows Vista also includes a device-driver setting feature that determines how device drivers are handled when they are downloaded with Windows Update. In short, this is a security feature that helps you use new drivers.

If you access System Properties in the Control Panel (or right-click Computer and choose Properties, and then choose Advanced System Settings), you can click the Hardware tab, and then choose the Windows Update Driver Settings. You see a single window that gives you three options:

- Check for drivers automatically.

- Ask me each time I connect a new device before checking for drivers.

- Never check for drivers when I connect a device.

Windows Vista recommends you use the first option, so Vista can check for drivers on Microsoft.com and download them automatically when needed.

Hardware Troubleshooting Tips

I wish I could say you will never have hardware problems with Windows Vista. Although many of you will escape hardware difficulties, I'm afraid some of you will have the same problems I have had. Fortunately, hardware problems don't have to be too difficult to solve if you take appropriate actions. Here's a list of my best troubleshooting tips regarding Windows Vista hardware:

- Relax. If a problem occurs or you can't get a device installed, work through the problem calmly and slowly. A hardware problem or failure won't cause your computer to disintegrate.

- If you're trying to install a new device, verify the device is Plug and Play and it is supported by Windows Vista.

- Check the device to make certain it's attached to the correct port or installed in your computer correctly. Reread the installation instructions and don't forget to power down and unplug your computer!

- Use Windows Help to access the Hardware Troubleshooter. This feature can often help you solve problems with a particular device.

- If a device is installed, but not working or not working properly, check the General and Resources tabs of the device's properties sheets in Device Manager. These tabs may tell you what is wrong with the device.

- If a hardware device is installed and not working well, odds are good a driver problem exists. Check the manufacturer's web site for an updated driver.

- If you cannot get the device to work properly, call the manufacturer for technical support. Often users are hesitant to seek telephone help, but these services are provided to help you solve problems. Take advantage of them!

If you're still having problems, call Microsoft Technical Support. You should find a telephone support number and related information with the documentation that came with Windows Vista. Again, don't hesitate to get help from Microsoft if you need it.

Chapter 7

Use Printers, Scanners, and Digital Cameras

How to...

- Install a printer
- Manage printers
- Use the print queue
- Install and configure scanners and digital cameras

Windows Vista makes external hardware easy to use. In Chapter 6, you learned about installing and managing hardware in Windows Vista. In this chapter, we explore some specialized hardware devices, specifically, printers, scanners, and digital cameras. For years, both desktop and home-based computing have supported printers, and later, scanners and digital cameras. Windows Vista makes using these devices easier than ever and, in this chapter, you learn how to install and manage them.

Check Out the Printers Folder

Windows Vista contains a *Printers folder* that stores information about any printers or fax machines connected to your computer and enables you to set up new printers and virtual fax machines. The Printers folder is found in the Control Panel. If you open the folder, you see a simple interface (shown in Figure 7-1) that gives you an icon for any existing printers set up on your computer. You also see options to open wizards to help you set up new printers and a setup icon for virtual fax machines.

Install a New Printer

You can use the Add a Printer Wizard in the Printers folder to help you install a new printer on your computer. Before tackling the wizard, however, you have a little work to do away from your keyboard. First, make certain your printer is compatible with Windows Vista. If you're thinking of buying a new printer, read the label carefully. The printer should explicitly say it is compatible with Windows Vista.

 The odds are good that if a printer is compatible with Windows 2000 or XP, it will work fine with Vista. The only potential problem could be an incompatible driver. Check out Chapter 6 for more information about device drivers.

Before starting the wizard, you also need to unpack, set up, and attach your printer's cable to the correct port on your computer. You'll probably be using a USB port on the back of your computer, and your computer may even have a picture of a printer next to the port where you should connect it. You may also use a USB printer, in which case you need to connect the printer USB cable to the USB port or hub. The important thing here is to break out the printer manufacturer's instruction booklet and take a few minutes to read through it. The instruction booklet tells you exactly how to attach your printer to the computer and how you should proceed

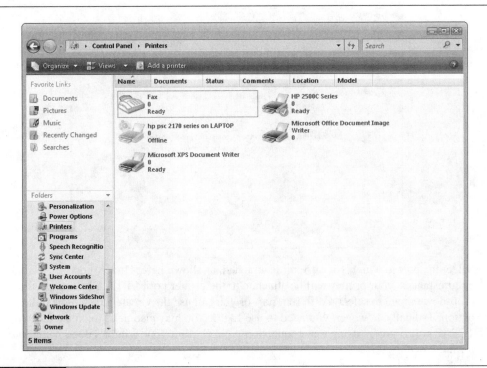

FIGURE 7-1   Printers folder

with the setup. In fact, some printers are shipped with their own setup program found on a CD-ROM. The key to success is to read and make sure you know what you should do to get the printer correctly installed on your computer.

Once the printer is attached to your computer and you have read the printer documentation, you may need to use the Add a Printer Wizard to get the printer installed (check the instructions that came with your printer). If you need to use the Add a Printer Wizard, it's easy. Make sure your printer is attached to your computer correctly and that it's turned on. Then, just follow these easy steps:

1. In the Printers folder, click the Add a Printer option on the toolbar.

2. The next window gives you two radio buttons for selecting either a local printer or a printer connection (network printer). A *local printer* means the printer is attached directly to your computer or you are using a remote TCP/IP printer that is using a local port to your computer (see Chapter 11 for more information about setting up remote printers). If you're on a network and you want to use a printer attached to another computer, click the Network option. Make your selection, and then click Next. (If you're installing a network printer, skip to Step 7.)

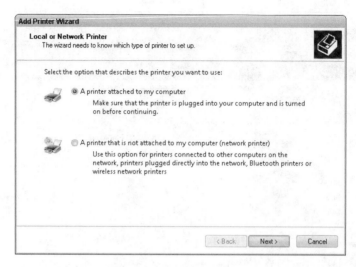

3. Select the port to which your printer is attached, as shown here. Under most circumstances, your printer will be attached to the printer port, LPT1. You can use the drop-down menu to select a different port or you can use the Create a New Port radio button. Typically, however, you need to use LPT1. You may also need to create a new TCP/IP port if you're using that connection type. Consult your printer's documentation for more details.

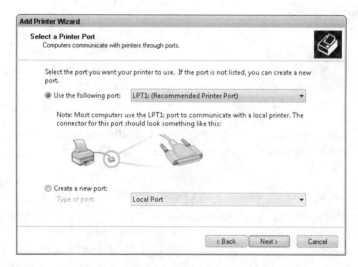

4. In the Install Printer Software window, shown next, select the manufacturer of your printer in the left-hand list, select the printer model in the right-hand list, and then click Next. If you have an installation disk, click the Have Disk button to install the printer software from a floppy disk or CD-ROM. However, remember, the drivers on the CD-ROM may have been updated, so you should check the manufacturer's web site for updated drivers.

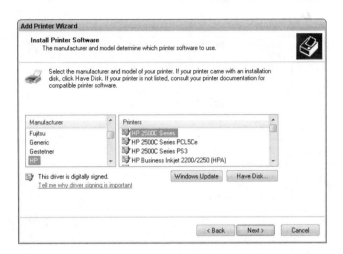

5. In the Name Your Printer window, type a friendly name, and then click either Yes or No to use the printer as the computer's default printer and if you want to print a test page. Click Next.

6. The next window asks you whether you want to print a test page. Simply choose either Yes or No, and click Next. Click Finish to complete installation.

7. If you chose to install a network printer in Step 3, a window appears, so Windows Vista can search for shared printers on your network. In an office network, consult your network administrator for the correct printer connection information. If Vista can't find a printer, the next page gives you the option to browse the network for it or to locate it by its UNC path. Make your selections and click Next.

8. Set up locations for the network printer. Enter a friendly name for the printer and click the Yes radio button if you want your Windows programs to use this printer as the default printer. Then click Finish.

Configure Your Printer

Once you install a printer, a printer icon appears in the Printers folder. You can use this printer icon to access the printer's properties sheets, so you can configure a number of different options for your printer. Several options are available, and some of them are a bit confusing. However, the following sections explain each of the options to you. To access the printer's properties sheets, right-click its icon in the Printers folder, and then choose Properties. You see a printer Properties window with several tabs. Depending on your printer, you may have more tabs than those listed here—consult your printer documentation for more information about configuration options for your printer.

General

The *General tab* gives you information about the printer, and it also gives you two button options. First, you have the option to print a test page by clicking the Print Test Page button. After you click the button, a window appears asking you whether the test page was printed correctly.

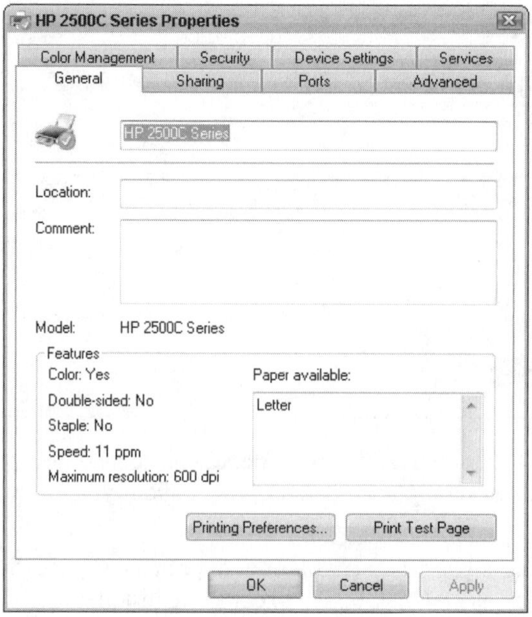

HP 2500C Series Properties

| Color Management | Security | Device Settings | Services |
| General | Sharing | Ports | Advanced |

HP 2500C Series

Location:

Comment:

Model: HP 2500C Series

Features
Color: Yes
Double-sided: No   Paper available:
Staple: No   Letter
Speed: 11 ppm
Maximum resolution: 600 dpi

[Printing Preferences...]   [Print Test Page]

[OK]   [Cancel]   [Apply]

FIGURE 7-2   Printing Preferences

If it wasn't, click No, and the Windows Help files open to help you solve the problem. The second option is Printing Preferences. When you click this button, the Printing Preferences window appears, as shown in Figure 7-2, where you can choose to print pages in portrait, landscape, front to back, and so on. You see both a Layout and a Paper/Quality tab, and the options here are self-explanatory.

TIP *Be sure to check your printer's documentation for special instructions about quality settings and features that may be available to you.*

Sharing

The *Sharing tab* enables you to share the printer. If you want to share the printer, simply click the Share Name radio button and enter a desired name. Network users will see this name when they want to connect to the shared printer. Windows Vista also has a feature that enables you to provide different drivers to network users. Remember from Chapter 6 that a driver is a piece of software your computer uses to communicate with some device. Different operating systems use different drivers. If you want to allow Windows operating systems other than Vista to connect to and use the shared printer, you can configure drivers for those systems. When network users connect to your computer, your Vista computer automatically downloads the printer driver to their computers. However, if a Windows 2000 / XP computer wants to connect, the drivers used for Vista probably won't be compatible. By clicking the Additional Drivers button on the Sharing tab,

FIGURE 7-3   Additional Drivers

you can choose to provide the appropriate drivers for that operating system (OS). Place a check mark in the check box next to the OS you want to select and click OK, as shown in Figure 7-3. You may need to provide your printer's CD-ROM, so Vista can get the needed driver files.

About Configuring Network Permissions and Access

Having your Windows Vista computer configured to use a network and share resources on a network is important. Also, the person who owns a network printer can let you use the printer or not—depending on what permissions he or she assigns. Just because you see a printer on your network doesn't mean you have permission to use it. When in doubt, ask a network administrator. If you're trying to connect to a printer in a home network, make sure the shared network printer is set up, functioning, and available. You can learn how to set up your computer for network service in Chapter 11.

If you download additional drivers from the manufacturer's web site, remember they may be in a compressed folder. You need to decompress the folder first before trying to use the drivers. Right-click the downloaded compressed folder and click Extract All.

Ports

The *Ports tab* enables you to make changes to the physical or logical port used for printing. For example, the typical printer port is labeled LPT1. However, configuration issues with your computer may make it necessary to connect the printer to a different port. If you're using a network printer, you may need to change the port that it is connected to as well. The Ports tab enables you to make these changes by changing the current port, as well as adding, removing, and deleting ports. All these actions tend to be more advanced and, under most circumstances, you should never have to make any configuration changes here. However, if you need to adjust or change ports that are in use, Windows Vista provides the Add, Remove, and Configure options to make port configuration easy.

It is important to remember you don't need to change printer ports unless you have physically moved your printer to a different port on your computer or the network path to a particular network printer has changed.

Advanced

The *Advanced tab,* shown in Figure 7-4, isn't all that advanced—it just provides you with a bunch of configuration options for printing that aren't necessarily related to each other. The following options are available on this tab:

- ■ **Availability**   Use the radio buttons to configure the time the printer is available. By default, the printer is always available, but you can place restrictions on when the printer can be used, if necessary. This setting is typically used in network environments in which you want to make certain that users can print only during work hours.

- ■ **Priority**   This setting can range from 1 to 99, with 1 being the default. This setting simply tells you that higher priority documents will print before lower priority documents (with 99 being the highest). Typically, you don't need to make any changes to this setting.

- ■ **Driver**   Occasionally, your printer manufacturer may produce a new driver for your printer. The new driver may increase performance or solve compatibility problems with a new version of Windows. If you need to update the printer driver, you can do so by clicking the New Driver button on this tab. This action opens a portion of the Hardware Update Wizard that can help you install the new printer driver. See Chapter 6 for more information about device drivers.

- ■ **Spooling**   This simply means that print jobs are stored on your hard disk while the computer waits for the printer to be ready. For example, let's say you print ten Word documents. It may take several minutes to print the documents, so while one document is printing, the others wait in the spool until their turn. Why? The answer is simple: *Spooling* moves the documents to the hard disk, so you get control over your application

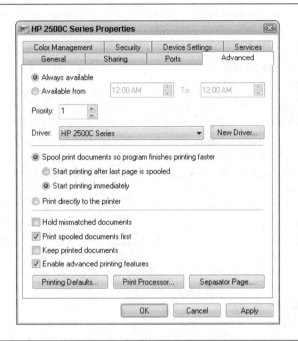

FIGURE 7-4   Advanced tab

without waiting for them to print. Without the spool, your application would be tied up until the print job finishes. With the spool, you can return to work or play and not have to wait for the file to print. You have the following spool options:

- **Spool Print Documents so Program Finishes Printing Faster**   This option is enabled by default and tells your printer to spool print jobs to your hard disk. You should leave this setting enabled.

- **Start Printing after Last Page Is Spooled**   This option holds the print job until the application spools all the pages. This frees up your application faster, but it delays printing longer.

- **Start Printing Immediately**   Printing begins as soon as the first page is spooled. In other words, printing starts faster because Vista doesn't wait until the entire document is spooled. This is the default setting.

- **Print Directly to Printer**   This option doesn't spool print jobs, but sends them directly to the printer. This setting causes your application to wait until the document finishes printing before you can work on other tasks. In other words, this setting doesn't use the spool. I don't recommend this setting, because you end up waiting for jobs to print before you can continue to work or play.

- **Hold Mismatched Documents**   Documents that don't match printer setup configurations are held in the queue instead of being printed. This setting can be helpful in troubleshooting mismatch problems.

- **Print Spooled Documents First**   Documents sent to the spool are always printed first. This setting is enabled by default.

- **Keep Printed Documents**   This setting tells the spooler not to delete documents out of the spool once they have been printed. Typically, you should not enable this setting.

- **Enable Advanced Printing Features**   This option, enabled by default, gives you advanced printing options, which vary with the type of printer. You may be able to manage page order, pages per sheet, and other printing options. Consult your printer's documentation for more information.

The final portion of the Advanced tab enables you to access printer defaults (Printing Preferences window) and print processor options; you can also set up a separator page here. You shouldn't make changes to the print processor configuration unless your printer documentation tells you to do so. The other setting options are self-explanatory.

Security and Device Settings

The *Security tab* enables you to configure the users and/or groups that can access your printer if it's shared on a network. If you're using Windows Vista Home edition, you won't see a Security tab because your system is configured for simple home networking. If you are a Windows Vista Ultimate user, you'll see the Security tab.

The Device Settings tab may contain additional configuration options, such as paper feed options, depending on your printer. See your printer's documentation for more details.

Depending on your printer, you may see additional tabs, such as Color Management and Services. These tabs apply specifically to your printer and, most of the time, they don't need to be edited. See your printer documentation for additional details.

Manage Print Jobs

Once your printer is set up and configured the way you want, you can print all kinds of documents and files—almost anything you like. As you are printing documents, a small printer icon appears in the Notification Area. This icon represents the *print queue,* which is the line of documents in your print spool waiting to be printed. You can manage the print queue by right-clicking this icon, and then choosing the printer's name. Doing this opens a small print queue window:

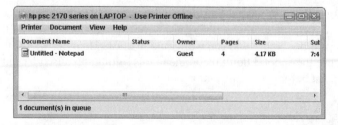

About Printer Pooling

In some network environments, printer pools are used. A *pool* is a collection of identical printers that are seen as one logical printer. For example, let's say you print to a printer named Company. To you and the computer, Company appears as one printer; but with pooling, Company can be five printers, for example, that are connected together. This feature enables all users to print to the same printer instead of five individual printers appearing on the network. If you need to enable printer pooling on your Vista computer and have several printers connected to different ports, you can select the check box option available on the Ports tab. Also refer to your printer's documentation for more information about pooling options.

7

As you can see, one file is printing while another is spooling and waiting to be printed. You can take several actions by using the menus to manage documents in the print queue. From the Printer menu, you can

■ **Pause Printing**   This action stops all printing.

■ **Cancel Print Documents**   If you send a bunch of documents to the printer and change your mind, you don't have to waste your paper and ink. Just use the Cancel option to dump everything out of the print queue.

From the Document menu, you can

■ **Pause**   Select a print job in the list and click Pause to stop printing.

■ **Cancel**   Select a print job in the list and click Cancel to cancel it.

If you use the Document menu, you can pause printing, resume printing, restart printing, and even cancel documents currently in the print queue. For example, let's say you want to print ten documents. You send all of them to the print queue, but you suddenly realize you do not want to print the ninth document. You don't have to waste your paper—just open this print queue window, select the ninth print job, and choose Document | Cancel.

TIP   *You can also remove any document from the print queue by right-clicking the document in the queue and clicking Cancel.*

Troubleshoot Common Printer Problems

Windows Vista includes better printer support than previous versions of Windows, so troubleshooting doesn't have to be a major chore. Remember, you should consult your printer documentation when you experience a problem, because some issues you need to resolve may be specific to your printer. The following sections tell you about some of the most common printer problems and their solutions.

NOTE   *You can use the Windows Troubleshooter tool to help you solve problems. See Chapter 20 for more information about troubleshooting.*

Printed Text Is Garbled

You have a document you want to print, it's nice and neat on the screen, but when you print the document, the text comes out garbled. This is a common problem typically caused by one of two things. First, the document you're trying to print may be damaged or corrupted. You can test this by printing a different document. Second, if the text still appears garbled, the most likely cause of the problem is your printer driver. Your printer driver may not be compatible, the wrong driver may be installed, or the driver may have become corrupted. Use the Details tab of the printer's properties sheets to reinstall the driver or install the correct driver.

The Printer Does Not Work

If your printer does not seem to work, make sure it's turned on and that it's attached to the correct port on the back of your computer. If this doesn't solve the problem, you may need to reinstall the driver and reboot Windows Vista. Sometimes internal issues can prevent a printer from working, and a reboot may take care of the problem. If these actions don't solve the problem, consult your printer documentation. You may have a printer hardware issue.

Printing Is Very Slow

If printing to a local printer is very slow, you may be running low on hard disk space. Remember, your printer uses part of your hard disk space to spool documents for background printing. You should have at least 10MB of free hard disk space available.

If you have enough free disk space, check your spool settings on the printer Properties window's Advanced tab to make sure spooling is enabled. Also, try defragmenting your hard disk to see if that helps. For more information about defragmentation, see Chapter 19.

A Certain Document Will Not Print

If a certain document will not print, try to print a different document from within the same application. If you can print another document within the same application, the problematic document is most likely corrupted. If printing is sporadic with the application or several applications, turn off the printer, wait ten seconds, and turn it on again. This may resolve the problems (you may try rebooting your computer as well).

Print Quality Is Poor

If your files will print, but the print quality is poor, you may need to make changes to printer-specific tabs within the printer's Properties window. Consult your printer documentation for help.

Use Fax Support in Windows Vista

Fax modems have been around for some time now, and support for fax modem capabilities continues in Windows Vista. Using a fax modem, you can fax documents to other fax machines, just as you would with a physical fax machine. Faxing tends to be application-specific, but I'll mention a couple of things about faxing with Windows Vista. If your modem is installed, you can double-click the Faxicon in the Printer folder in Control Panel. This opens the Fax and Scan application. The Fax and Scan console enables you to manage incoming and outgoing faxes, as well as send faxes from this simple console.

If you want to send a new fax, click the New Fax button and follow the steps you see. Overall, the Windows Fax and Scan application works a lot like a mail application and is rather intuitive to use.

Use Scanners and Digital Cameras with Windows Vista

During the past few years, the popularity of scanners and digital cameras has exploded. After all, we all like to use electronic pictures that we can print, e-mail to friends and family, or store on the computer's hard drive instead of in an album under the couch. Because of these devices' popularity, Windows Vista includes a Scanners and Cameras folder in the Control Panel that enables you to add a device and view its properties. You can use the Add Device option to add scanners and cameras to your system, and then manage them from this folder.

Install Scanners and Cameras

Installing a scanner or digital camera is a lot like installing a printer. Always consult the documentation and instructions that came with the scanner or digital camera for setup and management information. Some models include their own installation disk or CD-ROM, so be sure to check out the documentation carefully. Also, make sure any scanner or camera you purchase is compatible with Windows Vista.

You can use the Add Device option in the Scanners and Cameras folder in the Control Panel to install a new scanner or camera. You may not need to use the wizard, however. In many cases, Windows can automatically detect your scanner or camera via Plug and Play; but if it doesn't, you can use this wizard to assist you.

Like the Add a Printer Wizard, the Add Device option is easy to use. Just connect the scanner or camera to your computer, turn it on, and then follow these easy steps:

1. Click the Add Device icon in the Scanners and Cameras folder in the Control Panel.

2. Click Next on the Welcome screen.

3. Select the make and model of your camera or scanner, or click the Have Disk button to install it from a floppy disk or CD-ROM. Make your selection, and then click Next.

4. Select a port for the device (refer to your scanner or camera documentation) and click Next.

5. Give the device a friendly name, and then click Next.

Once you have your scanner and/or camera installed on Windows Vista, icons for them appear in the Scanners and Cameras folder, as shown in Figure 7-5.

Important to note here is, in many cases, you won't have to use this wizard to install a camera or scanner. Because of Plug and Play, you can often directly plug a scanner or camera into your computer's USB port, and Windows Vista will automatically detect the camera or scanner and show it to you as an external hard drive (which you can then open and access). Of course, you should read the camera or scanner manufacturer's installation instructions for Windows Vista and follow them—this can help reduce the likelihood of any problems.

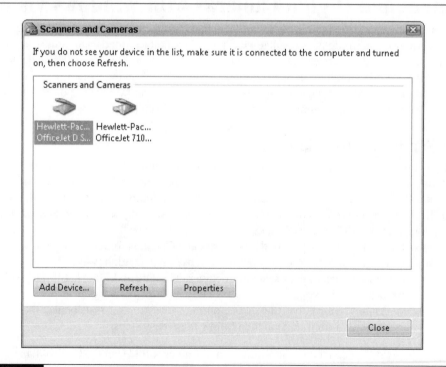

FIGURE 7-5   Scanners and Cameras folder

Manage Scanner and Camera Properties

You can right-click a scanner or camera icon in the Scanners and Cameras folder in the Control Panel and click Properties to access the device's properties sheets. As you might guess, the contents of the properties sheets depend on the type of device, as well as the make and model, much as with printers. Various options are available to you. For example, you can have a camera or scanner always save files to a certain folder and, for some devices, you can manage color settings here. Check your scanner or digital camera documentation for information about configuring these properties sheets.

Be sure to check your scanner or camera manufacturer's web site periodically. Often, you can find information about updates and how-to steps for troubleshooting common problems.

7

Part II

Get Connected

Chapter 8

Create Connections to the Internet

How to...

- Configure your modem
- Set up dialing rules and options
- Create Internet and dial-up connections
- Create broadband connections
- Edit dial-up connections

Simply put, Internet connections give you access to the Internet—a way to connect your computer to an Internet service provider (ISP), so you can use the Internet, and send and receive e-mail. In the past, connectivity to the Internet was one of those "extra" computing services—something only advanced computer users wanted. Not so today; virtually every computer is sold with the hardware and software necessary to connect to the Internet, and more and more computer users every day are joining the World Wide Web.

Like previous versions of Windows, Windows Vista provides the software you need to connect your computer to the Internet. Internet connectivity in Windows Vista is easier than ever, and some helpful wizards guide you every step of the way. In this chapter, you see how to set up your computer with an Internet connection, so you can be surfing the Internet in no time!

Internet Connections 101

Before we jump into the business of creating and managing Internet connections, let's first make sure you're up to speed about those connections. An Internet connection allows your computer to access the Internet: you can send e-mail, look at web pages, and download information with your Internet connection. An Internet connection is achieved through an ISP. The Internet itself is free but, generally, you must pay an ISP a fee (usually monthly, but annual and semiannual plans are also available) to access the Internet.

Think of the Internet as a busy freeway. To get on the freeway (the Internet), you must drive onto an access ramp (access the ISP), so your car (your computer) can enter the traffic. All information you send and receive over the Internet comes through server computers at your ISP before reaching your computer, so your ISP can also be thought of as the middleman that stands between your computer and the Internet. The *connection* to the Internet, then, is a physical connection that exists between your computer and your ISP. A few different types of connections exist, but they fall into two distinct categories—dial-up and broadband. The following sections explore both of these types.

Connecting with a Dial-Up Connection

The most common type of Internet access is *broadband,* but many people still use dial-up accounts in areas where broadband is not yet available. With a dial-up account, your computer uses a modem connected to your telephone line to dial an access number—just as you would make a telephone call.

Once the ISP answers the call, your computer sends user name and password information, so it can be authenticated (validated) by the ISP. After the ISP authenticates your information, you can use the Internet through the ISP. Dial-up access is the most common type of access, with 56 Kbps (or 56K) modems being the most common modem speed. Most new computers sold today are equipped with an *internal modem,* which is considered a standard piece of hardware. All computer operating systems, including Windows XP, give you software wizards and helpful information, so you can easily set up an Internet connection with your modem. You explore modem configuration in the section "Configure Modem Properties."

Connecting with a Broadband Connection

Today's Internet contains rich multimedia and surfing experiences. You can view all kinds of graphics, listen to music, and even watch movies and concerts over the Internet. Although a great addition, multimedia and the cool web pages of today are much larger in size than they once were—and 56K modems are quite slow. Therefore, many people are turning to broadband, "always on" Internet access. Broadband Internet access gives you much faster speeds than dial-up connections, and you do not dial any kind of access number to connect—because your computer is always connected to the ISP, it is always connected to the Internet. If you want to use the Internet or e-mail, you simply open your Internet browser or e-mail client and begin—there's nothing for you to connect to or anything else to do.

8

Connectivity Costs

As I mentioned, the Internet itself is free, but you must pay an ISP to provide you with a connection—and you'll pay more for a faster connection. A typical dial-up connection costs around $20 a month for unlimited access and an e-mail account. If you live in a city where several ISPs are competing, you may get unlimited access for as little as $10 a month.

Broadband solutions cost more than dial-up connections. Cable and DSL unlimited access with one e-mail account typically cost you between $20 and $40 a month, depending on competition in your area. Watch for special deals where the cable or DSL hardware and setup are free, and then shop around for the best deal. Finally, if you want satellite access, you can expect to pay around $60 a month for unlimited access and one e-mail account. However, the hardware and setup are often hefty—$400 or more, depending on your purchase plan.

Three main types of broadband connections are available:

- **Cable** *Cable Internet access* uses existing cable TV connections to provide Internet access over the cable line, just as television programs are accessed over the cable line. To use cable access, the cable modem is connected to your computer's Ethernet or USB port. You can then connect to a cable outlet and use the Internet at any time. Cable Internet access can provide speeds beginning around 800 Kbps and may be quite higher, depending on the cable company and the amount of activity of other users who are accessing the same cable network. Your ISP either provides you with a cable modem for your PC (which it likely rents to you) or you can acquire one yourself.

- **DSL** *DSL (Digital Subscriber Line)* typically provides a dedicated, secure line that connects directly to your ISP. This copper line connects directly to a switchboard of sorts at the phone company, which connects to your ISP. DSL is the most popular type of broadband connectivity available today, and it can give you super-fast speeds—often beyond 1.5 mbps. However, DSL must be supported by your phone company and ISP, so it is typically limited to more populous areas at this time. To use DSL, a special DSL adapter that uses the existing phone line in your home is connected to your computer via your computer's Ethernet or USB ports. You can either purchase the DSL adapter or rent it from the ISP.

- **Satellite** *Satellite* connections use a small satellite dish that mounts on your roof or to a pole in your yard. Information is sent and received over the disk to a satellite in orbit, which then beams data back to the ISP. Satellite connections are not that popular— yet—but they are especially helpful to people who cannot get cable or DSL. Satellite connections can give you speeds of around 800 Kbps and are currently offered by major ISPs, such as Starband (www.starband.com). To use satellite access, you must have a satellite dish, an adapter for your PC, and special software to run the connection. Your ISP provides all of this when you purchase the satellite access.

Configure Your Modem

As mentioned in the previous section, the most common type of Internet access is broadband, but you may need to use a dial-up account, which uses a modem in your computer, depending on where you live. Unless you have paid for DSL, satellite, or some other broadband service (and have the hardware to connect to your computer), you'll access the Internet via your internal modem.

Configuring modems has been a painful experience for Internet users in the past. I remember staying up late at night and literally pulling my hair out trying to get a modem to work correctly. Although modems can still be complicated, we're a long way from those days, and setting up your modem in Windows Vista should be no problem.

Before getting into the details, I do want to mention that dial-up connections tend to be problematic for computer users because you have to work with two different components. You have to configure the actual connection, which we do in the section "Create Connections to the Internet," and you have to configure your modem, which the connection uses. As you work with connections, just remember that successful Internet access requires the configuration of a connection and your modem. The following sections tell you how to configure your computer's modem.

Did you know?

Your Modem's Actual Speed

So, you're using a 56K modem—you should get 56 Kbps speed, right? Wrong! As a result of regulations, the highest speed you are likely to get with a 56K modem is about 48 Kbps. Even then, the speed must be matched with your ISP's modem, and telephone line conditions can lower the speed. If you have used the Internet, you may wonder why you get different connection speeds at different times. Local, ISP, and Internet traffic all affect modem speed, so you are often at the mercy of your ISP and phone-line traffic in general. This is one reason connections are often faster early in the morning or late at night. The distance your home is from your neighborhood's phone switch is also a factor with your speed.

Install a Modem

8

Your computer probably has an internal modem currently installed—after all, modems are a standard piece of hardware these days. You may have purchased a different modem, a particular one you want to use—that's fine, too. Windows Vista should automatically detect and install a Plug-and-Play modem, so modem installation works just like that of any other piece of hardware. Check out Chapter 6 for more information about installing devices.

Configure Modem Properties

To make modem configuration easier, a Phone and Modem Options icon is included in the Control Panel. If you double-click the icon, you see a Phone and Modem Options window that contains Dialing Rules, Modems, and Advanced tabs. The following sections show you what you can configure on each of these (and why you would want to).

Modems Tab

Today's modems do a good job of setting themselves up. You don't have to worry about inputting a lot of information to make the modem work, but you may want to adjust some of the settings to meet your needs. The *Modems tab,* shown in Figure 8-1, provides a simple interface that lists the modem(s) installed on your computer and provides you with a few buttons.

You can see Add and Remove buttons at the bottom of the screen. If you click the Add button, the New Modem Wizard appears and searches for additional modems attached to your computer. If the wizard finds one, it automatically installs the modem. If the wizard doesn't find one, you can select it from a list. This is the same type of installation wizard you see when installing various other hardware devices (see Chapter 6). If you select a modem in the list and click Remove, the modem's software is uninstalled from your computer. Under most circumstances, you don't need to use either of these buttons—unless you just love modems and want to use two or three of them on your computer.

Modems tab

You also see a Properties button. Select the desired modem in the list (if more than one appears), and then click the Properties button to see properties specific to that modem. Several properties tabs appear. The General tab, shown in Figure 8-2, tells you the status of the device (whether or not it is working). You can also use the drop-down menu at the bottom of the screen to disable the device if necessary.

Modem Tab   On the *Modem tab,* you have three basic options. First, you can adjust the slider bar for the modem's speaker volume. A lower setting is typically best here, unless you love to hear that familiar modem connection noise. Next, you see a Maximum Port Speed drop-down menu. You can use this drop-down menu to set a maximum speed at which you want the modem to connect. Typically, you leave this setting at the default, so you get the highest connection speed possible. Finally, a Dial Control section with a Wait for Dial Tone Before Dialing check box is probably enabled and, typically, should remain enabled, so your modem checks for a dial tone before dialing the number.

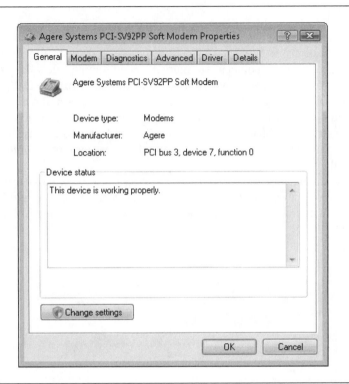

FIGURE 8-2   General tab

Diagnostics Tab   On the *Diagnostics tab,* you can run a query, which is simply a test your computer runs with the modem to make sure it's working properly. You can also view a log file. The information you see here is basically a lot of commands, and few will have any meaning to you. This information can be helpful, though, if you have to call technical support concerning problems with your modem.

Advanced Tab   The *Advanced tab* gives you a single Extra Settings field, where you can enter additional modem string commands. You don't need to do anything here unless your modem documentation or the technical support explicitly instructs you to make a change. The extra initialization commands entered here are most often used to solve problems with modem connectivity.

Driver Tab   Finally, the *Driver tab* is like all such tabs for hardware in Windows Vista. Use this tab to update or change drivers for the device. See Chapter 6 to learn more about drivers and the configuration options presented on this tab.

Dialing Rules Tab

In the Phone and Modem Options window, the *Dialing Rules tab,* shown in Figure 8-3, provides a place to configure locations. In Windows Vista, a *location* is a place from which you dial in to the Internet. For each location, you can configure different dialing rules. For example, let's say you use a laptop computer for your work. Some days you dial from the Dallas office, and some days you dial from the Seattle office. Depending on your location, the dialing rules and preferences you need will be different. Rather than having to reconfigure your dialing rules manually each time you travel, you can simply create different locations and use those locations as needed. By clicking the desired location, you can use the rules configured for that location immediately and easily.

To create a new location, click the New button. The New Location window appears with three tabs. Also, if you want to make changes to a location, select the location and click the Edit button, which gives you the same tabs that appear in the New Location window. Either way,

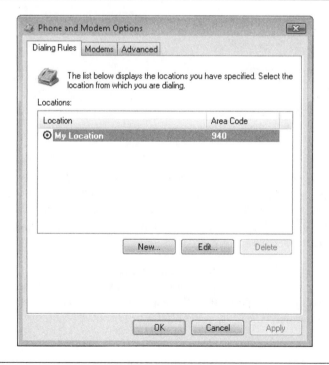

FIGURE 8-3　Dialing Rules tab

you can create new locations or edit existing locations using these tabs, which we explore in the following sections.

If you're using Windows Vista from a home or office on a desktop system that stays in one place, then all you need is the default "My Location," which you can edit as necessary.

General Tab   The *General tab,* shown in Figure 8-4, enables you to make some basic dialing rules configurations. First, you can name the location by entering a recognizable name in the provided text box. If you travel, you may consider naming the location after cities or areas, such as Dallas, Canada, Northwest, and so on.

Next, use the Country/Region drop-down menu to select the country or region for the location, and then enter the area code. You then see a collection of options called *Dialing Rules,* which are simply fields where you enter information, if necessary, that tells Windows Vista

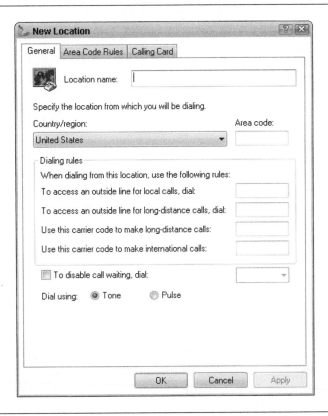

FIGURE 8-4   General tab

how to dial the connection. For example, if you need to dial 9 to access an outside line, a field is provided for entering this information. You also see configuration options to disable call waiting and to use either tone or pulse dialing.

Area Code Rules Tab In the past, dialing an area code typically meant you were making a long-distance call. However, in many cities, several area codes are now considered local. Windows Vista has to know how to handle different area codes, which is the reason for area code rules. If you click the *Area Code Rules* tab, shown here, you can generate a list of area code rules specific to a particular location. Obviously, area code rules from one location to the next may vary, so Windows Vista gives you the option to configure area code rules on a location-by-location basis.

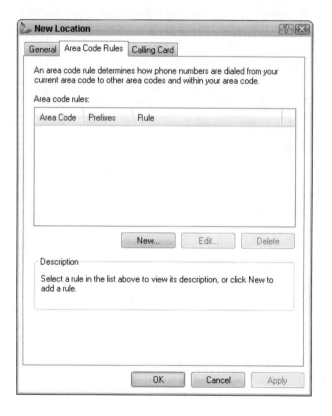

To create a new area code rule, click the New button, which opens the New Area Code Rule window, shown next. Enter the area code for this rule in the Area Code field. In the Prefixes section of the window, you can specify how prefixes are handled for the area code, such as to use all prefixes or to limit them to a specific set. Under the Rules section of the window, you can tell Windows Vista to dial 1 in front of the area code or include the area code for all numbers.

As you generate your list of area code rules, you can edit them or delete them at any time using the Edit and Delete buttons on the Area Code Rules tab.

> TIP   *Create only area code rules you need. Too many area code rules become more confusing than helpful.*

Calling Card Tab   The final New Location window tab is Calling Card. In the *Calling Card tab,* you can use the provided list to select the type of calling card you want to use, and then you can enter the account number and PIN. If you don't need to use a calling card for long-distance calls, you don't need to configure anything here, of course. If your calling card is not listed on the menu, click the New button and enter the necessary information about your calling card.

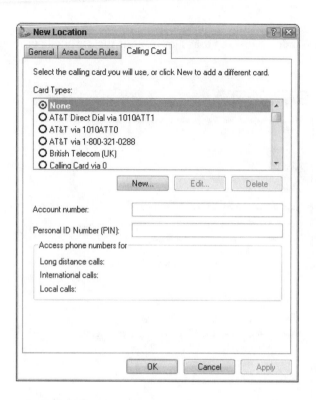

Using calling cards is a great idea when you're away from home, but the feature doesn't always work well. Your computer has to negotiate the call and the calling card number with the phone system, and depending on your location, that negotiation process simply doesn't work well all the time. It's still a good feature, though, and one you should consider working with if you travel a lot and need to dial in with a calling card.

Advanced Tab

The final Phone and Modem Options tab is the *Advanced tab,* which lists information about telephony software installed on your Windows Vista computer. You don't need to configure anything in this window for your modem connection.

Create Connections to the Internet

Once you're sure your modem is installed and you have configured any connection and dialing rules you need, you can turn to creating your Internet connection. If you're using a dial-up connection, remember your Internet connection uses your modem to dial a connection, and your modem uses the modem settings to manage the call. Think of these two items as a duet—two pieces that work together to accomplish one goal.

Fortunately, creating connections to the Internet is made rather easy by the *Connect to the Internet Wizard* included in Windows Vista. Once you start the wizard, it walks you through a series of steps, collecting information from you to create a connection. To use the Connect to the Internet Wizard, follow these steps:

1. Click Start | Control Panel | Network and Sharing Center.

2. In the left pane, click the Set Up a Connection or Network option.

3. In the wizard, choose the Connect the Internet option, shown in the following illustration. This starts the Connect to the Internet Wizard.

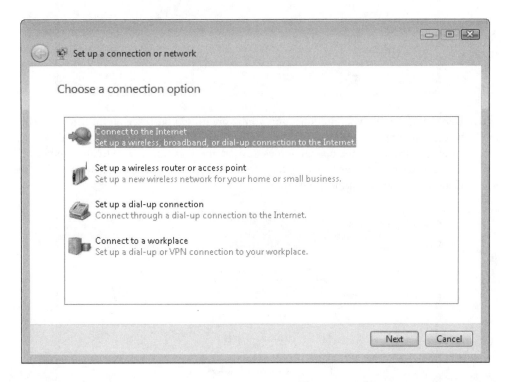

4. Click the option to set up a new connection. If you have an existing connection to the Internet and desire to create a secondary connection, you'll see an option to Browse the Internet now. Just click the Set Up a New Connection option to continue.

5. Choose how you want to connect to the Internet, either by clicking the Broadband option or the Dial-Up option.

6. Depending on the type of connection you're creating, you'll see an information window where you input the information provide by your ISP, such as user name and password. Note, you can name the connection as desired and you can choose to allow other people who use your computer to access the connection. When you're done, simply click the Connect button to test the connection.

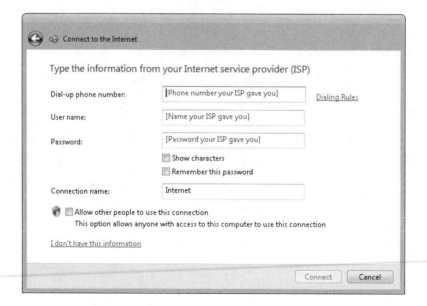

Are you having problems with your Internet connection? Open the Network Center in Control Panel and click the Diagnose Internet Connection option in the left pane. Windows Vista will examine your connection and attempt to offer a possible solution. Naturally, if you have problems with the connection that you cannot solve, you should call the technical support line for your ISP. They will be glad to assist you with the connection problem.

8

Chapter 9 — Surf the Internet

How to...

- Use Internet Explorer
- Access Internet Explorer features
- Configure Internet Explorer options

Windows Vista is an operating system (OS) designed for use on the Internet. As you learned in Chapter 8, creating connections to the Internet is quick and easy. And Windows Vista includes all the software you need to use the Internet, and to send and receive e-mail. In this chapter, we consider the new Internet Explorer browser. You can learn all about e-mail in Chapter 10. If you're new to the Internet and this is your first attempt to surf, don't worry. This chapter tells you everything you need to know!

Understand Internet Terms and Technology

Windows Vista includes a built-in tool called a web browser that enables you to use the Internet—Internet Explorer (IE). A *browser* is simply a program your computer uses to access and view web pages and content. At its core, the Web is made up of *Hypertext Markup Language (HTML)* documents. HTML is scripting language your browser reads to draw and create the nifty web pages you see. In today's Internet, several scripting languages are also used for added functionality. HTML documents are transferred from place to place using the Hypertext Transfer Protocol (HTTP). *HTTP* is a communications protocol that is a part of the *Transmission Control Protocol/Internet Protocol* (TCP/IP) suite of protocols. These common protocols and programming languages are universally used on the Internet. Now, do you really need to know anything about HTML, HTTP, or TCP/IP to use the Internet? Not at all, which is good news! However, it may help to know that just as you need Microsoft Word to read a Word document, you need a web browser to access and read web pages.

IE is built right into the Windows Vista OS. You can find the IE icon (a blue *e*) on the Start menu or on your Taskbar if Quick Launch is enabled (see Taskbar properties to turn it on).

Understand the Internet Explorer Interface

You can start IE by clicking the Internet Explorer icon on your Start menu. This action opens the web browser and, if you have a dial-up connection to the Internet, probably launches the connection automatically. If you haven't configured a connection for your computer, then Connect to the Internet Wizard instead of IE. (See Chapter 8 to learn how to configure an Internet connection.)

One thing you notice right away about IE is that it looks similar to any other folder on your computer. This is by design. Microsoft has made Windows Vista integrate closely with the Internet, so your computer can look and feel more like a web page. The IE browser, like your Vista folders, contains several menus across the top, toolbars, and a primary interface area, as shown in Figure 9-1.

FIGURE 9-1   Internet Explorer

At the top of the Internet Explorer window, you see your standard back and forward buttons, along with the Address bar where you type in the web address, and also a box to search for a subject on MSN. This option takes to you Windows Live, where you can browse for web sites that contain the desired subject. Below this area, you have a toolbar containing several important options, as well as some new ones in this version of IE. The following sections explore these features.

Favorites

The *Favorites Center* contains a few folders of generic favorites that Microsoft configures for you. You use this menu to add favorites you want to keep. For example, let's say you find a web page you like. You don't have to remember where the web page is located on the Internet—Favorites can do that for you. Click the Add Favorites button (the plus (+) sign over the Star on the toolbar) to save the web page to your Favorites list. The next time you want to visit the page, click the Favorites Center, and then click the page title you want to visit. You can also access

FIGURE 9-2   Favorites options

Feeds (a stream of data sent to you, such as a news feed) you've subscribed to and view your surfing history within this interface, as you can see in Figure 9-2.

NOTE   *A new and cool feature of Favorites involves the use of tabs, which you can read about in the following section. You can quickly open any favorite by pointing to it in the list with your mouse. You see a clickable arrow that appears, which enables you to open the favorite in a new tab, so you can have the favorite open without leaving your current web page.*

Tabs

Tabs are probably one of the best improvements in the usability of IE I've seen in a long time. In fact, I think the new tab feature is going to make your web surfing easier if you'll put them to work. If you look on the lower toolbar next to favorites, you can see the current web page tile residing on a tab. But, you can open additional web pages on other tabs, so you can toggle between them simply by clicking a tab, rather than surfing from page to page. As you can see in Figure 9-3, I currently have three web sites tabbed. You can also see a fourth tab, which is currently empty (an empty tab is always available). I can simply click the empty tab, type a URL or click a link, and the new site is added as another tab.

Once you place sites on tabs, simply click the different tabs to access the sites. If you want to close a site, click the little *X* on the tab you selected. You can add a new tab at any time by

FIGURE 9-3   Tabs in Internet Explorer

clicking the new tab and entering the URL, or you can press CTRL+T. Here are a few other things to remember about tabs:

- Press the CTRL key while clicking links or use your middle mouse button to open links on a new tab.

- Click any tab with the middle mouse button to close it.

- Press ALT+ENTER from the Address bar or Search box to open the result in a new tab.

- Click the Tab List button just before your tabs on the toolbar to see a quick list of tabs, or

- Click the Quick Tabs button (CTRL+Q) to see a minilook at each tab, shown in Figure 9-4. You can click any of the web pages in the Quick Tab interface to jump immediately to it.

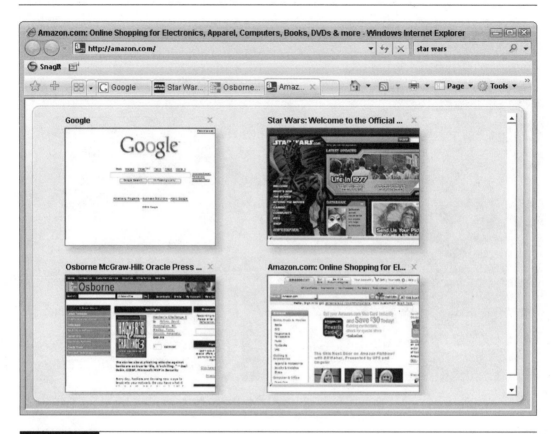

FIGURE 9-4 Quick Tabs

Home

The *Home button* enables you to jump to your home page, which is the page that opens when you first open IE, at any time. But you can also click the arrow for a drop-down menu that enables you to remove the current home page or change it to the currently selected tab. You can see a small Change Home Page dialog box, shown in the illustration on the right, where you can make your choice. Note, you can have more than one home page. Once you add them, you can simply use the Home drop-down menu to select the one you want.

Feeds and Print

The *Feeds button* enables you to access any current Internet feeds you subscribe to and, just like the Home option, you can click the drop-down menu to manage current feeds and add new ones. You can also print any web page by clicking the Print button. If you click the Print button drop-down arrow, you can also access Print Preview and Page Setup.

Page

The *Page button* enables you to open the currently selected web page in a new window, but you can also access some additional features here. If you have selected something on a web page, use this menu to access standard Cut, Copy, and Paste functions. You can save the web page, send it to someone to view via e-mail, or you can open the HTML code in Notepad, where you can edit it. Additional features are Zoom and Text Size, as well as View Source, Security Report, and Web Page Privacy Report features.

Tools

The *Tools drop-down menu* gives you access to several options, many of which are repeated in Internet Options, which you also see on this menu (these are explored in the next section). Here's a quick look at what you can access on the Tools menu:

- **Delete Browsing History**   This option deletes all history items.
- **Diagnose Connection Problems**   This option lets Windows diagnose a possible reason for connection problems if you're having problems surfing the Internet.
- **Pop-Up Blocker**   This option enables you to stop pop-up windows. You can use the option here to turn this feature on or off, or to access Pop-Up Blocker settings.
- **Phishing Filter**   *Phishing* is a technique people use on the Internet to trick users into revealing personal or financial information through an e-mail message or web site. The web sites look like legitimate web sites you would normally log into and reveal such information. The *phishing filter* works to identify these pages as false web sites to keep your personal information safe. The phishing filter is turned on by default and you should leave it turned on for your protection.
- **Manage Add-Ons**   You may use some add-ons to IE from various web sites, and you can manage them here.
- **Work Offline**   This option enables you to work without an Internet connection.
- **Windows Update**   Access Windows Update directly for possible updates to IE.
- **Full Screen**   See IE in full screen mode (you can also press F11 to access Full Screen).
- **Toolbars**   This option adjusts IE's default toolbars or creates a custom toolbar.
- **Windows Messenger**   This option opens Windows Messenger.
- **Internet Options**   Many other configuration options and features are available through Internet Options, which are explored in the next section.

9

Configure Internet Explorer Through Internet Options

You can make changes to the way IE behaves, so the browser looks and acts the way you want. You have a variety of useful options. I'll guide you through them, so you can decide which are the best for you. You can configure IE through Internet Options, which is found in your Tools menu. When you open Internet Options, you find seven different configuration tabs. The following sections show you what you can do on each tab.

General Tab

The *General tab,* shown in Figure 9-5, contains five major categories—Home Page, Browsing History, Search, Tabs, and Appearance.

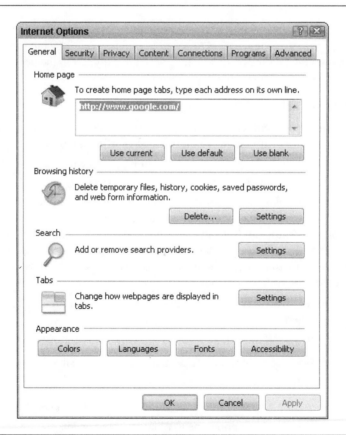

FIGURE 9-5   General tab

The *Home Page* is simply the Internet site to which you want IE to connect as a default site. Whenever you open IE, it always connects to this site first. If you want to change the site, type a new URL in the Address field. If you don't want to use a home page, click the Use Blank button. Also, if you're currently visiting the web page you want to make your home page, click the Use Current button on the General tab (which keeps you from having to type the URL).

The *Browsing History section* enables you to determine how temporary Internet pages are stored. When you surf the Web, your computer stores pages you visit in a Temporary Internet Files folder (including all the graphics and photos from that page). This speeds your access to those pages when you revisit them. You can change the default options by clicking the Settings button. Doing this opens a Settings window, shown here, where you can adjust how IE uses the temporary pages. If you have a fast Internet connection, temporary Internet files are unnecessary because they're designed to help speed slow-connection web surfing.

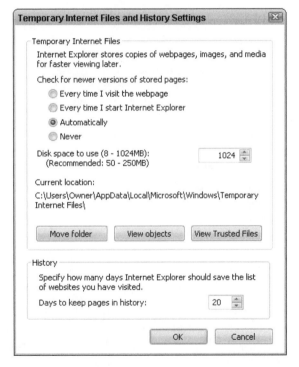

By default, IE automatically checks for new material. This setting ensures you're looking at the most current version of the web page—I recommend you leave this default setting. You also see you can adjust the amount of disk space used for temporary Internet files. You can increase this setting, if you like, but the default setting is probably all the space you need. And, you can use the buttons at the bottom of the Settings window to view your temporary Internet files and objects. You can also move the Temporary Internet Files folder to a different location on your computer, but this doesn't help anything, so it's best to leave it alone.

If you believe you're looking at an "old" page from your temporary file, click the Refresh button and the page is then re-downloaded from the web server. Remember, if you have a fast Internet connection, temporary Internet files don't help you and they junk up your system. You may consider turning off this feature.

You see a Search option on the General tab as well. You can click the Settings button and change the default search engine, which is MSN by default.

Under the Tabs section, you can make some changes to the way tabs behave and function in IE. Click the Settings tab and see the check box options, as shown in the following illustration. The options you see here are self-explanatory, and generally speaking, the default options are all you typically need.

At the bottom of the General tab, you see several buttons: Colors, Fonts, Languages, and Accessibility. These options enable you to change the way IE looks and displays web pages. These options are self-explanatory, so check them out if you want to make appearance changes.

Security Tab

The *Security tab* enables you to configure how IE handles security issues on Internet or intranet sites, as Figure 9-6 shows. A typical home user doesn't need to make any configuration changes on this tab. If you're using IE on a business network, you shouldn't make any changes here,

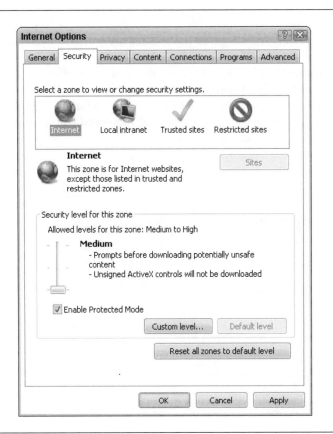

FIGURE 9-6   Security tab

unless instructed to do so by your network administrator. Click the Internet icon, and you see that, by default, the Internet option (shown in Figure 9-3) is set to Medium. This setting gives you all the browser functionality, but prompts you before downloading questionable content. You can change this level by using the slider bar to access different settings. For each slider bar movement, you can read an explanation of how the browser behaves. Typically, though, the Medium setting is best.

You can also use the *Trusted Sites and Restricted Sites options,* which enable you to list sites you know are safe or sites you know are questionable. This, in turn, affects how your browser acts when handling these sites.

Privacy Tab

The *Privacy tab,* shown in Figure 9-7, gives you a slider bar option, so you can set a privacy configuration for your computer (first click the Default button on the tab). Web sites have become more interactive in the past year or so, and many of them want to collect information from you and your computer. This setting enables you to determine whether web sites can set cookies with your browser and use personal information. By default, the Medium setting is used, which is typically all you need. You can click the Advanced button to alter the cookie settings, as desired.

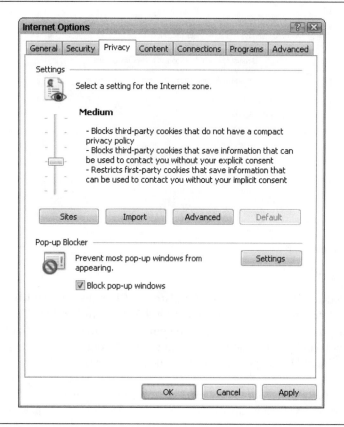

FIGURE 9-7   Privacy tab

You also see a Pop-Up Blocker, which can help IE prevent those annoying pop-ups. If you want to block pop-ups, select the check box option, and you can click the Settings button to create exceptions, if necessary.

Content Tab

The *Content tab* enables you to configure how IE manages different kinds of content from the Internet, as well as information about you. This tab has five sections—Parental Controls, Content Advisor, Certificates, AutoComplete, and Feeds, as Figure 9-8 shows.

You can configure Parental Controls that enable you to determine what web sites your children are able to access, as well as other items on your computer. You can find out more about Parental Controls in Chapter 13.

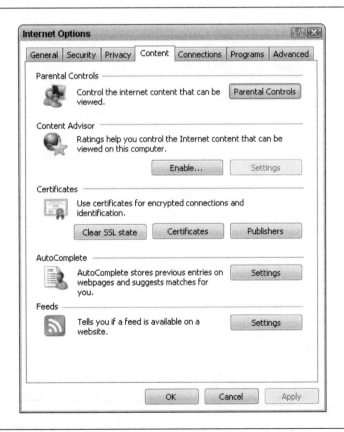

FIGURE 9-8 Content tab

The Content Advisor enables you to manage how (and if) IE handles different kinds of potentially offensive web content. If you click the Enable button, you see a Content Advisor window, shown here:

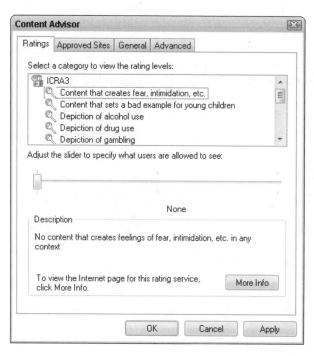

You see different categories of potential offensive material. You can use the slider bar to adjust the level of offensive content users are able to view. This feature is great if you have children who use the Internet on your computer. You can enable this feature to prevent accidental access to offensive web content.

NOTE   *These settings aren't foolproof. IE examines the requested web site for keywords that provide clues about offensive content. IE can also use a site's rating system to determine whether it is safe. As you can see, a lot of this is up to the individual site, so don't think your kids are safe when you enable these settings. You still need to monitor them, and you might consider investing in some third-party software, which can also help manage access to offensive web sites.*

Once you make some settings decisions, click Apply, and Windows Vista prompts you to enter a password. This prevents other users of your computer from changing the content settings. Also note, you can access the Approved Sites tab to create a list of approved sites, and you can make some basic changes on the General and Advanced tabs. Normally, however, you don't need to use these tabs. If you do, you'll find them self-explanatory.

You also see a Certificates option in IE. In some organizations, IE is configured to use various digital certificates to verify certain web site authenticity. Home users don't use certificate options, so you don't need to configure anything here. In some circumstances, you might want to use a digital certificate to communicate with a highly secure web site. In this case, you need to follow that web site's instructions about obtaining and using a digital certificate. If you're using Vista in a business environment, your network administrators manage these settings for you.

You can use the AutoComplete section of the Content tab to change or turn off AutoComplete. IE tries to learn what web sites and information you enter into web pages. If IE recognizes what you're typing, it tries to complete it for you. You may find this helpful or aggravating. At any rate, you can click the AutoComplete button to change the behavior. This button opens another window with some simple check box options you can consider. Also, you see a My Profile button, which you can click to change personal information about yourself that IE keeps.

Finally, you see a Feeds section that helps you manage Internet feeds from various web sites. You can click the Settings button to manage a default feed schedule.

Connections Tab

The *Connections tab,* shown in Figure 9-9, lists any Internet connections you have configured on your computer. You normally don't need to configure anything on this tab because you configure these options when you create a dial-up connection (see Chapter 8). However, you can use this tab to tell IE what specific connection to use if your computer has multiple connections. If you're on a network where your computer accesses another network computer (called a *proxy server*) to reach the Internet, you may need to perform some configuration here. Consult with your network administrator for specific setting information.

What Happened to Windows Messenger?

Windows Messenger was an instant messaging tool that was included in Windows XP. However, Windows Messenger isn't included in Windows Vista. To use instant messaging, you need to install an instant-messaging software product from another software provider. In the past, Outlook Express also provided instant messaging functionality, but Outlook Express has been replaced by Windows Mail in Vista, and it doesn't support instant messaging either. This means you need to install a compatible instant-messaging software package from a different software provider.

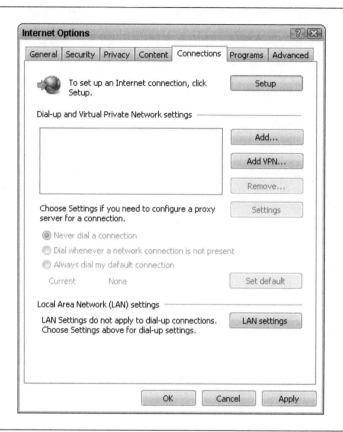

FIGURE 9-9   Connections tab

Programs Tab

The *Programs tab,* shown in Figure 9-10, enables you to choose which programs on Windows Vista perform what options. For example, by default, IE uses Windows Mail for Internet mail (in other words, if you are visiting a web page and click a "send e-mail" link, IE opens a Windows Mail message). However, you may want to use a different mail client you have installed on your computer. You can use this page to change the applications that IE uses for HTML editing, e-mail, newsgroups, Internet calling, your calendar, and your contact list. If you plan to use both IE and Windows Mail, you won't need to change any of these settings. The Set Programs button takes you to the Default Programs interface, which is also directly available in the Control Panel. This interface lets you choose the default programs that should be used for different kinds of files and media.

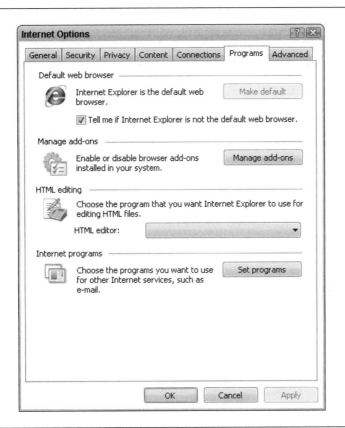

FIGURE 9-10   Programs tab

Advanced Tab

The *Advanced tab* contains a bunch of check box options for a variety of processes. For example, you can change some browsing behavior, multimedia settings, and printing settings (among others) just by checking or unchecking different options.

The real question, of course, is what do you need to change? In reality, nothing—under most circumstances. Don't start making changes on this tab unless you have a specific goal in mind. For example, as a way of sparing your color ink cartridge from printing unnecessary graphics, IE doesn't print background colors and images on web pages. However, if I want IE to print them anyway, I can select the Print Background Colors and Images check box under Printing. The key is to identify a goal you want to accomplish, and then determine whether you can enable or disable that option on the Advanced tab. The most common settings are already configured for you. If you make a bunch of changes you're unhappy with, use the Reset button that resets all settings in IE.

Chapter 10 Run Windows Mail

How to...

- Set up Windows Mail
- Send and receive e-mail
- Configure interface views
- Use identities
- Create and manage message rules
- Customize Windows Mail

If you are like many of us, you didn't have e-mail a few years ago, and the concept of e-mail didn't seem very important. Today, e-mail is a daily part of your life, and you don't know how you ever survived without it! That statement certainly describes me—I use e-mail every day for my work, and to keep up with friends and family. Checking and managing the e-mail I receive consumes a significant amount of my time each day.

Like previous versions of Windows, Windows Vista includes an e-mail client called Windows Mail. An *e-mail client* is a software program that enables you to send and receive e-mail, as well as manage the e-mail you receive. Windows Mail is an effective program, and if you've ever used Outlook or Windows Mail, you'll feel at home with this software product.

How E-Mail Works

E-mail is primarily sent over the Internet to reach a certain person. Businesses and organizations also use e-mail, which is sent over their local network instead of the Internet. But, most of us use e-mail that is sent over our Internet connection to the Internet. Like everything else on the Internet, e-mail uses a protocol to send mail between different computers.

Typically, e-mail uses Simple Mail Transfer Protocol (SMTP) to move mail from one place to another. An e-mail address is made up of a user name and a domain name, such as *myname@mydomain.com*. When you send an e-mail to someone, e-mail servers first examine the mydomain.com portion of the address to find a mydomain.com server. Once this server is located, the mail is sent to the server. This server recognizes mydomain.com as its own domain, so it examines the user name to see whether a user by that name exists. If myname is, in fact, a user, the mail is held on the server until it is downloaded. If the name doesn't match, the mail is sometimes sent back to the sender with a "user unknown" message. In many respects, e-mail is just like regular mail, where the address is inspected first, and then the name is inspected by the local post office. Of course, e-mail is a lot faster. You can send a message to any e-mail address anywhere in the world, and it normally arrives in a few minutes or less. Also, you can send any kind of electronic file as an attachment—pictures, documents, video, applications . . . you name it. Because it's so fast and can handle almost any kind of attachment, e-mail has become popular in our fast-paced world.

Set Up Windows Mail

When you install Windows Vista, Windows Mail is installed by default. You can access Windows Mail by clicking Start | All Programs | Windows Mail. To use Windows Mail, you need to set up your mail account, so Windows Mail knows how to connect to a mail server to send and receive e-mail. This information is available from your Internet service provider (ISP). You most likely received printed instructions about setting up your computer for a connection to the Internet (see Chapter 8). Once you make this connection, you then use your documentation to set up Windows Mail.

NOTE   *You don't have to use Windows Mail to send and receive e-mail with Windows Vista. You can use other POP clients, such as Mozilla Thunderbird, Eudora, or some other mail client instead. However, this chapter focuses only on Windows Mail because it is included with your Vista operating system (OS).*

Once you open Windows Mail, you see the basic Windows Mail interface. Choose Tools | Accounts. Click the Add button on the right side of the window, then click E-Mail account, and then click Next. The software leads you through a series of steps in which you enter your name, your e-mail address, your server type, and your e-mail user name and password. Have this information ready, and then follow these easy steps to complete the wizard:

1. Enter your display name. This is the name you want other e-mail users to see when you send mail. Typically, you want to use your real name here and not something that can't be recognized, such as "Biker Dad" or "Sweet Cakes." However, if you want to be known by a nickname, that's okay, too. Click Next when you're done.

2. In the next window, enter your e-mail address and click Next. If you already have an existing account, you can use that, or you can set up a free web-based e-mail account on the Internet with Hotmail, which is a part of MSN.

NOTE   *Hotmail is not the only free web-based e-mail account that is available. Yahoo.com, Netscape.com, Go.com, and many others also offer free e-mail accounts. However, these kinds of accounts are web mail accounts and may be incompatible with Windows Mail.*

3. In the next window, you need to enter your e-mail server information. Almost all e-mail servers use POP3 (Post Office Protocol 3) to manage e-mail messages, with the exception of free e-mail servers. Windows Mail needs to know whether your server is a POP3 server or a different kind of server, such as IMAP or HTTP. Check your ISP documentation. Then, enter the incoming mail server name and the outgoing mail server name. Typically, both of these names will be in the form of mail.mydomain.com. You need

10

to check your ISP documentation to know for sure. Enter the correct information, and then click Next.

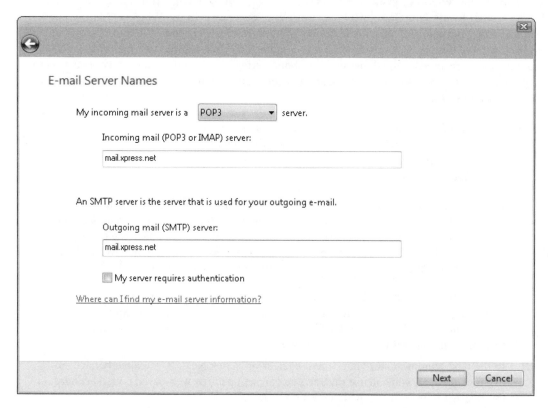

4. In the next window, enter your logon name and your password. Check your ISP documentation to make certain you are entering the correct information—and do remember that passwords are case-sensitive. Click Next.

5. Click Finish.

Windows Mail has the capability to support multiple accounts for the same user. For example, let's say you have a primary ISP with an e-mail address of myaddress@myisp.com. However, you also have an e-mail account at youraddress@youraddress.com. Can you use Windows Mail to access information on both of those accounts? Sure! All you need to do is configure both mail accounts using the previous steps. When you check your mail, Windows Mail will check both accounts.

Check Out the Windows Mail Interface

Windows Mail provides an easy-to-read and easy-to-use interface where you can quickly view e-mail messages. By default, Windows Mail uses four major *panes,* or views, to separate different mail components. These four panes make mail usage easy, and you can customize this interface as well (I show you how in the section "Change Windows Mail Views"). Figure 10-1 gives you a look at the default Windows Mail interface.

Let's first take a look at your menu options. At the top of the Windows Mail window, you see common menus: File, Edit, View, Tools, Message, and Help. You have the standard options on these menus, such as Open, Save, Cut, and Paste, but you also have quite a few options that are specific to Windows Mail. The following list highlights the most important features:

■ **File**   Using this menu, you can perform standard open and save functions, and you can create additional mail folders in which you can store mail. You can also import and export mail settings, messages, and address books to and from other e-mail programs. And, you can use the File menu to establish different identities. This way, two different people can send and receive mail using a single Windows Mail program. All these options are easy and self-explanatory, but I explore the Identities feature later in the section "Use Identities."

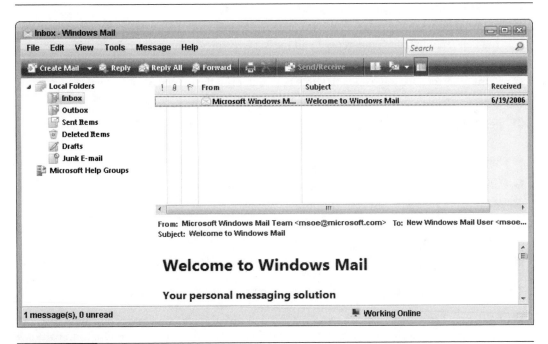

FIGURE 10-1   Windows Mail Interface

- **Edit** The Edit menu contains typical editing functions. Use the Edit menu to delete e-mail, move e-mail between folders, mark e-mail messages in various ways, and perform other standard editing tasks.

- **View** You use this menu to change how current messages are viewed, as well as how the entire Windows Mail interface appears. See the section "Change Windows Mail Views" for more information.

- **Tools** The Tools menu enables you to send and receive e-mail, configure message rules, customize Windows Mail, and manage Windows Contracts and Calendar. All these items are explored in more detail later in this chapter.

- **Message** The Message menu contains typical message functions, most of which you can perform by clicking a toolbar button. You can also use this menu to block senders, create message rules, and "watch" messages or discussions. You can use Windows Mail to connect to newsgroups and flag messages, so you can watch the message and all the replies. This is a great way to organize and keep track of information that is useful to you.

- **Help** Get help from the Windows Mail Help files or on the Microsoft web site.

Below the menu bar, you see the standard Windows Mail toolbar. You'll use this toolbar quite a bit when working with Windows Mail. You have the following standard buttons:

- **Create Mail** Click this button to start a new mail message.

- **Reply, Reply All, and Forward** If you select a message, you see these options appear. You can reply to a message, reply to all message recipients, and forward a message to someone else.

- **Print** Select a message and click this button to print the message.

- **Delete** Select a message and click this button to delete the message.

- **Send/Receive** Click this button to see a drop-down list of choices. You can Send and Receive, Receive All, and Send All.

- **Sign In to Microsoft Communities** Access Microsoft communities directly.

- **Contacts** Click this button to open the Address Book.

- **Windows Calendar** Access Windows Calendar directly.

- **Find** Click this button to find specific messages. You can search by sender, message subject, or keywords.

- **Folder List** Click this button to see your list of Windows Mail folders.

The final part of the Windows Mail interface is composed of the three primary panes:

- **Folders** The top-left pane shows your Windows Mail folder structure. You can easily move among your Inbox, Outbox, Sent Items, and Deleted Items, as well as additional folders you can create using the File menu.

- ■ **New Message**   The top-right pane contains a message list. These are messages you've received, but haven't deleted or moved into another folder.

- ■ **Preview**   The bottom-right pane contains the text of the selected message. This is an easy preview that enables you to skim through your messages without opening them.

Send and Receive E-Mail

Once you set up an account, you can send and receive e-mail. Sending and receiving e-mail is easy—the following sections show you how.

Send an E-Mail

To send a new e-mail message, click the Create Mail button on your toolbar. A new mail message appears, as shown in Figure 10-2. To send a new mail message, type the recipient's e-mail address in the To line and any additional e-mail addresses in the Cc line (if you want other individuals copied), enter a subject, and then type your message in the provided message box—it's that easy!

<table>
<tr>
<td>NOTE</td>
<td>When you enter a subject, be as descriptive as possible. E-mail users often receive many e-mails on any given day. Descriptive subjects help identify important messages. Also, if your message is important, you can attach a high priority notice with it. Choose Message | Set Priority | High, or click the Priority button and select a priority.</td>
</tr>
</table>

When you finish with your message, click the Send button. If you're currently connected to the Internet, the message is immediately sent. If you aren't currently connected to the Internet,

10

Advanced Message-Editing Features

Windows Mail supports advanced message-editing features. As you're typing your new message, notice you have bold, italic, bulleted lists, and other button features on the message toolbar. You can cut, copy, and paste message text, as well. You can use the Format menu to use different color styles in your message and even use a background picture or graphic with the Message menu. You can also check your message for spelling errors by choosing Tools | Spelling, or click the Spelling button.

All these features are nice, but be aware that not all mail clients can receive these formatting features. Even though you style your text and add a background, some of your recipients may see only plain text.

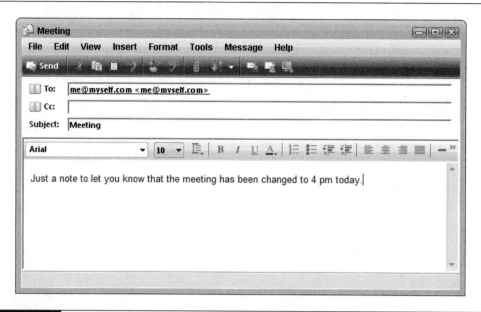

FIGURE 10-2 New mail message

click the Send/Receive button on your Windows Mail toolbar. Doing this launches an Internet dial-up connection, so the message can be sent.

Attach a File to an E-Mail

If you want to send an e-mail with an *attachment,* which is just a file of some kind, you can easily do so. Click the Create Mail button on your Windows Mail toolbar and follow these steps:

1. Enter the recipient's e-mail address, cc addresses if desired, and a subject, and then type any text in the message area.

2. To attach a file, choose Insert, and then choose either File Attachment or Picture. (You can also choose to include the text from a file, which enables you to browse for the file and copy-and-paste the text from it, although this isn't technically an attachment.) You can also click the Attach button.

3. A browse window appears. Browse to the location of the file, and then select it.

4. Click the Attach button. The file now appears in your New Message window as an attachment, as shown in Figure 10-3.

NOTE

Want to know an easier way to attach a file to a message? Shrink your message window, so you can see your Desktop, and then locate the file you want to include. Drag the file into the message portion of the window. The file's name appears in the Attach line and the file is attached to the e-mail.

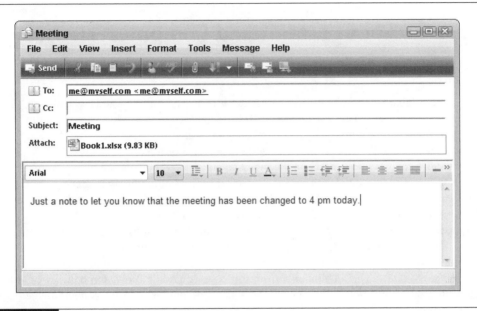

FIGURE 10-3 New Message window with attachment

Before sending attachments, you should consider putting the attachments in a new folder and compressing the folder. Doing this makes your transmission time shorter. To learn more about folder compression, see Chapter 4.

Receive Messages

When you're ready to check for messages, open Windows Mail and click the Send/Receive button on your toolbar. Doing this launches an Internet connection, so mail can be downloaded to your computer. New e-mail messages appear in the New Message pane. If you click each message, you can read its text in the Preview pane, but don't assume you see all of the message text in the Preview pane: scroll down with the slider bar to view the entire message. To open a message, double-click it. Doing this enables you to read the message in its own message window. Once you receive and read your messages, you can delete them, leave them in the Inbox, or drag them to a desired folder for safekeeping.

A great feature of Windows Mail is that deleted messages aren't really deleted—they are moved to the Deleted Items folder. You can click this folder and find a message that was previously deleted and reread it. You can also right-click the Deleted Items folder and choose Empty Deleted Items to delete the items permanently if you need to free up disk space. I don't recommend you choose this global delete option, however. Invariably, you will need to refer to a mail item you thought you no longer needed.

Did you know?

About E-Mail and Computer Viruses

There's a lot of talk and confusion about computer viruses and e-mail—and rightfully so. Generally speaking, computers do get viruses from e-mail. However, what's important to know is you cannot get a computer virus from the text of an e-mail. For example, let's say you download your mail, select a message, and the contents of the message appear in the Preview pane. Let's say you even open the message and read it. You cannot get a computer virus this way, but there's an exception to this rule: HTML e-mail messages. Because HTML is a computer language, it is possible to get a Trojan horse or other malicious code from an HTML message—this is why it's important to keep your antivirus software up-to-date.

Computer viruses typically come in the form of some kind of attachment. Opening an attachment can give your computer a virus. Virus attachments normally contain some kind of executable code that launches on your computer and does all kinds of annoying and nasty things. In short—don't open attachments from someone you don't know, and be wary of attachments from people you do know, who may have unintentionally sent you an infected file. Also, watch for the .exe and .vbs extensions on attachments (such as attachmentname .exe or attachmentname.vbs). These are executable files and are more likely to contain viruses than other attachments, such as a picture file. In addition, "macro" viruses can hide within word processing documents, such as a Microsoft Word document. All major brands of antivirus software include an e-mail scan feature that can check your e-mail attachments for viruses before you open them. This software is inexpensive and a great investment.

Receive Attachments

Any attachments sent to you are automatically downloaded with the mail message. Messages with attachments have a small paper clip beside them in the New Message pane. In the Preview pane, you see a larger paper clip on the right side of the window. If you click the paper clip, a pop-out menu appears where you can choose either to open the attachment or save it to your computer (such as in the Documents folder or on your Desktop).

Change Windows Mail Views

As discussed, Windows Mail has a three-pane option that *I* think is great. However, *you* may not think it's so great and you may want to change it. That's fine, and it's easy to do. To change the appearance of the Windows Mail interface, choose View | Layout. A window appears with a single Layout tab, as shown in Figure 10-4.

As you can see, two sections appear—Basic and Preview Pane. You can select or clear the various check boxes to display the panes you want. You can try different settings to find the ones

FIGURE 10-4   Layout tab

you like best. Also, if you click Customize Toolbar, you can add other toolbar icon features, which are discussed in more detail in Chapter 3.

In addition to using the Layout feature, you can also customize the current view, which enables you to determine which messages are displayed and which are hidden. You can use different views by choosing View | Current View. You can then select a desired option from the pop-out menu. As with an appearance configuration, you may need to play around with the settings to find the ones that are right for you.

Create Message Rules

Message rules enable you to control how various messages are handled by Windows Mail. Message rules are most helpful to people who receive a lot of e-mail or who receive a lot of *spam,* or junk e-mail. You can set up rules to help you manage messages, so Windows Mail can automatically delete certain messages or move certain messages to other folders.

Rules are easy to create, but be careful of overdoing it. Too many rules usually become more confusing than helpful, so plan carefully before you create a bunch of e-mail rules. Make sure you have a specific reason to create a rule or a specific problem you want the rule to solve.

Create a New Rule

To create a new rule, follow these easy steps:

1. In Windows Mail, choose Tools | Message Rules | Mail.

2. The New Mail Rule window appears. In the top portion of the window, select a condition for your rule. Scroll through the list and select the check box next to the desired condition.

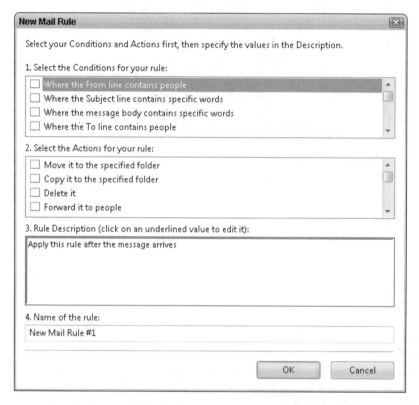

3. In the second portion of the window, select an action for your rule. Scroll through the list and select the check box next to the desired action.

4. Depending on your selection, you may need to enter a rule description or perform some editing. If a link appears (blue underlined wording), click it to enter some additional information that's needed for the rule.

5. In the bottom of the window, give the rule a friendly name, and then click OK.

Manage Message Rules

Once you create message rules, you can manage them from the same Message Rules interface. Choose Tools | Message Rules | Mail. A window appears, listing your current rules. You can use the provided buttons to create new rules, delete existing rules, edit existing rules, and perform related management features. This interface is easy to use and self-explanatory.

Block Senders

Let's say you meet Chatty Kathy in a chat room and you make the mistake of giving her your personal e-mail address. Now Chatty Kathy writes to you every day and sends you piles of junk mail. You decide you don't like Chatty Kathy and you don't want any more mail from her. What to do? No problem. You can block Chatty Kathy, so your computer automatically moves her mail to the Deleted Items folder without informing you of the mail's arrival.

To use the Blocked Senders option, select the message from the sender you want to block and choose Tools | Junk E-Mail Options, and then click the Blocked Senders tab. A simple window appears. Click the Add button, enter the e-mail address of the sender you want to block, and click OK. The sender appears in the Blocked Senders list, as Figure 10-5 shows. You can modify this list at any time.

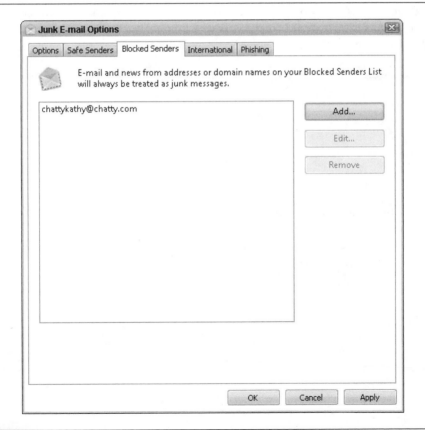

FIGURE 10-5   Blocked Senders list

You can also use the Message menu to add a new person to your Blocked Senders list immediately (and easily). When you get a message from someone and you know you don't want any more messages from that sender, select the message in Outlook, and then choose Message | Junk E-Mail | Add Sender to Blocked Senders List. That's all you have to do. Any mail sent in the future from this sender is removed automatically. Additionally, you can use the Message menu to create a rule from the message. Select the message, choose Message | Create Rule from Message, and you can see the New Mail Rule window appear. These options give you quick and easy access to the Message Rules and Blocked Senders features of Windows Mail.

What Happened to Identities?

If you look at the File menu, you can see an option for Identities. *Identities* were a way to use different e-mail accounts by different people accessing your computer. However, all that information is now tied to the user account and Identities are no longer used as they were in Outlook Express. The Identities option you see on the File menu enables you to import account information and messages from selected Identities into your mailbox. This way, if you need to import someone else's mail into your mailbox, you can do so here as a workaround to the user accounts. If you click File | Identities, you can click the Next button and choose an action you want to take in terms of importing identities and deleting old identities, as you can see in the following illustration.

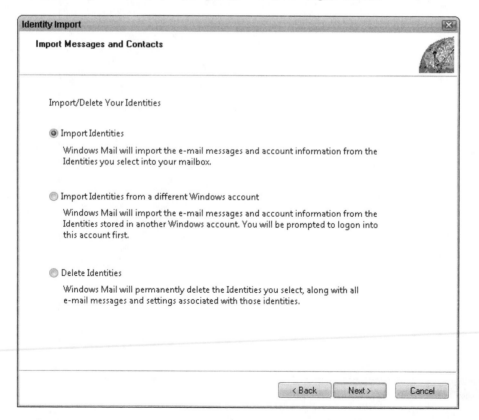

Manage Your Accounts

When you first begin using Windows Mail, you set up an account, so your computer can send and receive e-mail to and from your ISP. Over time, that account information may change, or you may need to add other accounts. You can make changes to your accounts by choosing Tools | Accounts. This action opens a window where you can view your current mail account, news account, or even directory service account. Use the provided buttons to create a new account, edit an existing one, and perform other related account-management tasks. Before making changes to an account or creating a new one, remember you need information from your ISP for the correct user name, password, and e-mail server information.

Customize Windows Mail

Windows Mail contains quite a few customization options you can access by choosing Tools | Options. You can see several tabs, but the good news is each tab is rather easy to use. Most present a list of check box options you can choose from. The following list gives you an overview of what you can do on each tab. Remember, you can try different settings and change them later if you don't like them, and one of the best ways to find the settings that work for you is to experiment.

- **General**   This tab contains information about the way your computer receives messages. Most of the default options on this tab are all you need. If you want Windows Mail to check for messages automatically by launching a dial-up connection at specified intervals, you can select the option on this tab and enter the amount of time you want to pass between checks (such as 30 minutes or so).

- **Read**   This tab contains settings for messages you have received. You can choose to view messages in various colors and fonts.

- **Receipts**   Some messages you receive (or send) can request a receipt—a return e-mail notification that the message was opened. Use the tab to enable this feature and determine how it should be used.

- **Send**   This tab contains basic settings for sending messages. Almost all options are enabled by default, and you should probably keep these options enabled for the best functionality.

- **Compose**   Use this tab to select font settings and business card settings and to attach stationery to your e-mail messages. Remember, not all mail clients can read these style features.

- **Signatures**   You can automatically add a signature—such as your name and phone number—to all new messages you type. Use this tab to enter the text you want for the signature.

- **Spelling**   Use this tab to enable automatic spelling and spell settings.

10

- **Security** If you want to use encrypted mail with digital certificates (which you probably won't), use this tab to enable the option. This feature is typically used by business individuals who need to send secure, encrypted files, and/or e-mail messages encrypted with a digital certificate.

- **Connection** This tab contains information about your dial-up connection. One item of interest here is you can tell Windows Mail to hang up the dial-up connection automatically once mail has been sent and received. If you use the General tab to dial a connection automatically to get mail, you should use this option on the Connection tab, so those dial-out sessions are terminated automatically unless you want your computer tying up the phone line all day.

- **Advanced** Use this tab to choose various advanced settings. In most cases, you don't need to make any changes on this tab, but you can look through these self-explanatory options for any configuration changes you might want.

Chapter 11

Create a Home Network

How to...

- Plan a home network
- Create your home network
- Use Internet Connection Sharing
- Create a wireless network
- Use Windows Vista on a large network

Windows Vista gives you plenty of home networking options. In fact, home networking in Windows Vista has never been easier. If you're interested in networking two or more home computers (or computers in a small office), this chapter is just for you. Let's get our feet wet by talking about home networks and small office networks, and then you can see what Windows Vista offers to make networking easy.

Windows Networking Basics

Before you jump into the home-networking arena, you need to know a few basics about what it takes to create a wired home network. Networks, on a simple level, require both hardware and software to allow one computer to communicate with another computer. First, computers must be equipped with a network adapter card, and these cards come in several forms. Most are integrated with the mother boards, but they can also be internal cards that fit into an expansion slot on your computer, similar to sound and video cards. Network adapter cards can also be built into the motherboard, or they can function as separate USB devices. The *network adapter card* enables information to flow to and from your computer.

A special cable, usually with an *RJ-45 plug* (this looks like a large telephone cable), connects to the network adapter card. The cables from all the computers connect through a device called a *switch*—a small piece of hardware with several places to plug in RJ-45 connectors. The switch routes information to and from computers, so the information travels to the appropriate computer.

Now, if all that sounds a little overwhelming, don't worry, because other alternatives are available. With the growth of home networking, a number of solutions are available where cabling and a switch aren't needed. For example, you can purchase network adapter cards that plug into your phone jacks. The computers use the existing phone wiring in your house to communicate with each other at no expense and interruption to you. Some versions also use power outlets, and you can easily create a wireless network (which you learn about in the section "Set Up a Wireless Network"), so your PCs and peripherals can communicate with each other. The key is to shop around and find a solution (and dollar amount) that works best for you. And, you can always use standard networking cabling and switches (as I do), which aren't terribly expensive.

NOTE
Many computers come equipped with a standard network adapter when you purchase them. Most new laptops even ship with a wireless network adapter. Check your computer documentation to find out what's included.

In addition to the hardware needs, your Windows Vista software must also be configured for networking. This can include turning on Microsoft File and Printer Sharing, and configuring the TCP/IP protocol, so the computers can understand each other. Fortunately, in Windows Vista, you get setup help from the Connect to a Network Wizard, which you learn about in the section "Use the Set Up a Network Wizard."

Plan Your Home Network

Before you try to configure your Windows Vista computer for networking, you need to complete a few tasks to make sure your home-networking experience will be a positive one. I've arranged these tasks into a quick and easy, step-by-step format, so make sure you perform these steps before moving on to the next section in this chapter.

1. If you have only one Windows Vista computer, it needs to be the primary computer. For example, if your computer is using Windows Vista and another computer uses Windows XP or 2000, Windows Vista will be the primary computer on your network. However, shared peripherals, such as a printer or scanner, can be connected to any other computer. If you want to share one Internet connection, it should be on the Windows Vista computer (especially if you're using a broadband solution, such as DSL)—although this isn't a mandatory requirement, it does make the entire process a lot easier. Of course, if you have multiple peripherals, other computers can share those. Just remember, Windows Vista will be your primary, or server, machine for your home network.

2. Make a list of all the hardware you will need. Inspect your computers to determine whether you have available expansion slots or whether some computers already have a network adapter card. You need to determine what kind of network you want (whether to use typical wiring, wireless, or phone wire, for instance). You can learn more about the different kinds of networks on the Web or from your local computer store. Remember, some solutions provide faster network transfer speeds. If your budget allows, always go for the fastest solution you can obtain. Also, many home-networking hardware components are sold as a single kit with a single instruction list. These kits are great solutions, as they make certain you have everything you need. Check out your favorite computer store for details.

NOTE   *Your computer has different kinds of expansion slots. The most common type used for a network adapter card are PCI and PC Cards for laptops (although you can use USB in all cases). More than likely, you will have available PCI slots, so you'll want to buy a PCI network adapter. Consult your computer documentation for more information.*

3. Once you determine which type of network you will use, buy the required hardware devices and install them. Follow the manufacturer's guidelines during the installation process. Note, you may be required to install the network drivers from the CD before you install the physical adapter.

11

Your computer must be powered down and unplugged from its outlet before you install a network adapter. See Chapter 6 for more information about managing hardware.

4. Check to make sure your computers and peripherals are connected together correctly, and check your Internet connection as well. Access the Windows Vista Help files and search under "Home Networking" for more information.

Understand Internet Connection Sharing

Internet Connection Sharing (ICS), first introduced with Windows 98, enables you to have one computer connected to the Internet and all other computers on the network share the Internet connection through that computer. This feature is specifically designed for home networks or small office networks with ten or fewer computers. Why is ICS so helpful? With ICS, you need only one Internet connection and one computer connected to the Internet—each computer doesn't need its own modem or broadband hardware (such as a cable modem or DSL connection). Through sharing, you save money and aggravation because you don't have to configure each computer for Internet use.

While you're designing your home network, you need to decide whether you want to use ICS. On a practical note, ICS is designed for use with broadband Internet access (such as DSL, cable, or satellite). Although you can use ICS with a 56K modem, your modem will operate slowly if several people are trying to use the Internet connection at the same time. (This effect results from the 56K modem's lack of sufficient bandwidth to perform at a desirable speed.) However, if users on your network don't access the Internet at the same time, the 56K modem's shared connection will probably be fine. You also need to decide if ICS is a better solution for you than a *router,* which is a device that serves as an Internet gateway. I use a router rather than ICS for my home network because of added security features and flexibility. In most cases, I'd say a router is probably a better solution than ICS, especially in today's market, where you can get a good router for less than $100. A router is much more secure and it is easier to use since there is no host computer for the connection.

When you use ICS, your Windows Vista computer should be the ICS *host.* Note, you don't have to use the Windows Vista computer as the host—you can use a different computer, such as a Windows XP computer, but you will have fewer operational problems if the Vista computer is the ICS host. All other computers on your network, called ICS *clients,* access the host to gain access to the Internet. Therefore, all Internet communications flow from your home network to the host computer, and then to the Internet, and vice versa. Using this setup, your host computer has a connection to the Internet and a connection to your home network. All the client computers need only a network adapter, so they can connect to the host. As far as the Internet is concerned, it appears as though only one computer is accessing the Internet.

ICS doesn't work with some versions of America Online (AOL). Check with AOL to see if your version is supported. Also, it's possible, although unlikely, your Internet service provider (ISP) will charge you for multiple computer connections to the Internet. Check with your ISP to make certain you won't receive additional charges (and if you do, I suggest you shop elsewhere).

Use the Set Up a Network Wizard

Once you connect all your hardware and your computers are connected to each other, you can run the Set Up a Network Wizard to set up home networking on your computers. The following steps walk you through the wizard.

NOTE

You may have a custom setup CD-ROM, especially if you purchased a home-networking kit. Refer to the kit's documentation about setup, but if you have a custom CD-ROM for the kit you purchased, you need to use the kit's setup program instead of the Set Up Network Wizard.

1. Turn on all computers on your home network, so they are booted and operational.

2. On your Windows Vista computer, choose Start | Control Panel. Double-click the Network and Sharing Center icon. In the left pane, choose the Set Up a Connection or Network link.

3. Choose the option to Set up a connection or network and click Next.

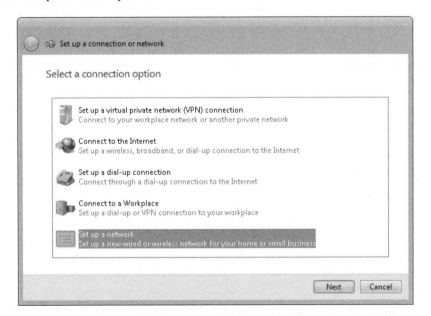

4. The next window gives you more information about home networking. Make sure you have completed the preparation tasks listed, and then click Next.

5. The wizard then detects the computer's connection to the network. Depending on the connection, you'll see additional screens that ask you to share files and printers. You may also see an option to manually configure your network adapter card if the wizard has problems configuring it automatically. This is especially true if you're a using a router. Again, make sure you read your networking hardware's setup instructions and follow them.

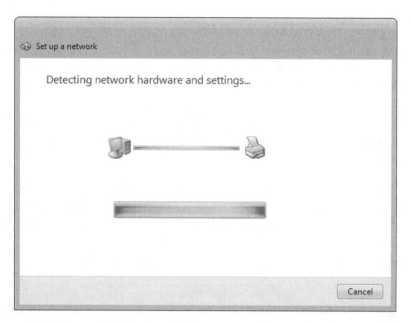

So, what do you do if you have problems connecting the computers together? Or, what if you're really curious and want to know what the Set Up a Network Wizard did to your computer? For either situation, check out the properties of your local area connection, which are found in the Network Connections folder.

What TCP/IP Is

Transmission Control Protocol/Internet Protocol (TCP/IP) is an advanced topic and one that even gives network administrators severe headaches occasionally. Fortunately, Windows operating systems have evolved to help humans deal with TCP/IP. In a TCP/IP network, each computer must have a unique Internet Protocol (IP) address, which is a series of numbers, such as 131.107.2.200. For computers to communicate, you must configure each computer with an appropriate IP address in the same IP class as the other computers. Actually, it's all more complicated than this, but you probably realize that having Windows Vista set this up for you is a great help. Windows Vista, like Windows XP/2000, can give itself a private IP address in an appropriate range reserved for small networks. Windows Vista does all the work, so you don't have to do anything—which is really nice!

Open the Network and Sharing Center and click Manage Network Connections in the Tasks pane. Double-click the Local Area Connection and click Properties. You see a Networking tab that gives you basic information about the connection, as Figure 11-1 shows. You can select an item in the list and click the Properties button for additional details. In most cases, all you'll want to see is the Local Area Connection Status information, which you can see if you cancel out of properties, shown in Figure 11-2.

Essentially, the communications protocol (TCP/IP) is configured, so your computer can talk with other computers, and the File and Printer Sharing software is configured, so your computer can function on a Microsoft network with other Windows operating systems. The computers on the network can share folders, printers, drives, and just about anything else. Right-click the item you want to share and choose Sharing to configure it. See Chapter 4 for more information about sharing folders.

If you open the Properties page for the Local Area Connection (see Figure 11-1), select Internet Protocol (TCP/IP) and click Properties, you can see the Home Networking Wizard has assigned your computer an IP address and a subnet mask value automatically (which is why you don't see any numbers in the window), as shown in Figure 11-3. I won't go into the intricacies of

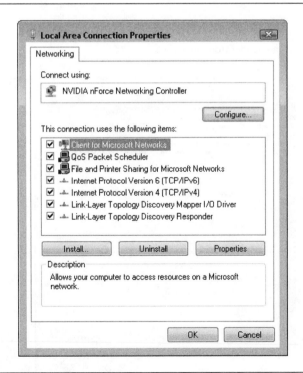

FIGURE 11-1   Local Area Connection properties

FIGURE 11-2   Local Area Connection status

FIGURE 11-3   IP address and subnet mask values

Burning a DVD

In the past, burning a DVD in Windows required additional software and, frankly, a lot of luck to get everything to work right. With Windows Vista, you put those problems in the past. You can burn DVDs of photos and other multimedia items or directly burn movies you create with Windows Movie Maker (see Chapter 16). The good news is, with the simplicity of Windows Movie Maker, you can burn DVDs quickly and easily. In this special section, you learn just how to do it.

What You Need

To burn a DVD, you need the following:

- Items you want to burn, such as movies or photos
- A DVD-R, DVD+R, or DVD-RW disc
- A Windows Vista computer with a DVD burner

NOTE

You can find DVD discs at most computer and department stores (look in the section where CDs are sold). Any brand will work with your Windows Vista computer. You can use DVD-R, DVD+R, or DVD-RW, depending on your DVD burner. Refer to your DVD burner's documentation for information about the kinds of DVD discs your burner can use.

Get Ready to Use the DVD Maker

Spend a few moments before you open Windows DVD Maker deciding what you want to include in your movie. If you've made a Windows Movie Maker movie, all you need to do is click DVD under Publish in Windows Movie Maker. This action transfers your movie to Windows DVD Maker. However, you can also add other items within the DVD Maker or simply build a DVD from scratch. The point is you need to stop for a moment and decide what you want the DVD to look like. When making a DVD, a good idea is always to start with a pen and paper. Map out the DVD on paper and you can use your notes as you move forward.

Checking Windows DVD Maker Options

When you first open Windows DVD Maker, you see a basic interface with no content, as shown in Figure 1.

Before using the DVD Maker, you may want to change one of the options that determines how the DVD Maker works. Notice the Options link in the lower right-hand corner. Click this link to open the DVD-Video Options dialog box, shown in Figure 2. Notice you can choose how your DVD is played back. You have the option to start with a DVD menu (this is the default), play video and end with a DVD menu, or Play video in a continuous loop. In most cases, starting with a menu is the easiest way to use a DVD and it is the standard DVD format you're already used to. You don't need to change the DVD aspect ratio or Video format. Keep the DVD burner speed set to "fastest." When you're done, click OK.

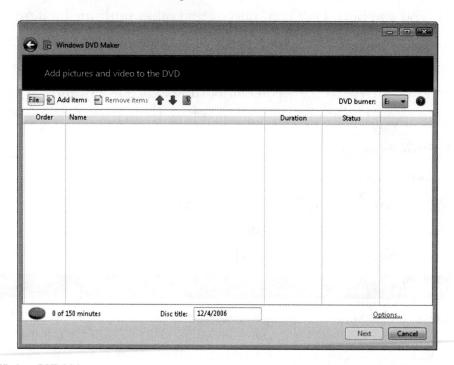

Figure 1. Windows DVD Maker

Figure 2. DVD-Video Options

Building Your DVD

Now that you understand the basic interface of the Windows DVD Maker, you're ready to start building the content in your DVD. This process is easy and fun.

Adding Items

The first thing you need to do is add media items to your DVD. First things first: if you're using a movie you created with Windows Movie Maker, just click DVD under Publish and it sends your movie to the Windows DVD Maker. Figure 3 shows you an example of a Windows Movie Maker movie added directly to Windows DVD Maker.

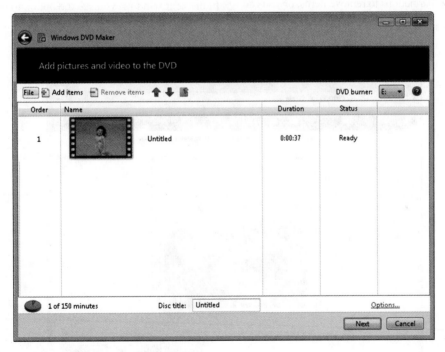

Figure 3. Windows Movie Maker movie in the DVD Maker

However, you can also add other items, or you can mix video and photos from scratch. Click the Add Items button on the toolbar. This opens a standard folder interface where you can browse for your movies, video clips, or photos. Windows DVD Maker can read and use most standard file formats. Locate and select your items, and then click the Open button, shown in Figure 4. Remember, you can select multiple items at the same time by CTRL-clicking them.

The new items appear in the DVD Maker. Note, if you choose photos, they are placed in a folder called "slideshow" within the DVD Maker interface, as you can see in Figure 5. You can double-click the folder to see the photos. When you're done, click the Back to Videos button on the toolbar.

As you're working on adding items, notice you can use the toolbar buttons to remove items, or you can select an item and move it up or down in the list. Make

sure the order of the items is as you want because the order you see here is the order for the DVD.

Before moving forward, notice a Disc title dialog box is toward the bottom of the window. By default, the title is set by today's date (see Figure 5). However, you can change the title to whatever you would like.

Now that everything is added and ordered the way you want, click Next.

Configure the Menu

In the next window, you see the option to burn your disc. Before doing so, though, you have some

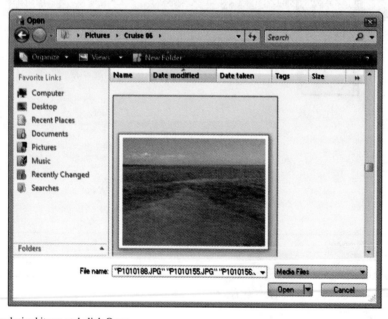

Figure 4. Select the desired items and click Open.

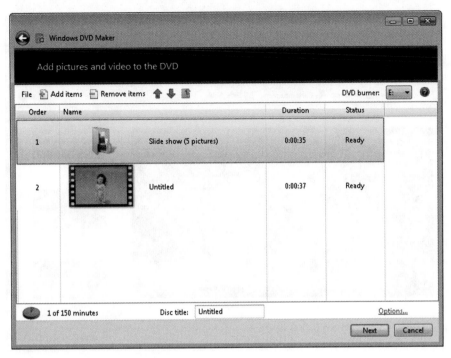

Figure 5. Photos appear in a folder called slideshow.

additional options you need to configure. The first is the DVD menu, which is what you see when you put the DVD into a DVD player. To create a menu, simply follow these steps:

1. In the right Menu Styles pane, click through the menu items to locate the one you want. When you click a menu style, you can see it in the interface. Notice the menus will use pieces of your DVD content, as shown in Figure 6.

2. As you might imagine, you'll want to change some things about the menu and you can easily do so. First, click the Menu text button on the toolbar. Choose the Font option, and then adjust the labels for the Disc title, Play button, Scenes button, and Notes button (if desired), as shown in Figure 7. Note, once you make your changes, you can click the Preview button to see your changes. Click Save when you're done.

3. Now, click the Customize button on the toolbar. You can use the provided dialog box and buttons to adjust the foreground and background video, menu audio, motion menu, and scene buttons, shown in Figure 8. The video option enables you to pull in other videos or photos to use within the menu, so the video looks just as you want. Make any desired changes here and click Save.

Configuring Your Slideshow

If your DVD includes a folder of photos for a slideshow, you can click the Slideshow button on the toolbar and make some adjustments as to how

Figure 6. Choose a menu option.

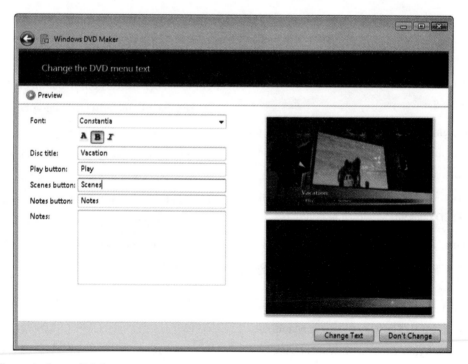

Figure 7. Change the font and labels.

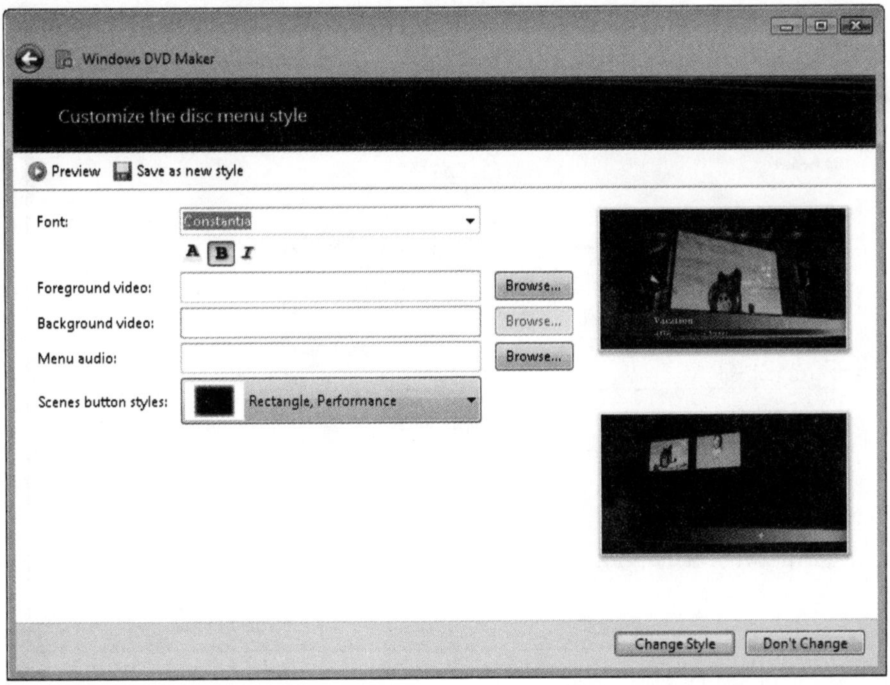

Figure 8. Customize the menu.

the slideshow looks when it's played. You'll see a slide show settings window, shown in Figure 9, where you can do the following:

- **Music**   Use the Add music button to add any music stored on your computer or a device connected to your computer to the slideshow. You see a standard Open interface where you can browse and select the music.

- **Slideshow length**   You can change the slideshow length to match the music clip you're using. You can also change the picture length, so each photo is displayed for a desired number of seconds. Typically, seven to ten seconds is enough.

- **Transition**   You can choose a transition between the photos. Use the drop-down

menu to make your selection. The transition you choose applies to all photos. In other words, you can't assign different transitions to different photos.

- **Pan and Zoom**   You can use this feature, so your photos appear to have movement with a panning and zooming feature.

Previewing Your DVD

Now that you have your settings and content configured, click the Preview button on the toolbar to see a preview of your DVD. After the preview, you can still make changes to the menu and slideshow, if necessary. When you click Preview, DVD Maker generates the movie and begins playing from the menu. Use the standard controls on the interface to view your movie.

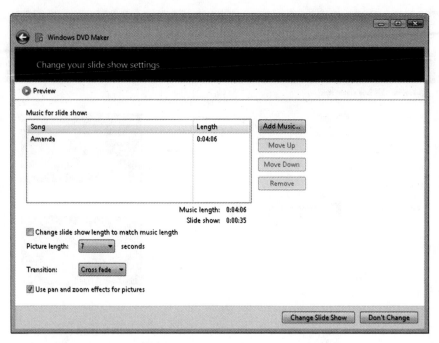

Figure 9. Choose the slide show settings and click Save.

Burn Your DVD

When you finish previewing your movie and have made final changes, then you're ready to burn your DVD. Make sure you're happy with your DVD before burning because you cannot stop the burn process to make changes. When you're ready, simply click Start Burn. The interface disappears and you see a Burning dialog box, shown in Figure 10. The burning process takes some time and it takes longer if your content is long. When the process is complete, you have a DVD that will play on any DVD player!

> ### NOTE
>
> Do you feel a lack of control? Remember, the DVD Maker simply helps you make the DVD. If you want to create a slideshow with more panning and transition controls, different music selections and such, use Windows Movie Maker to create the slideshow, and then simply burn the finished product using the DVD Maker. You can learn all about using Windows Movie Maker in Chapter 16.

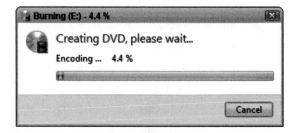

Figure 10. Your DVD is being burned.

TCP/IP here because Windows Vista does a good job of managing them on its own—which is a good thing since TCP/IP configuration can be really confusing.

Once you have run the wizard on your computers or have looked around at the settings, you can open the Network and Sharing Center in the Control Panel and click View Network Computers and Devices in the left pane and see the other computers available on your network, as the following illustration shows.

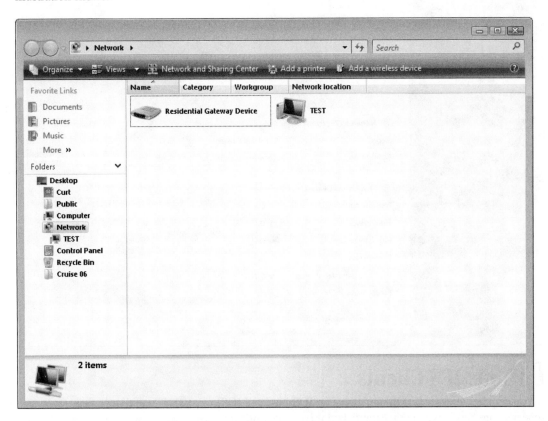

You can also access Windows Vista's new *Network Map,* which simply shows you a graphical representation of your network connection, shown in the following illustration.

You can find the Network Map by clicking View Full Map in the Network and Sharing Center.

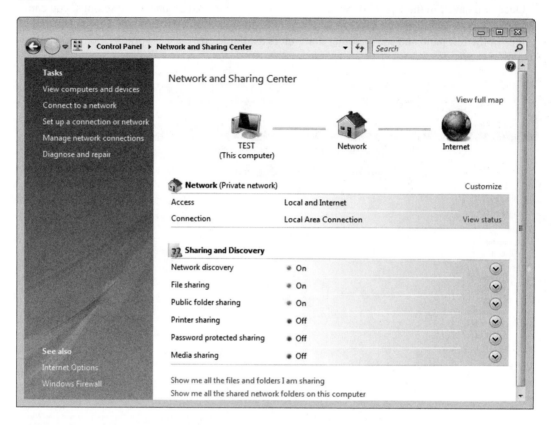

Set Up Your ICS Clients

If you decided to use ICS, you now have an ICS host and ICS client(s). If you didn't share your Internet connection when you established the connection, you can now turn on the feature by opening the Network and Sharing Center and clicking Manage Network Connections. Right-click the Internet connection and click Properties. On the Sharing tab, you can allow other people to access the connection to reach the Internet.

For your client computers to access the ICS host, you need to tell Internet Explorer how to access the Internet through the ICS host. Without this configuration, your applications will think your computer has a direct connection to the Internet. This configuration is easy, and this section shows you how to make the change with Internet Explorer. If you're using other browsers, e-mail clients, or applications, consult their documentation for specific steps—it will be similar to what you learn here.

Internet Explorer

To configure Internet Explorer to access the Internet through the ICS host, follow these easy steps:

1. Open Internet Explorer. If you get an error message about connecting to the Internet, click OK.

2. Choose Tools | Internet Options. Click the Connections tab.

3. On the Connections tab, select any existing dial-up connections in the window and click Remove.

4. Because you configured your computer for ICS with a host computer during the Home Networking Wizard, your computer should use the default LAN setting to find the shared connection.

Set Up a Wireless Network

Wireless networking has become popular over the past few years for the home and small office user, and rightly so. After all, it lets you create a network without needing to connect a bunch of cables. If you have a laptop computer, you can freely move around your home or office and stay connected to the network without being tied down (literally!).

If you visit your local computer store, you can find all kinds of home-networking cards, access points, routers, and other hardware provided by a variety of vendors. You can even find wireless home-networking kits designed to get you started. As you're thinking about creating a wireless network, here are a few pointers to remember:

■ Wireless networks require the use of a device similar to a hub, called an access point. Most *access points* are set up so you can connect a cable or DSL Internet connection directly to them for Internet sharing. While you can directly connect wireless computers using a method known as Ad Hoc, you'll probably be happier purchasing the access point.

■ If you buy an access point and wireless network cards for your computers, using the same brand for both is best. Although all wireless networking components work on a standard (so they *should* work well together), you'll have much better performance on your network and you're less likely to have problems if you stick with the same manufacturer.

■ Follow the manufacturer's setup instructions exactly. Wireless networks require all wireless cards to use the same channel and security key, so if you follow the manufacturer's installation and setup instructions, you're less likely to have problems.

■ Finally, make sure you change the default password on your wireless access point. This prevents someone else from changing the administrator password on your network, thus locking you out of your own network.

11

Once you install a wireless network card on your Windows Vista computer, you can use the Set Up a Network Wizard to configure the connection. However, once again, it's best to use the manufacturer's setup software and instructions. Once the wireless network is configured, you can view the properties of the connection and adjust them as necessary, using the wireless network connection in the Network Connections folder.

You should be able to get help from the wireless networking manufacturer's web site and, most likely, a toll-free help line. Do not call Microsoft for support because you are using hardware and software created by another company. If you're having problems, though, don't hesitate to call the manufacturer for assistance.

Use Windows Vista on a Large Network

It's no secret that Windows Vista is designed for high efficiency and operability in a Microsoft Windows network. *Windows Vista Ultimate* is designed to take full advantage of all Windows networking has to offer. You don't have to be a networking guru to understand this fact, and if you do work with Windows Vista Ultimate in a Microsoft network, you might hear some of these buzz words from time-to-time:

- **Web Integration** Windows Vista is designed to use the Internet or an intranet without any difficulty. When you jump to the Internet or an intranet, the information you see integrates with your folder views, so your Vista computer appears to be one with the Internet. With easy Web integration, networks can disseminate information to their employees more easily, and you can get what you need from the network more easily.

- **Active Directory** *Active Directory* is a powerful Microsoft networking feature that enables administrators to organize and manage a highly effective and large network. The benefit of Active Directory from your point of view is *simplicity*. You can easily search your network and find what you need, and then you can create a network place, so it appears right on your computer. Active Directory allows querying for all kinds of resources. For example, you can search for printers and find all the printers in your network, or even just those in your department. Windows Vista makes full use of Active Directory.

- **Group Policy** *Group Policy* is a feature network administrators use to manage user Desktops. Simply put, Group Policy lets administrators control the way your computer looks and what you can do with your computer. First introduced in Windows 2000, Group Policy is a powerful tool that allows administrators to configure your computer without any help from you and even to install software without your intervention. On the downside, Group Policy lets network administrators place restrictions on what you can and cannot do, as well. The good news is Group Policy is highly effective and makes computer environments easier to manage. Windows Vista takes full advantage of Group Policy in Windows networks.

Did you know?

How VPN Works

VPN uses a protocol called Point-to-Point Tunneling Protocol (PPTP). To send private communications over the Internet to and from a corporate network, PPTP hides the data you're sending inside a PPTP packet. A *PPTP packet* looks and acts like all the traffic on the Internet, but it hides the real network data inside. Think of a PPTP packet as a Christmas present: The wrappings and paper hide what's inside the box. The PPTP packet allows the data to traverse the Internet unharmed. When it reaches the private network, the PPTP wrapping is stripped away, revealing the real data hidden inside. To use PPTP, both your private network and your ISP must support VPN. Windows Vista also supports a new, more secure version of PPTP called Layer 2 Tunneling Protocol (L2TP). (This information may not be that useful to you, but you will sound cool throwing these terms around at the company water cooler.)

■ **Security**   In network environments, security is always a major concern. After all, you don't want intruders to gain access to computer data and steal company secrets. Windows Vista Ultimate provides the highest industry standards for security and, in a network environment, Windows Vista Ultimate can easily be configured to use the security standards in place for that network.

11

Virtual Private Networking

Virtual private networking (VPN) has been around for a few years, but it has recently become popular. As a home user, you probably won't use a virtual private network, but it *is* possible, and if you are a part of a small office, you may find VPN quite helpful. If you're in a larger network, you may use a Windows Vista laptop computer to connect to your corporate network using a VPN connection. You may want to connect to your office from home using a VPN connection.

VPN enables Windows Vista to create a private networking session using a public network. For example, let's say you work for a company based in Seattle. You travel to Atlanta for a conference. While you're in Atlanta, you want to access your company's network over the Internet. To ensure privacy, you can use a VPN connection. Or, what if your company has an intranet and you need to send private files to another employee? You can create a virtual private network over the intranet for the file transfer.

 *Your private network must support VPN for it to work. If your network uses an ISP to access the Internet, it must support VPN as well.*

Configure Your Windows Vista Computer for a VPN Connection

When you're ready to create the VPN connection on your computer, refer to the following steps:

1. Choose Start | Control Panel | Network and Sharing Center.

2. Click the Set Up a Connection or Network link in left pane.

3. In the window that appears, click the Connect to a Workplace option, and then click Next.

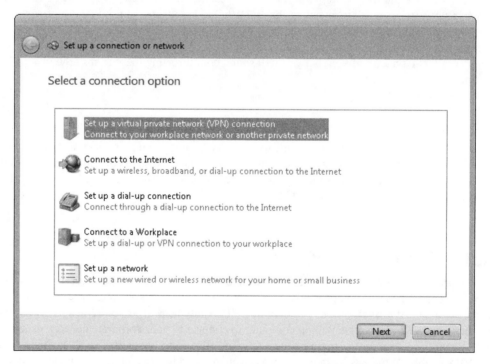

4. In the connection window, shown in the following illustration, enter the Internet address for the connection as provided by your network administrator. Notice you can connect using a smart card and you can also share this connection. Click Next.

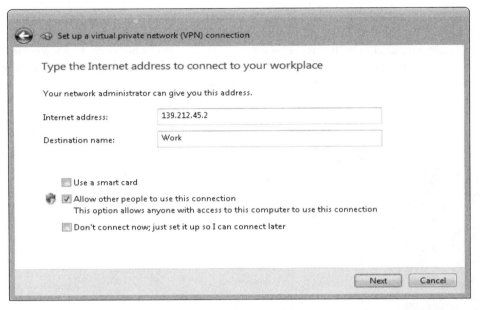

Type the Internet address to connect to your workplace

Your network administrator can give you this address.

Internet address: 139.212.45.2

Destination name: Work

☐ Use a smart card

☑ Allow other people to use this connection
  This option allows anyone with access to this computer to use this connection

☐ Don't connect now; just set it up so I can connect later

[Next]   [Cancel]

5. Enter your user name and password, and then click Connect to test the connection.

Network File and Printer Sharing

The purpose of networking is to share resources, which is true for home networking or even connecting to the Internet. The Network and Sharing Center icon in the Control Panel help you further control how you share resources on your network. If you open this applet in the

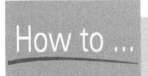

How to ...   Diagnose a Problem

Windows Vista includes a diagnostic tool for both Internet connections and your local area connection if you're having problems with connectivity. If Internet connectivity is the problem, open the Network and Sharing Center in the Control Panel and click the Diagnose and Repair link in the left pane. Follow any advice/instructions that appear.

Control Panel, you can determine settings for network discovery, file sharing, your public folder, printer sharing, password-protected sharing, and media sharing, shown in Figure 11-4. As a general rule, you want to be as flexible as possible, especially in a home-networking environment where access tends to be more important than security. Still, you can check the settings here to determine what permission levels you want to establish.

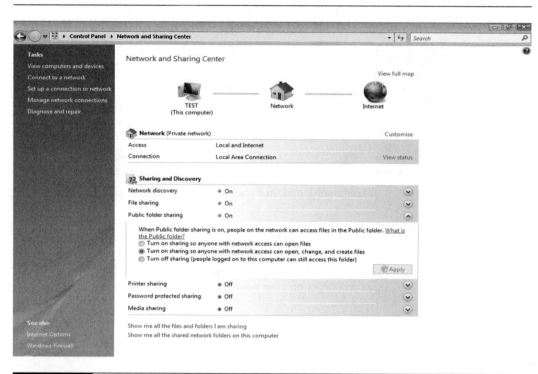

FIGURE 11-4 Network Sharing and Discovery

Chapter 12

Manage Users and Groups

How to...

- Understand Vista permissions
- Manage and configure user accounts
- Manage and configure group accounts

Windows Vista is designed to be a highly stable, highly secure desktop operating system (OS) for the home or office user. With Windows Vista, you can easily allow other people to use your computer, while preserving your personal settings and files. As far as users are concerned, each user can log in and log out of Windows Vista and use the computer as if it were his or her own PC. For both the home and the office user, this feature has far-reaching advantages. Managing permissions, users, and groups isn't a difficult task, but you must remember a number of concepts when working with these features of Windows Vista. In this chapter, you explore setting permissions, and managing and configuring user and group accounts.

Understand User Accounts

When Windows Vista is first installed, two default accounts are created: administrator and guest. The *administrator account,* which may be called Owner on your computer, has control of the entire Windows Vista computer—the administrator can perform tasks on the computer to make any changes he or she chooses. The administrator account cannot be deleted or disabled, so you (as the administrator) could never lock yourself out of your own computer unless, of course, you forgot your password.

The second default account, the *guest account,* is provided for users who don't have a user account on the computer. The guest account doesn't require a password, but it also has no permissions to make changes on the computer. The guest account is disabled by default, but it can be enabled if you need to use it.

Windows Vista provides these two built-in accounts, but from there, the issue of accounts and account configuration is up to you. As you are reading this section, you may be wondering how accounts affect you. If you are a home user and the Windows Vista computer is your primary home computer, you may be logging in with the default administrator account all the time (when I use Windows Vista at home, that is what I do). This account gives you complete control over the system. In addition to the default accounts, user accounts can be created to meet the needs of an administrator. For example, at an office, you may have your own user account, so you can use your computer as needed, but you can't change anything on it. With your home computer, you can, for example, use the administrator account yourself and configure other, more restrictive, accounts for your kids or others who borrow your PC. The choice is completely yours, and Windows Vista makes user management easy.

How to ... **Create a Password Reset Disk**

Windows Vista is geared for use in a multiuser environment in an office or in a home setting. To keep individual user's information private, user accounts should be set up with each account given a unique password.

If you want some added safety in case you forget your password, you should create a password reset disk. To do this, open the Control Panel and click User Accounts. Select the account for which you want to create a password recovery disk. From the Tasks list at the left, choose Prepare for a Forgotten Password and follow the wizard's instructions to create the disk.

If you forget your password, click the green arrow on the Windows Vista login screen, and you see a link to use your password recovery disk. This verifies your access rights and prompts you to create a new password, which you can use to access your account. The new password is written to your recovery disk at the same time you create it.

If you upgraded to Windows Vista from an older version of Windows, you need to create new recovery disks. The old disks you created on the previous version will no longer work.

Windows Vista offers two types of user accounts. The first is the administrator account created by default. The administrator can make changes or perform a variety of tasks on the computer. The second type is the *standard account,* which is good for most other users. With the limited account, the user can change desktop images and related personal data, as well as create, change, or remove his or her own password. The limited account user can also view any files he or she created and view files in the Public folder. This account type is great for kids, because it prevents them from adding or removing programs or hardware from the computer (which may end up with you being on the phone with technical support).

12

Rarely, games don't work well (or at all) under the limited user account. If you find this is the case, you need to use an upgraded account to run the games.

Manage User Accounts

You can easily manage user accounts from two different places within Windows Vista—from the User Accounts icon in the Control Panel and from the Computer Management console. We start with the UserAccounts icon in the Control Panel. If you click the icon, the User Accounts

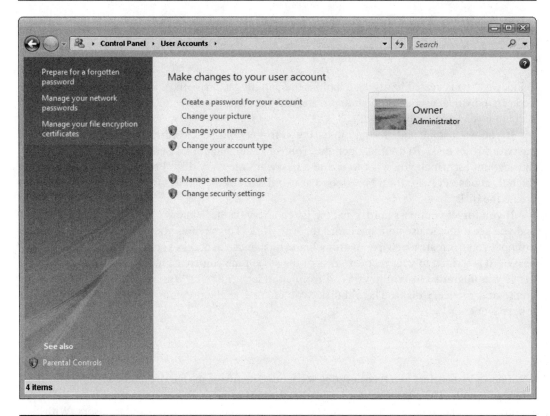

FIGURE 12-1 User Accounts

window opens, which gives you an easy-to-use graphical interface, as you can see in
Figure 12-1.

In the User Accounts window, you see some tasks you can perform and the current accounts
that exist on your computer. You can easily create new accounts or change existing accounts. The
following sections show you how to perform these actions.

Create a New Account

You can create new user accounts at any time, giving others access to your computer. To create a
new user account, follow these steps:

1. If you want to create a new account, click the Manage another account link in the User
    Accounts window. Then, click the option to Create a New Account, as the following
    illustration shows.

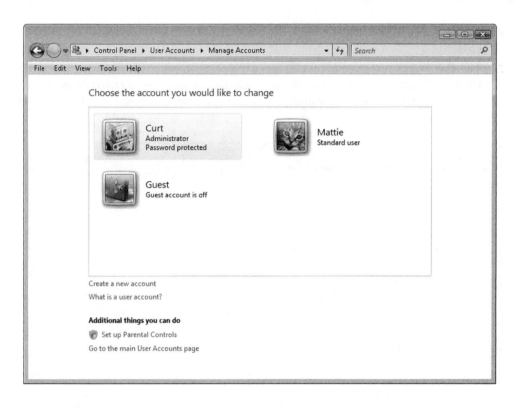

Did you know?

You Can Customize User Accounts with Pictures

By default, user accounts are represented with a picture that appears on the Welcome screen. At the Welcome screen, you click the user account picture to log on (and enter a password, if necessary). You can change these picture icons using the Change Picture feature. You can select another picture from those provided or browse and select your own. Virtually any type of graphics file can be used for your account icon picture (such as a GIF, JPEG, or BMP file). You can choose pictures that are interesting to you. For a family computer, it's fun to use a picture of each family member who has an account on the screen. When you see the Welcome screen, you see your family members, and you simply click your own picture to log on. This idea is great for computer users such as younger children who are just beginning to read. The possibilities are all yours—explore and have fun!

2. A New Account Name window appears. Enter the desired name for this new account and click Next.

3. The next window asks you to pick an account type, as shown in the following illustration. Choose either Administrator or Standard by selecting the appropriate radio button. If you're not sure, select each one and read the bulleted list of actions that can be performed by the account type.

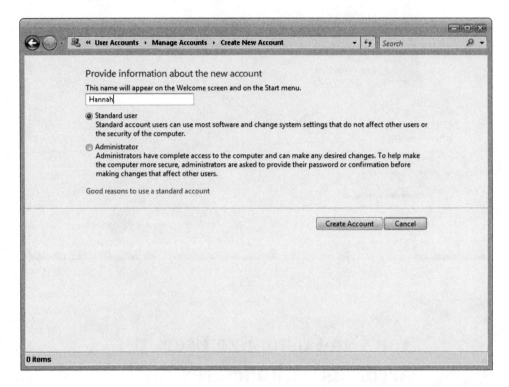

4. When you finish, click the Create Account button. The new account now appears in the User Accounts window.

Change an Account

Any account that has been created can be easily edited or changed from the User Accounts window. You can edit the password or create a password for an account that must be entered before a user logs on to the computer. Passwords provide security and prevent unauthorized individuals from logging on to a computer using someone else's account. Depending on your needs, you may not want passwords attached to user accounts (such as for home use), but you should always keep the administrator account password-protected, so little Johnny doesn't decide to log on as you and remove all your programs or delete your files!

In corporate environments, passwords are extremely important, and many highly secure environments go to great lengths to make sure passwords are so complex they cannot be easily broken. You may not need to worry about such matters, but if you're going to use passwords to protect your computer, you should use a combination of letters and numbers for the password and it should be at least seven characters long. Also, passwords are case-sensitive—so, for example, Windows Vista does not recognize CURT345 as the same password as Curt345. For security purposes, using a combination of letters (both uppercase and lowercase) and numbers is always best. The more random a password looks, the more difficult it is to break. Avoid using family names, pet names, phone numbers, birthdays, and other distinguishing words or numbers. Basically, avoid whole words, such as anything you might find in a dictionary. A combination of letters and numbers is always best.

If you create passwords, Windows Vista gives you the option of displaying a password hint that will appear on the Welcome screen. The purpose of the hint is to help you remember the password without giving it away to anyone else who accesses the Welcome screen (all users can see the hint). For example, you can use a password hint that reminds you of the topic of the password. On one of my Vista computers, my password is OldHOuse49. My wife and I own a historic home that is always in some phase of remodeling, so for my hint, I put "where my money goes." This reminds me of my old house and, hence, my password.

To make changes to an existing user account, follow these steps:

1. In the User Accounts window, click the account you want to change.

2. Another window appears that enables you to change the name on the account, change the picture that appears on the Welcome screen, change the account type, create a password, or delete the account. You can also set up parental controls here. Just select the option you want and follow the instructions. As you can see, each user account is represented by an icon. If you click Change Picture, a window appears, as the following illustration shows, where you can select a new picture or browse for a different one.

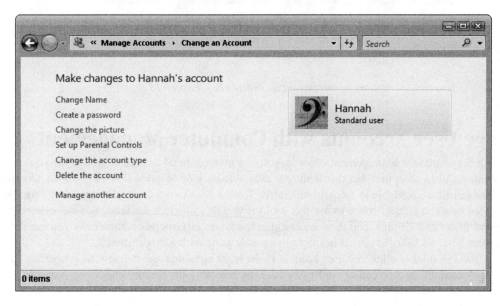

12

3. If you want to change a password for the account, click the Change Password option and enter the password as instructed in the Password window. You can choose to enter a password hint if you like, shown in the following illustration.

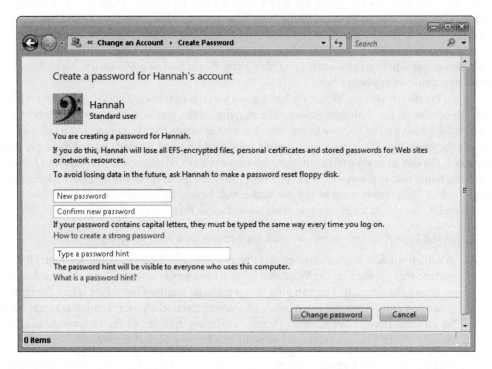

4. Use the Back button to return to the change list, and then make any additional changes you want.

   *You can learn more about parental controls in Chapter 13.*

Manage User Accounts with Computer Management

With the Computer Management console, you can manage local users and groups for your Windows Vista computer, but this feature is available only on Windows Vista Ultimate. Computer Management is available in the Administrative Tools folder in the Control Panel. (You must be logged on as an administrator to use this tool.) If you double-click the icon, you can expand Local Users and Groups, and then select either the Users or Groups container. As you can see in Figure 12-2, all users are listed in the right console pane with a description.

You can double-click any user account in the right console pane to open the properties sheets for the account. As you can see in Figure 12-3, by selecting the desired check box, you can make

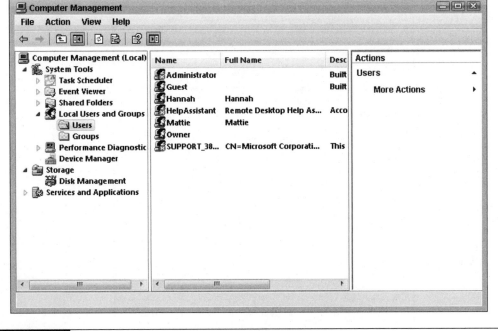

FIGURE 12-2   Local Users and Groups in Computer Management

a number of security-related changes, such as forcing a user to change his or her password at the next logon or restricting a user, so the password can never be changed. You can also disable the account from this location.

The Member Of tab lists the groups the user is a member of. To add the user to a new group, click the Add button and select the group. You can click the Remove button to remove the user from any group. (See the next section to learn more about groups.) Finally, from the Profile tab, you can use a few fields to configure a path to the user's profile (if profiles are used). Profiles are more widely used in larger networking environments, and this feature isn't something you would typically enable for home or small office use.

If you want to create a new user by using the Computer Management console, right-click the Users container in the left pane and choose New User.

Manage Groups

Groups are an effective way to organize users in terms of permissions. In fact, facilitating the permissions function is basically the only reason group accounts exist. Let's say ten people use your Windows Vista computer. Five of those users might be administrators, while the other five

FIGURE 12-3   User account properties

might have limited accounts. You can add those five limited users to the administrator group, and then manage them as one entity, rather than as five different accounts.

On a grander scale, groups are used in large networking environments for resource access in networks that use more complicated folder and file sharing methods. Let's say your department has one printer. You want everyone in your department, but not users from another department, to be able to use the printer. Sure, you can use the printer's Security tab and add each user from your department to the permissions list, but an easier way to manage the users is to create a group account for them once, and then use the group account to give them access to network resources, such as printers and shared folders.

If you click the Groups container in the Computer Management console, you see a list of default groups on the right side of the console. If you double-click a group, you see a listing of the members, which you can change using the Add and Remove buttons. You can also create a new group by right-clicking the Group container and choosing New Group. Doing this opens a New Group window, where you can name the group and add members to the group.

About User Account Control

Windows Vista includes a new feature called *User Account Control (UAC)*. UAC is an additional layer of security that greatly helps prevent unauthorized changes to your computer. If a program is trying to change something on your computer, you get a UAC message telling you so and requiring you to OK the change before proceeding. This feature, although somewhat annoying, is a helpful security step. You can turn off the UAC from the list of change options on your user account (click Change security settings), as you can see in the following illustration, but I strongly recommend you leave the feature enabled. UAC is enabled by default.

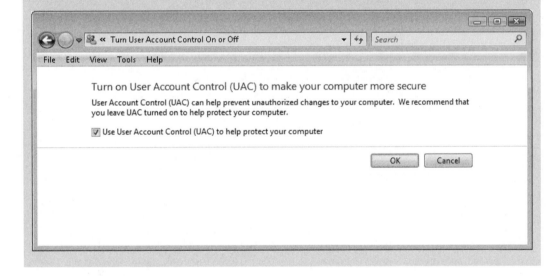

12

Chapter 13

Windows Vista Security and Remote Connections

How to...

- Use Windows Firewall
- Use Windows Defender
- Configure Parental Controls
- Configure Remote Desktop
- Use Remote Assistance

If the terms "firewall" and "defender" sound like worrisome things that reside on your computer, don't worry. A firewall is a good thing. In networks, a *firewall* is a piece of computer software or hardware that protects a network from intruders. For example, let's say you own a small company with a network of 200 computers. Each user needs to access the Internet every day, so a primary Internet link travels from your company to an ISP. Although you need to use the Internet each day, you don't want people on the Internet getting inside your private network and stealing information from you. What do you do? The answer is to use a firewall.

In this chapter, we look at Windows Firewall, as well as a new feature in Windows Vista called Windows Defender. You also see how to use Parental Controls in Windows Vista, as well as remote connections.

Use Windows Firewall

Firewalls use various kinds of protocol tactics to check traffic as it flows in and out of the network. Based on rules configured by system administrators, certain kinds of traffic are allowed or not allowed, and some kinds of traffic can even be seen as threatening. In short, the firewall acts as a paranoid traffic cop who makes certain no one gets inside the private network. Firewalls are nothing new. They have been around for years, and most large, private networks today use some kind of firewall technology (and they spend thousands of dollars on it each year).

You may think, "That's great, but what does that have to do with me and my Windows Vista computer?" Instead of firewalls that are limited to large networking environments, Windows Vista includes its own firewall to help protect your computer from malicious people when you're on the Internet, and even on a network at work and home. You can think of the firewall found in Windows Vista as a personal firewall. Other companies also produce firewalls for the typical home or small office user (such as Norton Internet Security), and you can even find good free products, such as ZoneAlarm (www.zonelabs.com).

The next question that may come to mind concerns the need for a firewall. After all, as a home user, you may have been connecting to the Internet for years without a firewall on your computer. Why do you need one now? Any time you are using the Internet, your computer is open to potential attacks. With a dial-up connection, the attacks are limited because you aren't connected to the Internet all the time. However, with the explosive growth of broadband connections (such as DSL and cable), the need for a firewall becomes important, because these computers are always connected to the Internet and, therefore, they're always exposed to danger. For this reason, Windows Firewall is included with Windows Vista and is a part of the Security Center.

Understand How Windows Firewall Works

Windows Firewall is a software solution in Windows Vista. A *software solution* means Windows Firewall uses code built into the Windows Vista OS to monitor and manage Internet and local network traffic. As you might imagine, the process of managing traffic can become a rather complex topic, so I'm going to give you the important aspects of the process here and skip the boring technical details.

Windows Firewall is considered a *stateful* firewall, which means Windows Firewall works with your Internet connection and/or local area network (LAN) connection to examine traffic as it passes through the firewall, both to and from your computer/network. Because Windows Firewall is stateful, it examines traffic in terms of its live use. If something not allowed attempts to enter the firewall, Windows Firewall steps in and blocks the traffic from entering. Basically, no disallowed traffic ever passes the firewall. To use stateful inspection, Windows Firewall examines the destination of every piece of traffic coming from your computer or computers on your network. Whenever something is sent to the Internet (such as a URL request) or even a local request on your local network, Windows Firewall keeps a routing table to track your requests. When data comes to the firewall, Windows Firewall inspects it to see if it matches with requests found in the routing table. If so, it's passed on to your computer or the requesting computer on your network. If not, it's blocked from entering the firewall. The end result is this: any traffic you want from the Internet or your LAN can enter the firewall, and anything you haven't requested is blocked.

Issues with Windows Firewall

Before we get into more detail about Windows Firewall configuration, let me point out a few issues concerning the firewall's default behavior. You should remember these issues as you set up Internet connections or home/small office networks:

- Windows Firewall should be enabled on any shared Internet connection in your home or small office network. You don't have to use a home or small office network to use Windows Firewall. If you want the protection, Windows Firewall works great on one computer, too.

- Windows Firewall works on a per-connection basis. For example, let's say your computer has a DSL connection and a modem connection (you use the modem connection in case the DSL connection goes down). You need to enable Windows Firewall on both the DSL and modem connections to have full protection. Windows Firewall is enabled per connection—not per computer.

13

■ In a small network setting using Internet Connection Sharing (ICS), you should certainly enable Windows Firewall on the ICS connection. However, if other computers on the network have other ways to connect to the Internet (such as through modems), you need to enable Windows Firewall on each of those connections as well. Again, Windows Firewall works on a per-connection basis.

Checking Windows Firewall

Windows Firewall is enabled by default when you install Windows Vista. You make sure it's turned on and access additional Firewall settings by opening the Windows Vista Security Center, found in the Control Panel. When you open the Security Center, you can click on Firewall and see Windows is actively defending your computer, as shown in Figure 13-1.

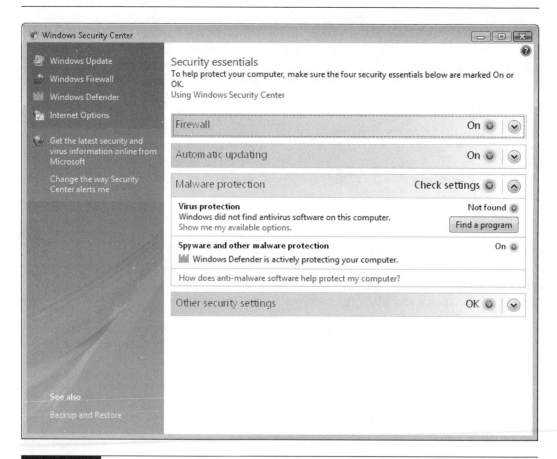

FIGURE 13-1   Windows Firewall in Windows Security Center

Configure Windows Firewall Settings

The default Firewall settings are typically all you need but, in some cases, you may need to change the normal way Windows Firewall works or even some advanced options to enable certain programs to work. You can do all these actions by clicking the Windows Firewall link in the left pane of the Windows Security Center and clicking the change settings link. This action opens the Windows Firewall properties.

The first tab you see is the General tab, shown in Figure 13-2. All you can do here is either turn the firewall on or off. Under the On setting, notice you have a Block All Programs check box option. This setting should be used when you're connected to public networks, such as those found in airports, coffee shops, and such. This feature blocks any and all programs coming from the network, which is an additional security feature. Otherwise, you can leave this check box alone. In terms of firewall use, you should always leave the firewall enabled. Only disable the firewall if you're using a third-party firewall solution instead.

If you open the Exceptions tab of the Windows Firewall dialog box, you see settings that govern how Windows Firewall works and what kinds of applications and services it allows. Again, you typically don't need to configure anything here if you're simply using the Internet and accessing Internet mail. However, if you're using certain applications or providing certain

13

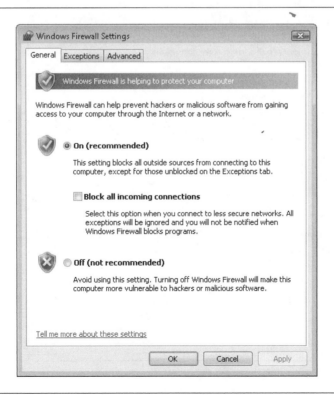

FIGURE 13-2   General tab

types of content to the Internet, you may need to configure some of these settings. The settings here can get a little complicated and tricky, however, so be forewarned!

Check out the Exceptions tab, shown in Figure 13-3. The *Exceptions tab* provides a list of programs and services running on your computer or network that you are allowing Internet or network users to access. For example, let's say you want to use Remote Assistance on your Windows Vista computer. (We explore this in the section "Use Remote Assistance.") If Windows Firewall is in use, you need to check the Remote Assistance check box, so a Remote Assistance user can contact you. Selecting a check box unblocks the program. When you click this check box, and then click OK, Windows Firewall reconfigures itself to allow certain kinds of content to pass through the firewall to meet these needs. Or, for example, let's say you want to use Remote Desktop (covered in the section "Configure Remote Desktop") with someone on the Internet. By default, Windows Firewall won't allow this kind of communication, but if you enable it here, Windows Firewall understands Remote Desktop should be allowed.

If you aren't offering any services to Internet clients, but you want to use the Internet only for Web surfing and e-mail, you don't need to do anything in this tab. Make sure none of the check boxes is selected.

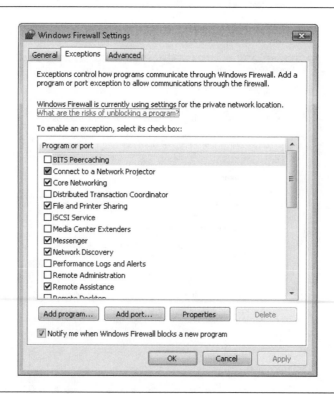

FIGURE 13-3   Exceptions tab

However, you can customize the exceptions by adding a program to unblock or adding a port to unblock. For example, let's say you have some application installed that uses the Internet in some way, but this application doesn't seem to work. You click the Add Program button and Browse your computer to locate the program, and then click OK. Furthermore, you can be even more specific by clicking the Add Program button, locating and selecting the program in the Browse list, and then clicking the Change Scope button. Here, you can specify that any computer (including those on the Internet) can access the program, or you can limit it to your local network or even local computers on your network if you like, as shown in the following illustration.

Change Scope

To specify the set of computers for which this port or program is unblocked, click an option below.

To specify a custom list, type a list of IP addresses, subnets, or both, separated by commas.

◉ Any computer (including those on the Internet)

◎ My network (subnet) only

◎ Custom list:

Example: 192.168.114.201,192.168.114.201/255.255.255.0,
             3ffe:ffff:8311:f282:1460:5260:c9b1:fda6

[OK]   [Cancel]

If you have a program that needs a particular port number open, you can click the Add Port button, give the exception name, and enter the port number. Certain programs use certain ports on the network to communicate. Consult your program's documentation to determine if this is something you need to do.

About Keeping Your Network Secure

Windows Firewall is designed to keep your computer or network secure, but it can do its job only if you keep it enabled and configured effectively. For this reason, you should never make any changes to the Exceptions and Advanced tab that you don't clearly understand. For example, let's say you enable the web server (HTTP) feature. This setting tells Windows Firewall your computer is a web server and that it should allow web server requests and messages to pass through the firewall. However, if your computer is not a web server, then selecting this check box opens the door for intruders to get into your computer or network for no reason at all. Windows Firewall is one of those great features where less is more—do *not* enable anything extra unless it's absolutely necessary.

13

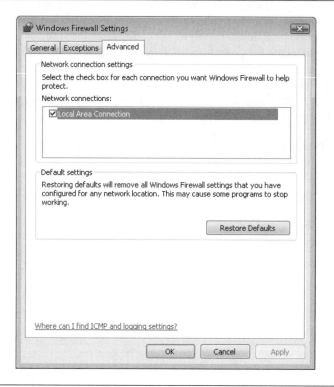

FIGURE 13-4   Advanced tab

If you click the Advanced tab, you can see which network connections Windows Firewall is protecting, as Figure 13-4 shows. If you want to allow more or less connections, select or deselect the check boxes as necessary. However, remember, every Internet connection on your computer should be protected by the firewall.

Use Windows Defender

Windows Defender is a new tool included in Windows Vista. *Windows Defender* is a spyware tool that looks at data and information flowing to your computer from the Internet, your local network, and even CDs or DVDs. Essentially, *spyware* refers to a collection of different programs that can install on your computer without you knowing it. These programs gather information about you and how you use the computer, and they send this information to a web server. Spyware can also change settings on your computer without your consent and cause your computer to run slowly. In the end, spyware is a program that installs without your consent or control and does things you don't want.

This leads us to Windows Defender, which is a software solution designed to scan programs that try to install on Windows Vista, identify spyware threats, and either keep them from installing or at least alert you to the possibility.

Tale-Tell Signs That Your Computer Has Spyware

How can you tell if your computer is infected with spyware? Here are some tale-tell signs you should be aware of:

■ You notice new toolbars, links, favorites, or even buttons in Internet Explorer (IE) that you didn't put there.

■ You type a web site address in your browser, but you end up at another web site you didn't want instead.

■ Your home page in your browser changes to a different home page.

■ You see pop-up adds appear, even when you're not using the Internet.

■ Your computer starts to run much more slowly than normal.

Spyware can come from any kind of software installation or download, but it most commonly gets on your computer by installing so-called "free" software from the Internet, such as file-sharing software, screen savers, and utilities, or by adding new search toolbars to your browser.

The good news is Windows Defender is software that can identify spyware and get rid of it. Like Windows Firewall, Windows Defender is managed from the Security Center, and it is enabled and runs by default. To protect your computer, Windows Defender uses real-time protection in that it is constantly watching programs that get installed on your computer. Defender can also connect you with the Microsoft SpyNet community, so you can check for the latest possible threats that may not yet be classified as "risks." You can also run scans yourself and schedule them to run on a regular basis. The following sections show you how to configure Windows Defender.

Run a Scan

Windows Defender is always at work, but you can run a scan yourself by clicking the Windows Defender link in the left pane of the Windows Security Center. This opens the Windows Defender interface. You have a few button options. If you click the Scan button, you can have Defender run a scan of your computer (see Figure 13-5). You can also check the History and see when the last scans were run and what spyware threats Defender has encountered. You can also click the drop-down menu next to Scan to run a quick scan, full computer scan, or scan selected drives and folders.

13

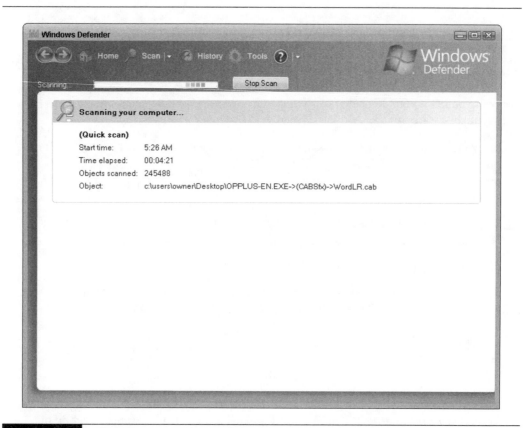

FIGURE 13-5   Click Scan to run a complete scan

Use Windows Defender Tools

If you click the Tools option, shown in Figure 13-6, you can choose from a few important features. The following sections outline these options.

Options

The *Options button* enables you to configure several options and features that are self-explanatory for the most part, shown in Figure 13-7. You can create a schedule when a scan should occur (a daily scan is recommended). You can also determine what the default actions should be for each kind of alert level. You can choose to use or not use real-time protection (I recommend you leave this setting enabled) and you can choose to scan certain archived files and folders for potential threats. Finally, you also have some administrator options that enable Windows Defender and allow users that don't have administrator privileges to run a scan. Make any desired changes and click the Save button.

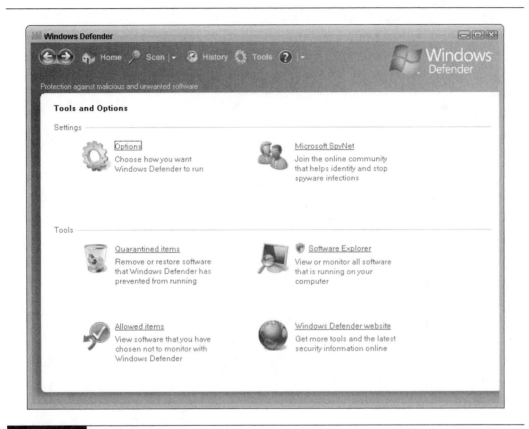

FIGURE 13-6   Tools and Options

Microsoft Spynet

This option enables you to join *Microsoft Spynet,* which is a community of users that submit information automatically to Microsoft. This program is free and it's a good idea to be a part of it. You can join with a basic membership, where information about detected items and the actions you take are sent to Microsoft, or you can join with an advanced membership where information about unclassified software is collected as well. Some personal information about you may be collected with the advanced membership, but it isn't used to contact you. To help in the threat against spyware, you should at least join with the basic membership. Click the desired radio button and click Save.

Quarantined Items

When Defender stops a program from installing, that program is placed in *quarantine,* which is basically a holding area. If you click Quarantined Items, you can see what software is being held here. At this point, you can remove the desired items or even restore quarantined items that shouldn't be there.

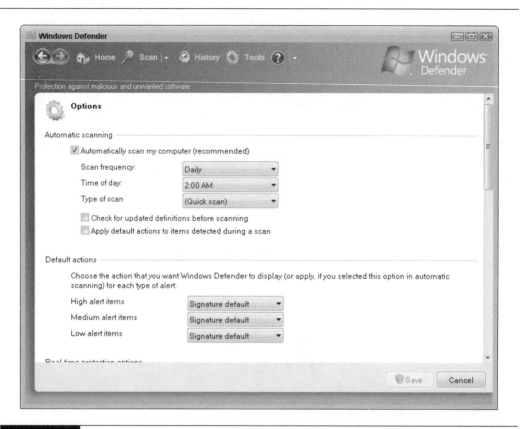

FIGURE 13-7   Options

Software Explorer

The *Software Explorer,* shown in Figure 13-8, is a cool feature that enables you to examine every piece of software running on your computer at the moment. Simply scroll through the list, select a software item, and you can see details about it in the right information pane. You can remove software by clicking the Remove button or stop it from running by clicking Disable.

Allowed Items and Windows Defender Web Site

If you click Allowed Items, you can see what software items Windows Defender has allowed installation. There isn't anything you can do here except view the items on the list. You can also click the Windows Defender web site option to get the latest tools and security information.

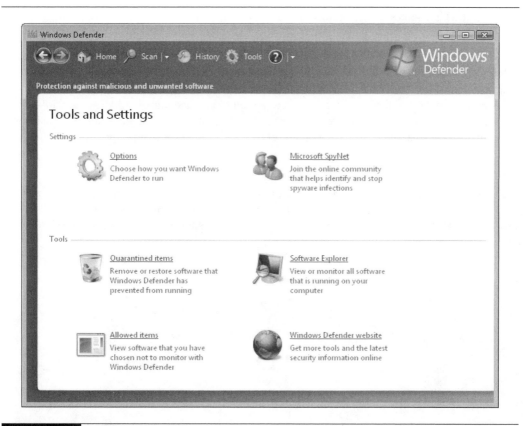

FIGURE 13-8   Software Explorer

13

Configure Parental Controls

Parental Controls are a great new feature in Windows Vista, and as a parent with young children who are just starting to use the computer and the Internet, I found this feature to be one of the more exciting ones in Windows Vista. After all, every parent wants his or her children to be safe, and in an information-exchange society, safety when using the computer and the Internet is of vital importance. In the past, you could purchase parental software that could help, but with Parental Controls in Windows Vista, you now have the necessary software provided directly to you through the OS.

First things first: What can you do with parental controls? A lot. Here's a rundown of its features:

■ Parental Controls are tied to each user account. You can create different user accounts for each child or teen and configure different settings for each.

■ Limit your child's access to the Internet.

■ Limit the hours your child can log on to the computer.

- Limit which games and programs your child can use.
- Override these settings at any time using your administrator account password.

Before you start to configure parental controls, each child needs his or her own user account. That account must be a standard account because parental controls cannot be applied to an administrator account. So, for basic security, your administrator account should be password-protected with a password your children don't know, so they can't override the settings by using your password. See Chapter 12 to learn how to set up user accounts and apply passwords.

Setting Up Parental Controls

To set up parental controls for a child, click Start | Control Panel | Parental Controls. Remember, you must be logged on with an administrator level account to configure these settings. In the Parental Controls window, choose the user account you want to configure, as shown in Figure 13-9.

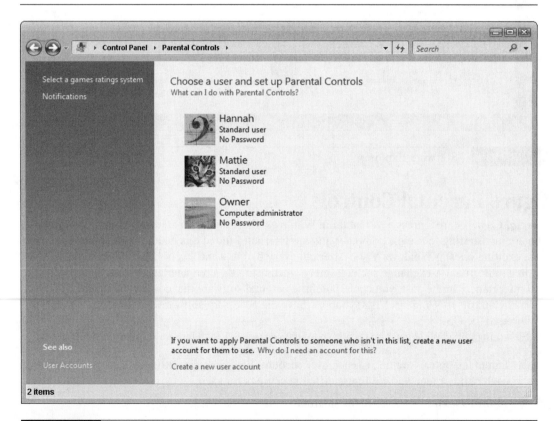

FIGURE 13-9 Choose the child's user account to which you want to apply parental controls

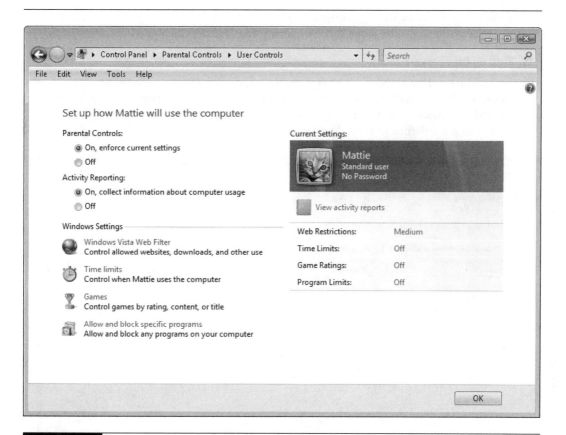

FIGURE 13-10   Turn on Parental Controls and Activity Reporting, if desired

13

In the Parental Controls window, turn on Parental Controls by clicking the On button, as shown in Figure 13-10. You can also turn on Activity Reporting, so you can view a report of everything your child is doing on the computer. This feature gives you accurate information about how your child is using the computer and I recommend you enable it, as well.

Configure Web Restrictions

One of the main features of Parental Controls is you can configure restrictions for your child, essentially determining what he or she can do on the Internet. Because Internet usage tends to be a major area of concern for parents (and rightfully so), you certainly want to place some restrictions on your child's Internet use.

Click the Windows Vista Web Filter option in the middle of the Parental Controls interface. This opens the Web Restrictions window, shown in Figure 13-11. You can do the following:

- Turn on the option to block some web content by clicking the Block button.
- Under Allow or Block Specific Websites, choose allow or block specific web sites that you choose to allow or block, as the following illustration shows. Simply type the desired web site and click Allow or Block. The options here override other general settings, so you can strengthen the web filter or override it for some sites.

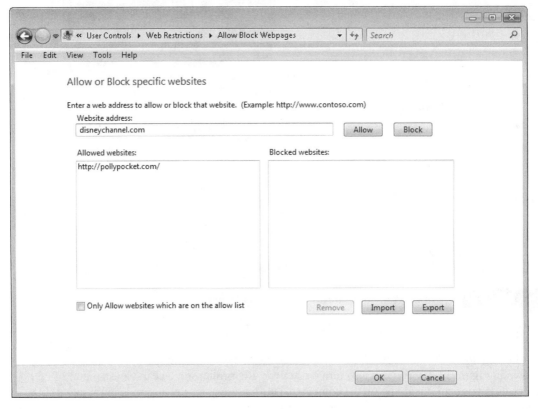

- Choose a restriction level. If you click a level of restriction, you'll notice different content categories are selected. However, you can customize this option by simply clicking the categories you want to block. This setting causes Parental Controls to look at each web site and block sites with this content, assuming the sites are rated. However, this feature is not foolproof, so if you want to make sure your child does not access any non-rated sites, simply click the "Block Websites that Parental Controls Cannot Rate" check box.
- Under Block File Downloads, you have the option to block file downloads or not. For younger children especially, this is a good setting to use.

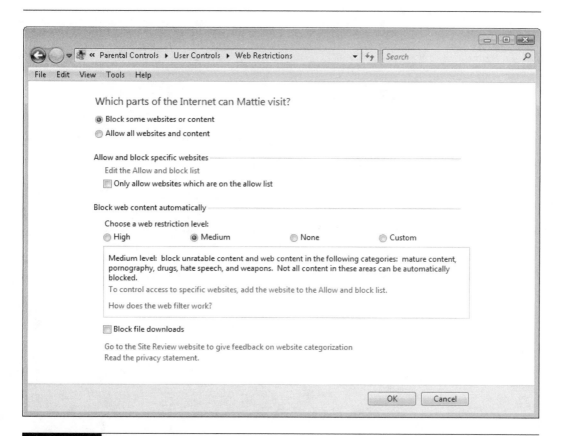

FIGURE 13-11 Configure the web filter

Set Time Limits

If you click the Time Limits option, you see a simple interface where you can click-and-drag to allow time that your child can use the computer each day. Red areas are blocked time, so your child will be unable to use the computer during blocked out hours of the day, as Figure 13-12 shows.

Games

Click the Games button to determine what types of games your child is allowed to play, shown in Figure 13-13. You can first allow games, and then you can choose to set the game rating limits for your child, and block or allow specific games found on your computer. If you click the Set Game Ratings option, you see a window, shown in Figure 13-14, that enables you to allow or block games with no ratings. You can then choose rating levels your child can play, as well as any online game content. Choose the desired options here and click OK.

13

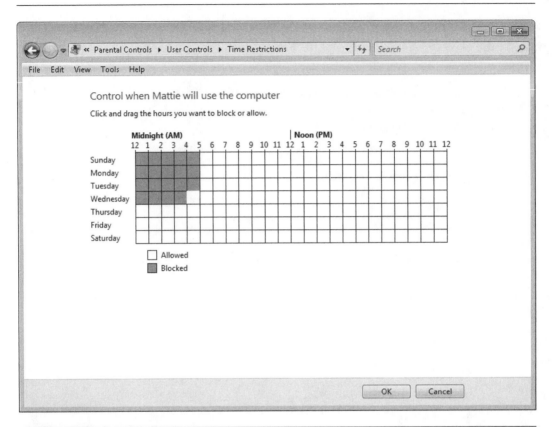

FIGURE 13-12   Time Limits

Allow or Block Specific Programs

You can allow your child to use programs on your computer, but you can also block any programs on your computer that you don't want your child to play. Simply click the Allow or Block Specific Programs option and, in the provided window, restrict the programs your child can use to the allowed programs on the list. Make your selections and click OK.

Activity Reports

At any time, you can return to the Parental Controls page and click Activity Reports to see your child's web browsing activities, file downloads, system events, and applications that were run, as shown in Figure 13-15. As you can see, this report can be helpful in determining what your child is doing on your computer.

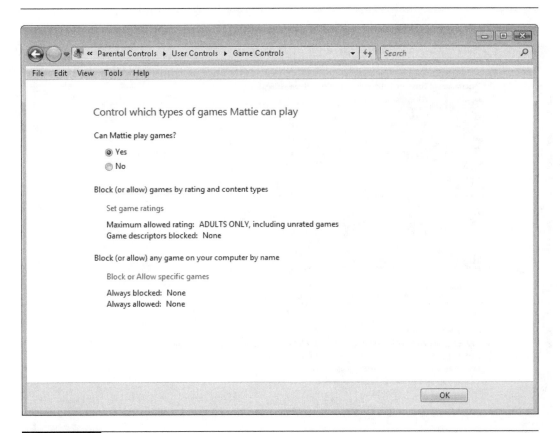

FIGURE 13-13   Games options

13

Configure Remote Desktop

Windows Vista supports a cool feature called Remote Desktop. Consider this scenario: You use Windows Vista at the office, which is half an hour from your home. When you get home, you realize you left some important business unattended on your work computer. You also have a Windows computer at your home—now, what can you do? No problem—you can use your home computer to connect with the office computer, and then you can use the office computer with Remote Desktop just as if you were sitting there. Sound too good to be true? It's true, and this new feature works great.

Remote Desktop has a number of potentially exciting applications. You can access a remote computer, and then use the applications and information found on that computer seamlessly, just as if your hands were on the computer's keyboard. You can even use Remote Desktop to connect to another person's computer and help him or her solve problems through Windows Vista's

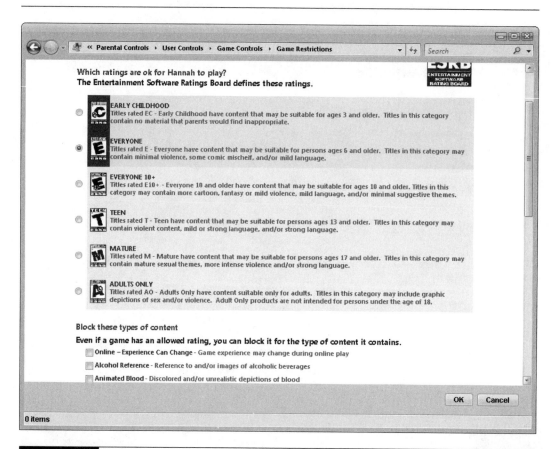

FIGURE 13-14 Choose the desired game ratings

Remote Assistance feature, explored in the section "Use Remote Assistance." The possibilities are endless. With Remote Desktop, a remote computer is always at your fingertips.

The Remote Desktop client updates an older technology called Terminal Services Client. Essentially, your computer can connect with a remote computer and, assuming proper permissions are in place, your computer can use the remote computer in a "dumb terminal" manner, as though you were sitting at the computer's location. Remote Desktop obviously works on Windows Vista as well as Windows XP, but by using the Vista installation CD-ROM, you can also add the Remote Desktop Connection tool to other Windows operating systems, such as Windows 9x, Me, NT 4.0, or 2000.

TIP

If you access a computer remotely, don't worry about onlookers. The remote computer is locked, so no one can walk by and see what you're doing on the computer in your physical absence. In other words, you aren't logged on to the local computer and another person cannot use it locally. However, a local administrator can disconnect you simply by logging on to the computer.

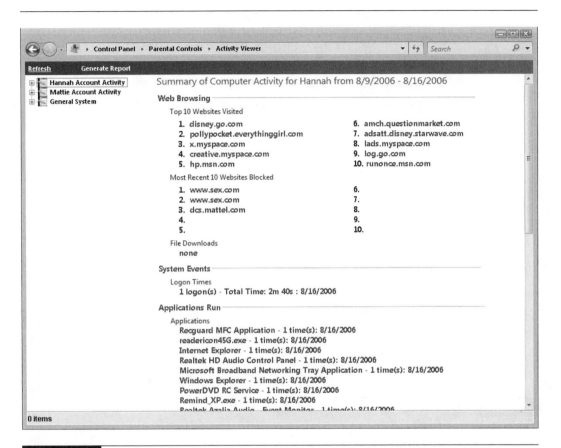

Control Panel ▸ Parental Controls ▸ Activity Viewer | Search

Refresh   Generate Report

Hannah Account Activity
Mattie Account Activity
General System

Summary of Computer Activity for Hannah from 8/9/2006 - 8/16/2006

Web Browsing

Top 10 Websites Visited

1. disney.go.com   6. amch.questionmarket.com
2. pollypocket.everythinggirl.com   7. adsatt.disney.starwave.com
3. x.myspace.com   8. lads.myspace.com
4. creative.myspace.com   9. log.go.com
5. hp.msn.com   10. runonce.msn.com

Most Recent 10 Websites Blocked

1. www.sex.com   6.
2. www.sex.com   7.
3. dcs.mattel.com   8.
4.   9.
5.   10.

File Downloads
none

System Events

Logon Times
1 logon(s) - Total Time: 2m 40s : 8/16/2006

Applications Run

Applications
Recguard MFC Application - 1 time(s): 8/16/2006
readericon45G.exe - 1 time(s): 8/16/2006
Internet Explorer - 1 time(s): 8/16/2006
Realtek HD Audio Control Panel - 1 time(s): 8/16/2006
Microsoft Broadband Networking Tray Application - 1 time(s): 8/16/2006
Windows Explorer - 1 time(s): 8/16/2006
PowerDVD RC Service - 1 time(s): 8/16/2006
Remind_XP.exe - 1 time(s): 8/16/2006
Realtek Azalia Audio - Event Monitor - 1 time(s): 8/16/2006

0 items

FIGURE 13-15   Activity reports

13

Enable Remote Desktop

If you're currently logged on as the computer's administrator, you can enable the Remote Desktop feature on your Windows Vista computer, so others can connect to it. Access System Properties in the Control Panel and click the Remote Settings link. As you can see in Figure 13-16, you can enable both Remote Assistance and Remote Desktop from this tab.

Once you enable Remote Desktop, you should consider two issues. The first is a user account. The remote computer must log on to your computer with a user name and password, just as if you were sitting at the local computer. When you log on locally, you may be able to use a blank password, but the Remote Desktop connection requires a password. Think about the account you will log on with and make sure a password is configured for the account. If it isn't, configure one using the User Accounts option in the Control Panel (see Chapter 12 for specific instructions). You may also consider creating a specific Remote Desktop account to use just for the Remote Desktop connection.

FIGURE 13-16   Remote tab

The second issue you need to consider is Windows Firewall. Remote Desktop won't work over Windows Firewall if Windows Firewall is enabled and not configured to pass Remote Desktop traffic. You can easily configure Windows Firewall to pass Remote Desktop traffic on the Exceptions tab of the Windows Firewall properties dialog. (See the earlier section "Configure Windows Firewall Settings" for instructions.) However, your company may be using an additional firewall as well. Check with your network administrator about additional settings that may need to be configured.

Once you address these two issues, you need to determine which users are allowed to connect from a remote location. Let's say you use Windows Vista at your office, and three other people use that computer with Limited accounts. You want to make certain that only your account can connect remotely. No problem. To configure the user(s) who can connect, click the Select Remote Users button on the Remote tab of the System Properties window, and then click the Add button on the Remote Desktop Users dialog box. A Select Users dialog box appears, as shown next.

Enter the user account to which you want to give permission, or click the Advanced button and choose the user from the list. When you're done, click OK.

Remote Desktop Users

The users listed below can connect to this computer, and any members of the Administrators group can connect even if they are not listed.

Administrator

Owner already has access.

[Add...] [Remove]

To create new user accounts or add users to other groups, go to Control Panel and open User Accounts.

[OK] [Cancel]

Configure the Remote Desktop Client Computer

Once you enable Remote Desktop on the host computer, you can then configure the remote computer to connect to the host. I have some great news—if the remote computer is running Windows Vista or XP, you have nothing to do! The Remote Desktop Connection software is already built-in and ready to go. Move on to the next section, "Make a Remote Desktop Connection."

If you're using an earlier version of Windows or a Macintosh, you need to install the Remote Desktop Connection software. This tool, called Remote Desktop Client, is found on your Windows Vista installation CD-ROM, or you can download it directly from www.microsoft.com/windowsxp/ downloads/tools/rdclientdl.mspx. The Remote Desktop Client software works on any version of Windows 95, 98, Me, NT, or 2000. (And a Remote Desktop version is also available for the Macintosh.)

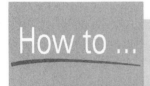

13

How to ... Connect Through a Corporate Firewall

This may be more information than you want to know, but if you're trying to connect to a work computer over a corporate firewall, you may encounter problems. Your corporate firewall may have blocked TCP/IP ports that Remote Desktop needs for the connection. In this case, a network administrator needs to open TCP port 3389. (That may not mean anything to you, but your network administrator will understand.) The point is this: Your corporate network will have to allow Remote Desktop connections if your work computer is protected by a network firewall. Typically, in this case, you'll connect remotely using the company's virtual private network (VPN) connection.

To install the software from your Windows Vista CD-ROM, insert the CD and click the Perform Additional Tasks option on the Welcome screen. Then, choose the Remote Desktop Connection option that appears. Follow the simple instructions that appear in the next How To.

Make a Remote Desktop Connection

Once you configure the host computer and the remote computer (if necessary), you are ready to make the Remote Desktop connection. On the remote computer, choose Start | All Programs | Accessories | Remote Desktop Connection. In the Remote Desktop Connection dialog box that appears, as shown in the following illustration, you can enter the name of the computer you want to connect to if the computer resides on your LAN or, if you're connecting over the Internet, enter the TCP/IP address of the computer you want to connect to and click the Connect button.

When the connection is made, you see a standard Windows dialog box where you enter a user name and password, and then click OK. Once you log in, you can use the host computer just as if you were sitting at it.

Manage Remote Desktop Performance

At first glance, it might not seem that Remote Desktop performance would be much of an issue. And, if you're using Remote Desktop over a LAN or DSL/cable connection, Remote Desktop performance isn't an issue. However, if you're using a dial-up connection from your home computer to your office, downloading all your remote computer's graphics and other Desktop features can be time-consuming, so Remote Desktop gives you some options to help you use less bandwidth. Using less bandwidth equals better performance, so if performance is an issue, you need to adjust the Experience settings of the Remote Desktop connection. Using the *Experience tab,* you can select your connection speed to optimize performance. Depending on your selection, the performance options will change. For example, if you're using a modem, the Desktop background isn't displayed because it tends to use a lot of bandwidth.

Choose Start | All Programs | Accessories | Remote Desktop Connection. In the Remote Desktop Connection dialog box, click the Options button, and then click the Experience tab. As you can see in Figure 13-17, you can choose the speed of your connection. If you choose the Modem option, not all the Remote Desktop features are used. The good news, however, is the default settings provided here are just suggestions. You can change any of them by enabling or disabling the check boxes, as desired. You may need to experiment with these settings to find those that work best for you. You should always leave Bitmap Caching enabled (checked), though, because this helps speed your connection. This feature allows images to be saved in your local cache, so they can be reused during the session, instead of having to download them individually each time.

FIGURE 13-17 Experience options

Manage the Display

The *Display tab,* shown in Figure 13-18, enables you to modify the options for the window containing the remote session. The supported resolutions range from Low to Full Screen. You may also specify the color depth to use for the connections, as well as decide whether to display the connection bar when in full-screen mode. The connection bar enables you to see the name or address of the computer hosting the session and to minimize or close the window.

Configure Local Resources

The *Local Resources tab,* shown in Figure 13-19, enables you to configure some of the newer features available with Remote Desktop. Three categories of options exist: Remote Computer Sound, Keyboard, and Local Devices. The *Remote Computer Sound* category enables you to specify one of three options: Leave at Remote Computer, Do Not Play, and Bring to This Computer (referring to the Remote Desktop client). In other words, depending on your choice, Windows event sounds can be heard on your remote session. Remember, though, that sounds also increase bandwidth, so you may want to choose the Do Not Play option if bandwidth is an issue.

The *Keyboard category* allows the use of keyboard strokes (such as ALT-TAB) so that they will operate when the remote session is open. The special key commands can be configured to work only on the remote computer, only on the local computer, or only when in full-screen mode.

13

FIGURE 13-18   Display options

FIGURE 13-19   Local Resources

The *Local Devices option* enables the mapping of the client's disk drives, printers, and serial ports to the Remote Desktop host. For example, let's say you're connected to your work computer from a home computer. You need to print a document on your work computer to your home computer's printer. This option enables you to do that. Or, say you want to access information stored on drives on your local computer while in the Remote Desktop session. Selecting the Local Devices option Disk Drives makes your disk drives appear in the My Computer window of the remote computer, so you can access them. This also enables you to copy-and-paste files or text from one computer to another.

Use Programs

The *Programs tab* can be used to launch a specific program when the user connects to the Remote Desktop host. In some cases, users will want to launch processes when they connect to the remote host, such as batch files or custom applications. This tab enables users to specify the location of the files that should be started.

Use Remote Assistance

Remote Assistance, a feature first introduced in Windows XP, enables users to help each other over the Internet. With this tool, one user who is deemed the "Expert" can view the Desktop of another user, deemed the "Novice." When properly authorized by the Novice, the Expert user can remotely use the Novice user's system to fix problems for the Novice user.

For a Remote Assistance session to succeed, both users must be connected to the same network (the Internet, typically), must be using Windows Vista or XP, and the account requesting assistance (the Novice) must have administrative rights to the computer. Unfortunately, no other operating systems work with Remote Assistance—both computers must be running Windows Vista or XP. The good news is Remote Assistance is easy to use and configure, and it can be helpful in the following situations:

- ■ It can be used on a company network where help desk personnel connect to remote computers and provide assistance.

- ■ It can be used as a workaround for Remote Desktop. In actuality, Remote Assistance uses Terminal Services, just like Remote Desktop. The difference is, with Remote Assistance, a person must be at each PC, and both Windows XP and Windows Vista can use the feature. This can be a quick and easy way to share data between two people over the Internet.

Remote Assistance works by sending Remote Assistance invitations. The Novice's computer uses either Windows Messenger (*not* MSN Messenger) or e-mail to send a Remote Assistance invitation to another, Expert, user. The Expert user accepts the invitation, which opens a terminal window showing the Desktop of the novice. The Expert can see the Novice's Desktop and exchange messages with the Novice. If the Novice wants the Expert to fix the computer, the

13

Novice can give the Expert control of the computer. From this point, the Expert can manage the Novice's computer remotely.

As with Remote Desktop, firewalls can pose a problem for Remote Assistance. The good news is Windows Messenger can typically get around the firewall, so use Windows Messenger instead of the e-mail option if you're having trouble.

Turn On Remote Assistance

Before your computer can use Remote Assistance, you must turn on the feature. Open the Control Panel and double-click System Properties. Click the Remote Settings link. You see an Allow Remote Assistance Invitations to Be Sent from This Computer check box. Select the check box to enable it.

Once you enable Remote Assistance, click the Advanced button. As you can see in the next illustration, you can use the Remote Assistance Settings dialog box to allow remote control of your computer. Remember, if you don't enable Remote Control, the Expert user can see your computer, but cannot make any configuration changes. You can also specify a period of time the invitation remains active.

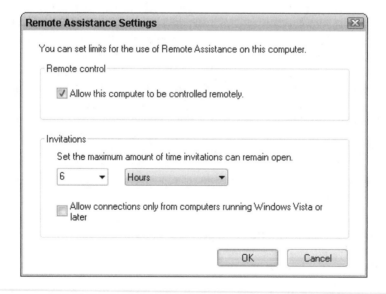

You need to enable Remote Assistance only if you plan on asking for assistance. You can accept Remote Assistance invitations from other people without enabling the feature on your computer.

Request Remote Assistance

If an end user (Novice) is ready to toss their computer through the nearest window, it's probably time to request some assistance. The Novice user needs to be able to send files to the Expert user who will be answering the call for help. This may mean using one of several methods, from using messaging software to saving a file to a floppy disk and hand-delivering it to the Expert. The logical place for the Novice to start is the Windows Vista Help and Support Center. A component of this help feature provides easy access to the various methods of requesting a Remote Assistance session.

Follow these steps to create a Remote Assistance ticket:

1. Choose Start | Help and Support.

2. In the middle to upper portion of the window that appears (the Help and Support Center), notice the section titled Use Remote Assistance. Click the option and in the window that appears, click Invite Someone You Trust to Help You, as you can see in the following illustration.

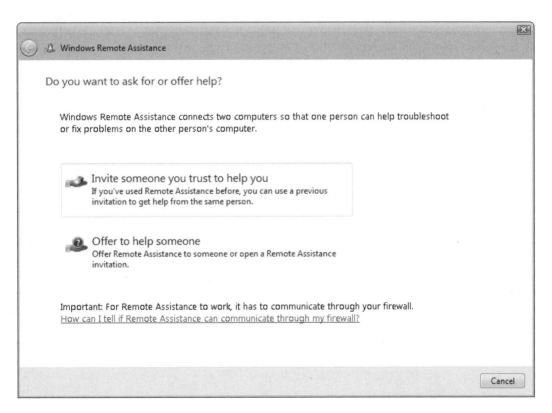

13

3. In the next window that appears, choose the way you want to send the Remote Assistance invitation—either through e-mail, or by using a disk. Once you click the desired option, follow the rest of the instructions to complete the invitation.

Once the invitation is sent and received, the Expert user is able to connect to your computer using the invitation and begin the help session.

Part III

Cool Things You Can Do with Windows Vista

Chapter 14 Play Games

How to...

- ■ Play games
- ■ Manage game controllers
- ■ Use Volume Control and Sound Recorder

Windows Vista provides a stable system for game playing and multimedia. In fact, as game playing and multimedia have become so popular over the past few years, Windows Vista is the best operating system (OS) Microsoft has produced to date for these purposes. In this chapter, you learn about two types of entertainment in Windows Vista—game playing and sound recording. As you see, playing games and working with gaming hardware is a snap in Windows Vista.

Manage Game Controllers

Game controllers are hardware devices you attach to your computer. These devices enable you to play a certain type of game that requires the device. A typical example is a *joystick*. Joysticks have been around for some time now. If you're as old as I am, you remember owning your first joystick and trying to play the home version of PacMan on the Atari 2600 or some related game system (that dates me a little). In today's gaming market, all kinds of game controllers are in use—different kinds of yokes, gamepads, virtual reality devices, and many others.

No matter what type of device you want to use, you need to install it on Windows Vista to work with the device. Installing a game controller is similar to installing any other piece of hardware in Windows Vista. Typically, you attach the game controller to the correct port on your computer (following the controller's instructions). Windows Vista normally recognizes the added device and automatically installs it without any intervention from you. Some advanced game controllers may include an installation CD-ROM. If so, just follow the instructions for installation and you'll be all set.

Make sure any game controller you purchase is compatible with Windows Vista. The device should tell you about compatibility right on the box.

Once you attach the game controller to your computer, you can manage and troubleshoot the device using Game Controllers in the Control Panel. Simply open the Control Panel and double-click the Game Controllers icon. The Game Controllers window, shown in Figure 14-1, shows you a list of game controllers currently installed on Windows XP.

If you don't see a Game Controllers icon in the Control Panel, switch the Control Panel to Classic view.

FIGURE 14-1   Game Controllers

Using this window, you can access an Advanced selection option to choose what device you want for older games by clicking the Advanced button (see Figure 14-2), and you can access properties for the device—which may or may not have configurable options, depending on the game controller.

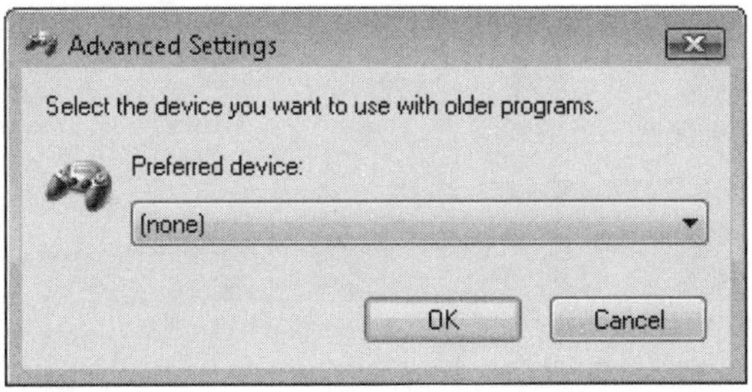

FIGURE 14-2   Advanced Settings

14

 *Windows Vista should automatically detect and install game controllers. Under most circumstances, you shouldn't have to add controllers manually to your system. You can, however, try manually adding an item if you're having installation problems.*

Play Games with Windows XP

Let's face it, for all the great tasks a PC can do, one of the most common reasons we use the PC is to play games. Gaming technology has come a long way in the past few years. With rich PC multimedia support, you can be transported into different worlds, create your own civilizations, race a car—you name it—you can do it in a game and experience awesome graphics and sound while playing. You can play games on Windows Vista in three major ways: you can play the basic games included with Windows Vista, play Internet games, or install other games you purchase. The following sections explore these options.

Playing Games Installed with Windows Vista

Unfortunately, operating systems don't offer a bunch of powerful games free. You have to purchase those on your own and install them on your computer. However, Windows Vista does include a few basic games you can play to pass the time, such as Chess Titans, Freecell, Hearts, InkBall, Minesweeper, Solitaire, and so forth. If you want to play one of these games, choose Start | All Programs | Games. If you click the Games option found here, you see a folder listing all available games, including any you have installed, as shown in Figure 14-3. Simply click a game to start it.

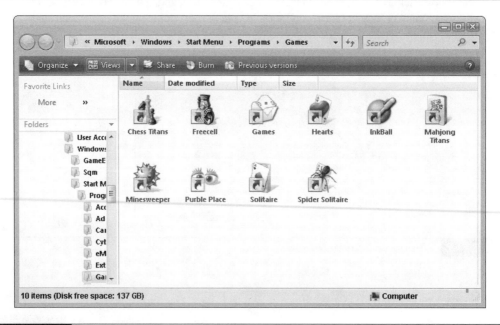

FIGURE 14-3   Games folder

Playing Games on the Internet

You can play a plethora of games on the Internet if you have a broadband Internet connection. Typically, the games are played directly on the web site, just as you would access resources on the Web at any other site. For some, you're required to download additional software that will let you to play the Internet games.

At www.zone.com (an MSN site), information about your computer is gathered and an ID is sent to you. Once you sign up, you can play a lot of free games. Other sites work in a similar way, but be sure you're accessing reputable gaming sites. You can also search on any Internet search engine about Internet games, and you'll find all kinds of sites and information to get you started.

Installing and Playing Your Own Games

You can purchase many different kinds of games at your local computer software store or on the Internet. As you might guess, virtually anything you want is available. The trick when purchasing any game is not to get caught up in the excitement until you're sure the game is right for your system. As you consider purchasing a game, keep these points in mind:

- Check the minimum RAM requirements and make sure your computer meets them. A typical game lists the system requirements on the side of the box.

- The game may require certain graphics and sound capabilities. Make sure your current video and sound cards can support the requirements (such as True Color).

- The game may require you to purchase certain gaming peripherals, such as joysticks and other controllers. Make sure you know what you need before buying the game.

- Make sure the game is compatible with Windows Vista.

With these considerations in mind, buy the game you want, and then read and follow the installation instructions. Most games include one or more CD-ROMs that guide you through the installation process. Once you finish, refer to the owner's manual for information about playing the game, game options, and solving problems with the particular game.

Troubleshooting Game Problems

Naturally, it's impossible to offer every solution to every problem you might encounter with a game, particularly one you install. Always begin with the game's documentation. Sometimes the documentation can help you solve known issues or common problems. In addition, you can use the Windows Vista Troubleshooter to help you solve a problem. The following sections list some of the more common problems and their solutions.

A Game Controller Doesn't Work

If you have a joystick or some other kind of game controller that doesn't work or is working erratically, first check the documentation for the hardware to see whether any immediate solutions are recommended. Check the Game Controllers icon in the Control Panel for the presence of the device.

14

If you don't see it listed there, Windows Vista doesn't think it's installed on the system. Check to make sure the device is plugged in correctly, and follow the manufacturer's instructions for installing the device. If the device works sporadically, you may need to access its properties in Game Controllers. Click the Settings tab and click Calibrate to try to resolve the problem. If calibration doesn't solve the problem, the odds are good the device driver is incorrect, corrupted, or needs to be updated. Try to reinstall the device driver or obtain an updated one from the manufacturer's web site.

DirectX Problems

DirectX is a graphics software component used by many games. If you get DirectX error messages, the odds are good you need to install the latest version of DirectX (found on the Windows Update Web site) or you're using a newer version of DirectX that your game doesn't support. Check your game documentation for more information. If you're using an older video card, you may also experience incompatibility problems with DirectX.

Game Lockup

Lockups are generally caused when a game attempts to use hardware in some way that violates the integrity of the Windows Vista OS. This can cause a "hard lock." Press CTRL-ALT-DEL on your keyboard to get control of your system, or you may have to restart your PC. If this continues to happen with one particular game, it probably indicates software problems with the game. Consult the game documentation or manufacturer's web site for more information.

Set Display Mode: DDERR_GENERIC

This error message can commonly occur if your video card resolution settings are too high for your video card to handle. You need to lower them to 256 colors on the Settings tab of the Display properties sheets.

Tired of playing a game, but you can't seem to make it stop? Just press the ESC key on your keyboard. This is a universal control that almost always halts a game and gives control of the OS back to you.

Use Volume Controls and Sound Recorder

Volume Controls and Sound Recorder are two tools you may use frequently. These are simple to use, and I just want to mention a few things about each of them.

If you double-click the sound icon in the Notification Area, you see a basic volume control, as shown in the following illustration. You can also right-click the Notification Area icon and click Playback Devices to access a management window, shown in Figure 14-4. You can double-click a device in this window, and then configure individual volume controls and settings. The options you find are self-explanatory.

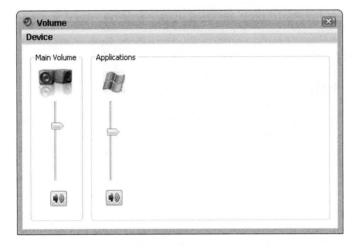

FIGURE 14-4   Audio Devices

 *You can also access these options using Audio Devices and Sound Themes in Control Panel.*

One additional setting you can configure is Windows Sounds. If you right-click the Sound icon in the Notification Area and click Sounds, you see a basic configuration window, as shown in Figure 14-5, which enables you to click through a list of sounds Windows makes for certain events. Use the Sound Scheme drop-down menu to choose a different sound scheme, or you can create your own by altering the sound events and using the Save As button to save your personal scheme.

Sound Recorder is a little utility that helps you record your voice (or whatever sound you want) using a microphone attached to your computer. This tool is located in Start | Accessories. The controls for Sound Recorder, shown in Figure 14-6, are similar to those on a tape recorder.

FIGURE 14-5   Windows Sounds

FIGURE 14-6   Sound Recorder

Click the record button to start recording. Once you finish, you can save the recording as a file. The menu options offer standard choices, and you can play around with these settings to see which ones work best for you. Like Volume Control, Sound Recorder is easy to use—just spend some time with it and you'll be a recording pro in no time.

14

Chapter 15

Use Windows Media Player

How to...

- Play media with Windows Media Player
- Rip CD tracks and other media
- Create and manage playlists
- Manage a Library
- Configure Media Player

Windows Me introduced Windows Media Player 7, which was a gigantic improvement over previous versions of Media Player. Windows XP saw several revisions of Media Player, which takes us to Windows Vista's version, which is a nice improvement over the past versions. If you've used Media Player 10, the new Media Player in Vista won't need much of a learning curve. With Media Player, you can play and manage all kinds of multimedia, from CD/DVD music and movies to all kinds of downloadable multimedia files. Media Player also gives you great media management features, and in this chapter, you learn about them.

You can start Windows Media Player by choosing Start | All Programs | Windows Media Player. Depending on your system configuration, you may also see a shortcut to Media Player on your Desktop or on your Taskbar.

When you first use Media Player, it asks you to choose either an express setup or a custom setup. Choose one to complete the setup. Once you open Media Player, you see a default interface. I say *default interface,* because you can completely change the interface using a variety of skins (you learn about skins in the section "Skin Chooser"). The default interface provides you with a primary media area, and a list of buttons on the top bar of Media Player (called features). If you click a button, you can see the contents displayed in the window. Figure 15-1, for example, shows my Library.

You use Media Player by accessing the features on the top of the Media Player interface. Each feature does something different, of course; the following sections explore the primary features and other aspects of working with Media Player.

Now Playing

Now Playing is your media play area and the primary area you'll use—it lists or shows whatever type of media you're currently playing. When you insert most types of media into your PC, Windows Media Player automatically launches. For example, let's say you want to listen to your favorite CD. All you need to do is put the CD into the CD-ROM drive. Windows Vista scans the CD, recognizes it as a music CD, and launches Windows Media Player. Media Player begins playing the CD, and information about the CD appears in the Now Playing area, as Figure 15-2 shows. If you decide to watch a home movie you made with Movie Maker, the home movie is also displayed in the Now Playing window.

FIGURE 15-1 Media Player Library

FIGURE 15-2 Now Playing area

15

You can change and configure the Now Playing interface. Because the primary purpose of Now Playing is to provide a quick-and-easy interface to view and hear multimedia, specific configuration options for the media cannot be changed here. Instead, you can adjust what's displayed in the Now Playing area and how the display looks.

If you click the Now Playing button drop-down menu, you see a few important Enhancements options:

■ **Enhancements** The *Enhancements option* turns on an enhancements interface that begins with a graphic equalizer, as the following illustration shows. If you click the next button in the upper-left corner, though, you can also access a media link for e-mail, play speed settings, quiet mode, SRS WOW effects, video settings, color chooser, and crossfading and auto volume leveling. All these settings help you customize your media experience.

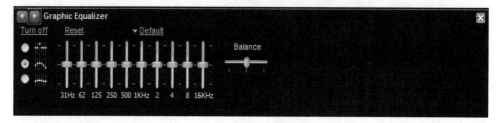

■ **Show List Pane** The *Show List pane,* which appears on the right side of the Now Playing area, gives you additional information about the media you're viewing, such as the album name and songs, or information about the DVD. You can toggle this feature on or off here.

■ **Visualizations** A *visualization* is a graphical display that moves with the music you're playing. You can use the pop-out box here to choose a different visualization or access options for them.

■ **Plug-ins** A *plug-in* is additional software that works with Media Player. If you have plug-ins for Media Player, you can manage them here.

■ **More Options** The *More Options* feature opens a tabbed properties interface with a lot of settings. We explore it later in the section "Media Player Configuration Options."

■ **Help with Playback** The *Help with Playback* feature lets you access the Media Player help file.

You can also use the Urge button to access URGE, the site of choice for Media Player. Here, you can download songs and videos, and find out nearly anything else you want to know about popular media. Remember, you must have an Internet connection to access this feature.

Use the standard control buttons in the lower area of Media Player to play the media, stop playing the media, skip tracks forward and back, adjust the volume, and use related stereo or video controls. At the bottom-right of the interface, you also see button options to switch to skin mode and full-screen mode. You learn about skin mode in the section "Skin Chooser."

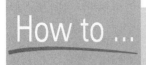

Get Visualizations from the Internet

Media Player offers quite a few visualization options when you choose Now Playing |
Visualizations. However, if you're a visualizations junkie, you can also get more from the
Web. Here's how:

1. In Media Player, choose Now Playing | Visualizations | Download Visualizations.
   This action launches an Internet connection and takes you to the Windows Media
   Player site.

2. In the Web browser, inspect the visualizations available, and then click the one you
   want, which starts the download process.

3. When the File Download dialog box appears, choose to run the program from its
   current location, and then click OK.

Once the download is complete, installation is automatically started. The visualization is
installed and now available in Media Player. That's all there is to it!

Library

All your saved music and video files are stored in the Library under different categories, so you
can easily access them, as shown in Figure 15-3.

On the left side of the interface, you see various categories with plus (+) and minus (−) sign
boxes next to them. Click a category, and you can see the songs or videos in your Library for that
category. For example, when I expand Album, I can select an album and see a list of songs I have
copied to my computer from that album in the right pane. Just double-click a song or video clip
to hear or see it.

So, how can you use the Library? Remember, the purpose of the *Library* is to help you
keep track of files you want. The Library is able to detect the type of multimedia you are
using and add it to the appropriate category. You can search your Library by clicking the
Search button at the top of the interface, and you can perform standard add, remove, and
delete functions.

You can also use the Library to create a playlist of your favorite tunes or videos. The
following sections show you how to use these options.

*You can see the old-style classic menu options by simply clicking the Layout Options
drop-down menu (near the Search box) and clicking Show Classic Menus.*

15

FIGURE 15-3   Library

How to ... Use URGE

URGE is essentially an online music store that ties into MTV, CMT, and VH1. Here you can access music, videos, Internet radio and such. To setup and use URGE, follow these steps:

1. Click the URGE button on the Windows Media Player toolbar. A download process will begin for you to download and install the URGE software. The download is rather large and will take some time.

2. Once installed, simply click the URGE button on the toolbar to access the music store directly within Media Player. You can try URGE for free for fourteen days, after which you'll need to pay for a subscription (currently $14.95 per month).

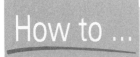

Configuring CD Audio Options

You can control how songs are recorded and managed in Media Player by choosing Rip | More Options. You see a Rip Music tab, shown in the following illustration.

Under most circumstances, the default options configured on this tab are all you need but, at times, you may want to change the default behavior. The following options are found on this tab:

- **Rip Music to This Location**   By default, the location is My Documents\My Music. If you want to change this default location, click the Change button and select a different folder on your computer's hard drive.

- **Rip Settings**   You can choose to copy music in either the Windows Media format or MP3. The Copy Protect Music check box simply means Windows Media Player is keeping a license for you to copy the music and play it on your computer. E-mailing copies of music to other people is illegal, however, as is redistribution by any other means. The other options are obvious. You can choose an Audio Quality setting by adjusting the slider bar. The higher the quality of the copy, the more hard drive space is consumed. Even at a lower quality, several megabytes of storage space are needed for only a few songs.

15

Adding an Item to the Library

To add a new item to the Library, switch from the Library to the Rip tab, where you can copy a CD or certain songs to the Library. You learn about the Rip option in the section "Rip."

Creating a Playlist

At any given moment, I have about ten favorite songs. The problem is each song is by a different artist on a different CD. Media Player can solve that problem by enabling me to copy each of those songs and create a playlist, so each song is played in the order I want directly from my hard drive. Sound interesting? Here's how it works:

1. In Library, click the Playlists option to expand it, and then click Create Playlist.

2. Type a name for the playlist. Then, browse the Library for the desired songs you want on the playlist. When you find a song you want to add, right-click it and use the Add To option to add it to your playlist, or you can simply drag-and-drop the song to the playlist.

3. As you add items to the playlist, they appear in the list pane on the right side of the interface. You can right-click a song in the list to move it up or down in the list or for song order purposes, or you can remove a song you added this way. The following illustration shows you a playlist I built. When you're done, click the Save Playlist button.

Rip

The *Rip* feature gives you information about the music CD you're currently listening to, so you can rip, or copy, the songs to your Library. If you're connected to the Internet, you see the names of the songs, artist name, and album name, if the CD is an original CD or an exact copy of an original. If not, the tracks are simply listed as Track 1, Track 2, and so on, as you can see in Figure 15-4.

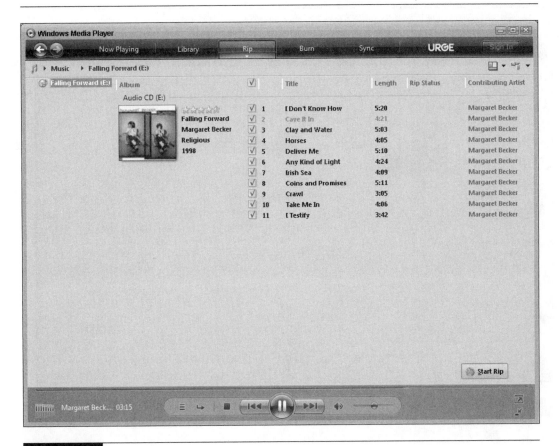

FIGURE 15-4 Rip feature

Choose the songs you want to rip by checking the boxes next to the songs (or unchecking them if you don't want certain songs ripped). Next, simply click the Start Rip button found on the lower-right portion of the screen. The ripping process takes a few minutes, depending on how many songs you're ripping from a CD. Remember, your ripped songs are added to your library.

Burn

The *Burn* interface enables you to choose songs or playlists you want to burn to a CD. First, though, your computer must have a CD-RW drive to burn CDs. Click the Burn button feature and drag items you want to burn, such as individual songs or whole albums, to the right pane. Once you finish, place a CD-R disk in your CD-RW drive and click the Start Burn button, as you can see in Figure 15-5. If you want to burn a data CD, used for backing up songs, instead of an audio CD, click the Burn drop-down menu and choose Data CD or DVD.

15

FIGURE 15-5   Burn your CD

Sync

The *Sync* interface looks almost exactly like the Burn interface, except you use this interface to synchronize songs with a portable device instead of burning them to a CD. Simply drag the songs or albums you want to sync with your device to the right pane, make sure your device is connected and turned on, and then click Start Sync.

Skin Chooser

Media Player includes a number of different *skins*—or interface overlays—you can apply to Media Player. These skins give Media Player completely different looks, which you may find either appealing or aggravating—depending on your point of view. For example, you can choose a skin that looks like the inside of an alien's head, as shown in Figure 15-6, one that looks like a heart, or a number of other interesting options.

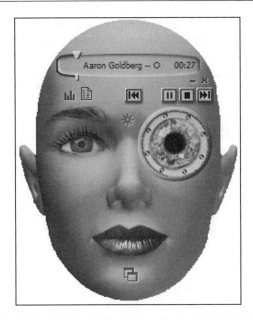

FIGURE 15-6   Personalize Media Player with a skin

As you can see, these are just for fun—you still have the same functionality in Media Player, regardless of what skin you choose to use. To use a skin, first turn on Classic Menus. Right-click on an empty area of the toolbar, such as the space next to the Now Playing button, and click Show Classic Menus. Then, Choose View | Skin Chooser. You can then choose the skin you want to use.

How to ...   **Download a Skin**

To download a new skin, follow these easy steps:

1. In the Skin Chooser feature, click the More Skins button.
2. Windows Vista launches an Internet connection and your web browser, connecting you to www.windowsmedia.com.
3. Check out the skins available. When you find one you want to download, click it. Download begins automatically, and the skin is installed in Windows Media Player.
4. When the installation is finished, click the Apply Skin button to start using the new skin.

15

In the Skin Chooser, you can click More Skins to connect to the Media Player web site, where you can download other skins. You can find several other skins available on this site.

Although most skins are fun, I've found some of them can be aggravating. Sure, you maintain the same Media Player controls in each skin, but some of them seem more of a hindrance than a help. Experiment with the available skins and download some new ones, so you can find the one that's right for you—and, remember, you don't have to use a skin at all.

Media Player Configuration Options

In addition to all the fun and frills of Media Player, you can do a few more substantial things. Click any toolbar button menu and choose More Options. If you have Classic Menus turned on, you can also choose Tools | Options, and you see several different tabs with a number of options on each tab.

The default options are typically all you need, so this isn't an interface where you need to wade around and make configuration changes. However, instances may occur when you need to use these options.

The following list tells you what's available on each tab:

- **Player**   The *Player tab* contains a number of basic check boxes. By default, your Media Player checks the Media Player web site monthly for updates to Media Player. This setting is all you need. By default, Media Player opens and starts the Media Player Guide. You can change that behavior by clearing the check box on this tab.

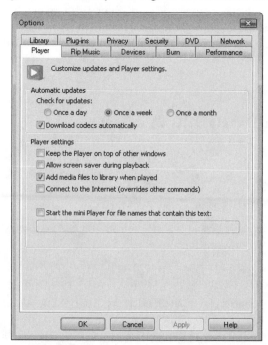

- **Rip Music**   The *Rip Music tab* enables you to make setting adjustments when you copy CD music.

- **Devices**   The *Devices tab,* shown in the following illustration, lists all devices found on your computer that can be used for media playback, such as your CD-ROM or DVD drive. If you select a drive and click Properties, a window appears where you can choose whether to use analog or digital playback and copy. Typically, this tab is set to digital, but if you're having problems, you can try the analog setting. The *Error Correction feature,* available only with digital playback, allows Windows to attempt to resolve problems found in the digital media. This setting can be used, but you may notice a negative effect on the performance of your system. I recommend you skip it unless you're having problems with digital media.

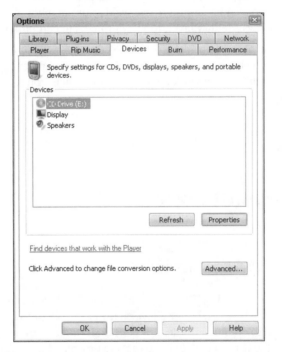

- **Performance**   *Performance settings* affect how Media Player uses your Internet connection. You don't need to configure anything here, but note, by default, Windows Media Player can detect your connection speed to the Internet. This allows Media Player to determine how best to handle media downloads. Make sure you leave this setting as is, because Media Player performs better if it can detect your Internet connection speeds. See Chapter 8 to learn more about Internet connections.

- **Library**   By default, *Library* gives other applications that tap into it read-only access, and no access is granted to anyone on the Internet. You should leave these settings alone.

- **Plug-Ins**   The *Plug-Ins tab* enables you to manage plug-ins by adding or removing them and accessing any available properties sheets.

15

- ■ **Privacy**   *Privacy settings* are designed to keep you anonymous while you're connected to the Internet. You can peruse this list and make any changes concerning what Media Player can and cannot do, but in most cases, the default settings are all you need.

- ■ **Security**   The *Security settings* you have with Media Player simply determine whether Media Player can run scripts from the Internet and what Internet Explorer (IE) zone Media Player should use (you can configure IE security zones within IE using Tools | Internet Options). Generally, you don't need to change these settings.

- ■ **File Types**   The *File Types tab* lists every file type Media Player can read. You don't need to do anything here unless you don't want Windows Media Player to be the default player for a particular file type. In that case, clear the check box next to the file type's name. This feature can be helpful if you want to use another player, such as RealPlayer instead of Windows Media Player, to view or listen to certain kinds of content.

- ■ **Network**   This tab contains protocol usage settings and proxy server enabler settings. You don't need to change anything here unless your computer is on a network that uses a proxy server. Unless a network administrator instructs you to make changes, best leave this tab alone.

About Codecs

Notice the Download Codecs Automatically check box option on the Player tab, which is selected by default. A *codec* is a compressor/decompressor mathematical algorithm used for audio, video, and image files. The codec allows the file to be compressed, and then uncompressed, so it can be read. Media Player must have codecs to be able to play files.

If a codec is used to compress a file, the same codec is used to decompress it. If Media Player doesn't have the correct codec, it attempts to download it automatically for you. If you clear this check box option, Media Player will be unable to get the codecs it needs—so leave this check box selected!

Chapter 16

Create Movies with Windows Movie Maker

How to...

- Use Windows Movie Maker
- Import data into Windows Movie Maker
- Create and edit movies
- Add audio and titles to movies to movies

Over the past few years, computer users have demanded more from their computer systems. We want computer systems to perform the important tasks we need to accomplish, but we also want to use our computers as digital playgrounds. Windows Vista helps meet the latter need by providing great digital media support, including support for digital video editing, DVD burning, and home movie making. That support is accomplished through a free application included in Windows Vista called Windows Movie Maker.

First introduced with Windows Me, *Windows Movie Maker* is a basic video-editing tool that enables you to manage segments of video and even create your own video production. It has a number of useful features and, in this chapter, you explore Windows Movie Maker to see how it can help you manage and create video files.

Why Use Windows Movie Maker?

If you're like me, you tend to use a lot of videotape. You shoot everything from Aunt Ruth's birthday party to little Johnny's latest shenanigans. You may also have piles of still pictures—most of them not even in an album. Windows Movie Maker is designed to help you both manage and edit your home videos and pictures. You can use Windows Movie Maker to organize the data and to edit, save, and even share it with others over the Internet. In short, Movie Maker gives you a way to manage those precious moments electronically and reduce the clutter around your house.

Naturally, you can import digital video from digital video cameras and DV tapes. You need a video capture port or a Fireware or a USB2 port on your computer that corresponds with your camera or video camera.

One of the greatest benefits of Movie Maker is you can take analog video (such as your typical camcorder or VHS tape), import the analog video into your computer, and then manage it electronically. For example, you can store video data electronically and tuck the media disks away for safekeeping. Once the video (and even pictures) are stored electronically, you can create multiple copies of them, store your movies on CDs or DVDs, and even share them through e-mail.

Another great feature of Movie Maker is ease of editing. In any given videotaping session, you're likely to have some dull spots on tape. Consider this personal example: during the writing of this book, my wife gave birth to our daughter, Mattie. A few weeks after the commotion of the new birth, we sat down to watch the hospital video. We saw heartwarming moments and memories we never want to lose, but we were also faced with miles of boring videotape. Not wanting to miss anything on that special day, we filmed *everything*. Although *everything* seemed important at the time, in retrospect, I don't want to watch hours of videotape that shows "Here we are, waiting for the baby. . . ."

With Windows Movie Maker, you can easily edit away the boring sections of video and keep the good stuff. By trimming clips and performing other editing tasks, your movies can become more interesting and entertaining, as well as shorter. The editing features can also help reduce the amount of storage space needed for the footage, and you can use it to join unrelated clips of video for a montage or another project.

Finally, you can have lots of fun with Movie Maker—create your own home movies and edit in transitions, voice, background music, and much more. Get creative and stretch your brain. As you can see, you have tons of possibilities.

With that said, remember, Windows Movie Maker is a free application included with your Vista system—this should indicate to you that video-editing software is not Microsoft's main focus, and Movie Maker is, in fact, a *basic* video-editing package. This isn't an advanced application. I've used video-editing software from other vendors that was much, much better, so I don't mind telling you up front that if you're interested in getting into movie editing and production, you might want to look for a different software package that offers the power and tools you need. However, Windows Movie Maker is free and readily available, and if you have basic video-editing needs, Movie Maker works just fine. Overall, the software is intuitive and easy-to-use, as you discover in this chapter.

Opening Windows Movie Maker

You can open Windows Movie Maker by clicking Start | All Programs | Windows Movie Maker. The Movie Maker interface provides you with a few important and distinct work areas:

- ■ **Menu**   Movie Maker contains a standard *menu* of options, including File, Edit, View, Tools, Clip, Play, and Help, as you can see in Figure 16-1. Use these menus to access Movie Maker features as you create movies.

- ■ **Toolbar**   The *toolbar* provides quick-and-easy access to common features. The toolbar options you see change, depending on your current task.

- ■ **Tasks**   The *Tasks pane,* located on the left side of the interface, is your quick-and-easy access point for all kinds of functions and features. The content of the Tasks pane changes, depending on what you're working on at the moment.

- ■ **Monitor Area**   The *Monitor* enables you to watch your movie in progress and also manage your clips.

- ■ **Storyboard/Timeline**   The *Storyboard and Timeline* views enable you to assemble your movie and work with various pieces of it.

16

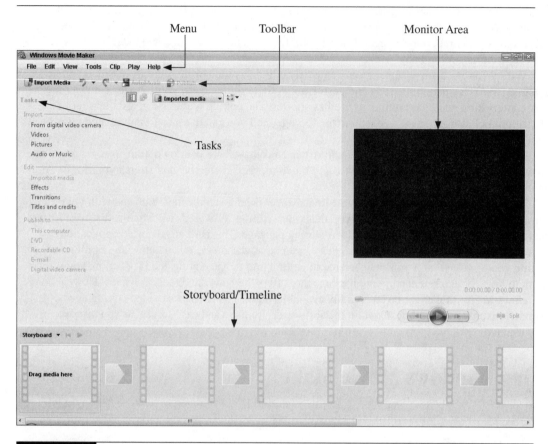

FIGURE 16-1 Windows Movie Maker

Windows Movie Maker looks for and expects to find both a video and sound card or other capture device. If it doesn't find these, you receive a message telling you your computer doesn't meet the Movie Maker requirements.

Importing Digital Data

You can import digital video and photos directly from your video camera or from your computer, if the files already reside there. You can also import music to use in your movie in the same way. Before we start importing, you need to know a few things first.

For the best performance, your computer needs an *IEEE 1394* (also called FireWire) card, so you can import movies from a digital camcorder into your computer (especially important if you'll be using any streaming media devices). This type of card provides fast transfer from the camcorder to the computer and is highly recommended by Microsoft. You need to do a little investigative work to determine if your computer has this card, if your digital camcorder supports it, and if this transfer card is right for you. Consult your computer and camcorder documentation for more information.

Windows Movie Maker can recognize all kinds of movie files, such as asf, avi, mpeg, wm, and so forth. Additionally, it can recognize and use essentially all kinds standard of picture and audio files.

Importing from a DV Camera

You can import directly from your DV camera. Simply connect your camera to your computer and turn it on. Then, follow these steps:

1. In the Tasks pane click Import From Digital Video Camera, and then click the Import button.

2. In the Name box, type a name for the video file.

3. Choose a location from which to save your video file to the Import to list, or click Browse and choose another location.

4. In the Format list, choose either the Windows Media Video (WMV) file format or you can choose the AVI format.

5. Click either Import entire videotape to my computer or Only import parts of the videotape to my computer, and then click Next.

6. Start importing, according to the directions on your screen.

Importing Existing Video or Pictures on Your Computer

If you already have video files and/or picture files on your computer, you can import them directly into movie maker. Do this:

1. In the Tasks pane under Import, click the Videos option.

2. In the Import Media Items dialog box, shown in the following illustration, browse to locate the desired video files. Select them, and then click Import.

3. Repeat this process, but this time in the Tasks pane, choose Pictures.

Once you import your items, they appear in the Collections pane, as you can see in Figure 16-2.

FIGURE 16-2   Your media appears in the Collections pane.

Make Movies

Now that you know how to import data, it's time to turn your attention to making movies.
Using Windows Movie Maker, import the clips you want to use, organize them, edit them
as desired, and then save the project. You're now ready to begin editing your video or still-
shot clips. Remember, you can combine video and still shots into one move and blend them
together as you like. You can also import background music and narrate a movie by recording
your voice. The following sections show you how to perform all these tasks.

Splitting Clips

Windows Movie Maker creates clips for you, but you may need to split those clips into more
manageable pieces. You can perform this function by using the *split* command. The following
easy steps show you how:

1. Select the clip you want to split in the Collections area.

2. In the Monitor area, click the Play button.

3. When the clip reaches the point at which you want to split it, click the Split Clip button in the Monitor area, as shown in Figure 16-3. You can also choose Clip | Split, or simply press CTRL-M on your keyboard. In the Collections area, the clip is split in two—the first part of the clip retains its original name, while the second clip contains the original name followed by *1*. You can change the name as desired.

Combining Clips

Just as you can split a clip into two or more clips, you can also combine clips as needed. If you want to combine two or more clips, follow these steps:

1. In the Collections area, select the clips you want to combine: select the first clip, hold down SHIFT on your keyboard, and select the remaining clips you want to combine.

2. Choose Clip | Combine. The clips are combined, using the first clip's name for the new file.

1/1/2001 6:00 AM

0:00:00.00 / 0:00:00.00

Split

FIGURE 16-3 Split Clip button

16

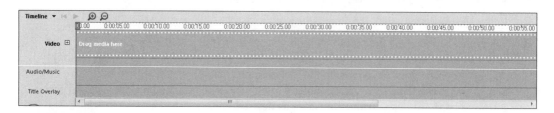

The Workspace

Getting Familiar with the Workspace

The *Workspace* at the bottom of the interface is where you edit and assemble movies. If you examine the interface, shown in Figure 16-4, you see a few buttons in the top left that correspond to areas in the Workspace. You can access volume controls, narration options, zoom controls, play and rewind buttons, and toggle between Timeline view and Storyboard views.

Creating a Storyboard

You can use the Workspace to create a storyboard or to sequence your clips together. You drag clips onto the Workspace area to create the storyboard. Begin by dragging the first clip in your movie to the video area of the Workspace. Once in position, you see the first frame of the video displayed in the Monitor. If you change to Timeline view, you can see how much time is consumed by the clip. By using the timeline, you can connect pieces of clips, while monitoring the time frame of the whole movie. However, you'll probably find Storyboard view, shown in Figure 16-5, is initially easier to use when you're assembling your movie.

The zoom in and zoom out buttons at the top of the Workspace let you see more detail concerning the timeline (click the Storyboard drop-down menu and choose the Timeline option) (see Figure 16-6). While zoomed out, the storyboard is shown to you in increments of ten seconds. You can zoom in and zoom out more to see the clips in whatever time measure you want.

Storyboard view

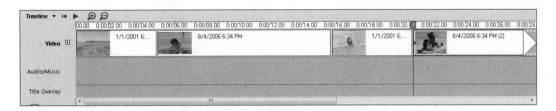

FIGURE 16-6 Timeline view

Feel free to mix video and still shots together on the storyboard. By default, imported still shots are given five seconds of time on a storyboard. You can change that value on the timeline by grabbing the edge of a photo and dragging to increase its duration.

Trimming Clips

As you're working with clips in the storyboard, notice areas of your video that you want to cut out, or trim. These are often dull spots in the video where not much is happening. For example, let's say you've been videotaping your dog. Your dog does this great trick, but to capture the trick, you end up filming a boring minute or two waiting for the dog to perform. Now you want to lose the boring time when you create the movie—no problem—just trim off the excess.

In reality, the *trim feature* is powerful because it gives you a fine level of control over your clips. You can use the *timeline feature* in the Workspace and trim away seconds of a clip that you don't want to use. You can trim clips in two ways. Here's the first:

1. In the Timeline view, select the clip you want to trim. The first frame of the clip appears in the Monitor.

2. The trimming process *keeps* the portion of videotape you trim and discards the rest. That seems a little confusing, but it might help to think of it as trimming a piece of paper. You trim away the pieces you don't want to keep the primary piece. With the trim feature, you set a beginning and an end trim point, and everything outside of the area is trimmed away. To begin, click Play in the Monitor area.

3. Watch the clip until it reaches the place where you want to begin making the trim. Choose Clip | Set Start Trim Point. (Remember, anything *previous* to the beginning trim point is discarded. The trimmed part is kept.)

4. When the clip reaches the point at which you want to stop trimming, choose Clip | Set End Trim Point. All video outside the trim area is cut away.

5. If you don't want to keep the trim points you just set, choose Clip | Clear Trim Points.

16

 *As you can probably guess, the trim feature is useful—but a little confusing at first. Spend a few moments playing with this feature until you get the hang of how it works.*

Creating Transitions

Windows Movie Maker provides several *transitions* you can use between clips. For example, say your movie contains clips of your vacation in Hawaii. You can use Movie Maker to assemble the clips and place transitions between them, so the flow from clip-to-clip is more natural and less choppy.

You can easily create transitions in the Storyboard. Follow these steps:

1. In the Workspace, make certain Storyboard view is enabled.

2. In the Tasks pane under Edit, click Transitions. You can see the available transitions in the content area of the interface, shown in the following illustration.

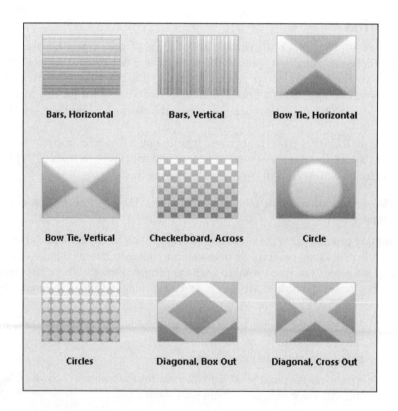

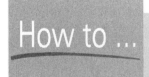

Add Effects

Movie Maker also includes a number of effects you can add to any clip or photo. Effects cover all kinds of video/photo effects, such as blurring features, lighting features, and even an old-age film effect. These features aren't necessary, of course, but they can add some cool features to your movies. To add an effect, follow these steps:

1. In the Tasks pane, choose Effects under Edit. You see the effects options in the collections area, as you can see in the following illustration.

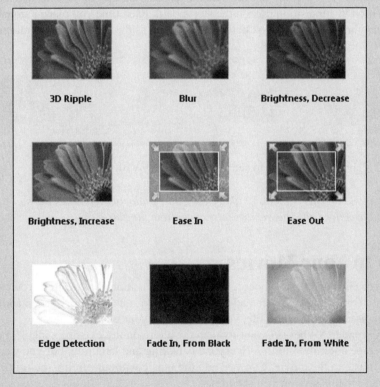

2. Scroll through the effects and locate one you want to use.

3. Drag the effect to the star icon on the desired clip in the storyboard, as shown in the following illustration. Repeat this process for other clips to which you want to add effects.

(continued)

16

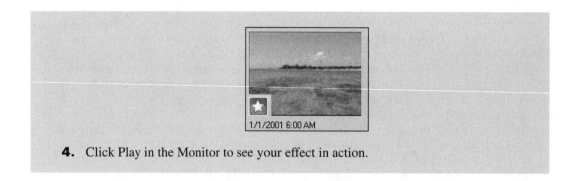

4. Click Play in the Monitor to see your effect in action.

3. A transition box appears between each clip/photo on the storyboard. Drag a desired transition to a transition box on the storyboard. Each time you place a transition, an icon appears in the transition box between each clip, as the following illustration shows.

4. Click Play in the Monitor to see your movie play with the transitions.

If you add an effect you don't like, click Edit | Undo, or right-click the star area of the clip, and then click Cut. This removes the effect from the clip.

Add Audio to Your Movies

Once you place clips on the storyboard, trimmed and transitioned as desired, you can add audio to your movie. For example, you can add narration, background music, or even additional background noise. If it's an audio file, you can add it to your movie.

You may wonder, "What if I want to keep the audio on my existing video?" For example, let's say you tape a family reunion. Everyone is talking and laughing, but you want to add soft background music to the movie. Can you add the music without ruining the original audio? Absolutely, and in this section you see how.

Adding Audio

If you switch to the Timeline view, you see an Audio/Music section on the Timeline. You can drag-and-drop music clips to this area to use in your video. (Remember, you import audio files in the same way you import photos and video clips.) The following illustration shows the Timeline with an audio clip added.

Just like trimming a video clip, you can click-and-drag the audio file on the timeline to trim off the beginning or end, as the following illustration shows. To adjust the level of the audio volume, click Tools | Audio.

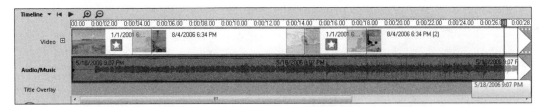

To record your voice, or some background music or sounds, click Tools | Narrate Timeline. You should already have your computer microphone connected and tested, or make sure any other sound input device you want to use to record is ready.

To record an audio file, follow these steps:

1. Click Tools | Narrate Timeline. A window appears above the Workspace, listing the sound device you will use to record the audio. If you have more than one sound device installed on your computer, use the drop-down menu to select a device as desired.

2. When you're ready to record, click the Start Narration button.

3. Name the file and save it. The file now appears in your Workspace timeline.

> NOTE
> *Recording narration or other background music or sounds doesn't erase the original video soundtrack—it simply adds another stream of sound to the existing movie.*

Adding Titles and Credits

You can easily add a title to the beginning of the movie, titles before or on a selected clip, and credits at the end of the movie. In the Tasks pane, click Titles and Credits under the Edit category and your workspace changes, so you can select the kind of title you want to add. Follow these steps to create your title:

1. Click Titles and Credits in the Task pane.

2. In the window that appears, choose the kind of title you want to add, such as a title at the beginning.

16

3. Type the desired title or credit in the box that appears, shown in the following illustration.

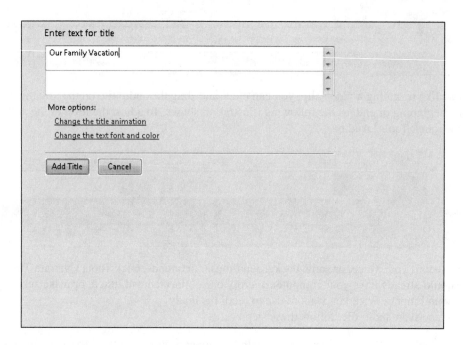

4. Play the title in the Monitor window, and view the animation, text font, and color. If you want to make changes, click the desired More Options under your text and make any desired changes.

5. When you're done, click Add Title. Note, if you decided to use a title overlay, so a title rolls over a clip as it's playing, you can adjust the position of the overlay on the Title Overlay line in the Timeline view.

Save Movies

As you work on your movie, you can save and close the entire project. When you're ready to begin working again, you can open the project and continue.

When you finish your movie, you can save it as a movie file, so Windows Media Player and other media software can read and play the movie. To save the movie, choose File | Save Movie File. Once you save the movie, you can view it with Windows Media Player.

Publishing Your Movie

After you finish your movie, you can publish it. When you publish your movie, you can save it to your computer, burn it to a DVD or recordable CD, save it in a smaller format so you can e-mail it to someone, or you can record it back to your digital video camera.

In the Tasks pane, simply click the desired option and follow any saving instructions that appear. Note, if you want to burn your movie to a DVD, the Windows DVD Maker appears. You can find out how to use the Windows DVD Maker by turning to the color insert that appears in the middle of this book.

16

Chapter 17

Manage Digital Photos and Use Windows Slideshow

How to...

- Work with digital photos
- Print digital photos
- Share and store digital photos
- Use Windows Slideshow

Digital photography has become an industry unto itself in the past few years. Digital cameras are better now than they have ever been, and millions of digital cameras are sold every year. Just take a walk into your favorite department or electronics store and glance at the available models. In many cases, you'll find digital cameras are pushing regular film cameras off the shelves! Although no one expects the film camera to die any time in the near future, the digital camera is here to stay. Windows Vista gives you built-in tools and capabilities that can help you manage digital photos and print them with greater ease and more flexibility than ever before. In the past, working with digital photos on a Windows computer, not to mention printing them in an effective manner, could be a difficult task. With Windows Vista, however, you can enjoy spending time and working with your photos, and this chapter shows you how.

In addition, Windows Vista also includes a new feature called Windows Slideshow. *Windows Slideshow* is a hardware feature that enables you to connect another device to your computer to display things like your calendar, e-mail messages, or scan news stories, even when your computer is off. We discuss Windows Slideshow in this chapter.

Connect to Your PC

Before you can use digital photos on Windows Vista, you need to connect your camera, card reader, or memory stick to Windows XP and download your photos. Most cameras, card readers, and memory sticks connect to your computer through a USB port. Because most of these products are Plug-and-Play, typically all you have to do is connect the device to a USB port and you're ready to go. You may have to install drivers or other software to connect your camera, though, so the best advice is to follow the manufacturer's instructions for downloading photos from your camera. Also, Windows Vista has a wizard you can use to install the camera on your system if you're having problems. See Chapter 7 for more information about installing a camera.

View and Manage Your Photos

Once your photos are downloaded to your Windows Vista computer, you can begin using them in any way you want. Before doing so, a good idea is to find out what's available to you, and how you can view and manage your photos. The good news is Windows Vista is rather flexible and gives you several different options you'll find helpful.

First, remember, you can organize photos in any way you want. This means you can download all your photos to a single folder, or you can create multiple folders and move them around as you like. Your photos may be downloaded to the My Pictures folder by default, and that's fine. But let me point out that the My Pictures folder doesn't have any magical powers—it's simply a folder like any folder on Windows Vista. I often organize my photos into various folders, so I can identify them more easily. I typically organize them by event (vacations, birthdays, holidays, and so on), but you can create any kind of system that suits your needs. People who take a lot of digital photos often create a new folder for each month and put all the photos for that month in one folder. There is no right or wrong answer, of course, but you'll want to decide on an organization method that works best for you. After all, there's nothing worse than taking a great digital photo and not being able to find it on your computer!

Second, once you open a folder that has photos stored in it, you're ready to begin using your photos in a number of ways. As you can see in Figure 17-1, a folder containing photos has

17

FIGURE 17-1 Thumbnails view

task features on a toolbar that give you several options. We explore the features you see here in upcoming sections, but I focus on a few direct features here. A good idea is to open the Views menu and find a View option that works well for you. Essentially, all views are thumbnails of the photos. Move the slider bar on the Views menu to choose a size you like.

On the Views menu, you find the following options:

- **Extra Large Icons** This option presents your photos as miniphotos. You can scroll through your folder list and see a larger view of each photo. If you hover over the photo with your mouse, you see file information appear, such as the size, date taken, and so forth. If you want a good look at your photos, as you can see in Figure 17-2, Extra Large Icons is the way to go.

- **Large Icons** This option shows you a smaller photo view, as shown in Figure 17-1. This is a good way to see photos and file names at the same time.

- **Medium Icons** This option shows you icons and the file name, only smaller. The good news is you can see more photos at one time in this view.

- **Small Icons** This option shows you smaller icons with only the file name.

FIGURE 17-2   Extra Large Icons view

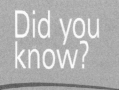

Make Sure You Back Up!

As with any file, photos can get corrupted or accidentally deleted from your system. You should have a backup plan in place, so you always have additional copies of your favorite photos stored elsewhere. This can be as simple as copying photos to a CD and putting that CD in a safe place, or it can be a full backup plan using the Windows Backup utility. You can learn more about using Windows Backup in Chapter 20.

■ **Details** This option shows you even smaller icons and the file name. You also see additional information for each photo, such as the date taken, date modified, file size, and so on.

■ **Tiles** This is the same as Medium Icons, but it provides more information about each photo, such as size, type, date modified, and so forth.

In addition to these basic viewing options, you can also quickly access some features by right-clicking a photo. You see a context menu (the same one that appears when you right-click just about anything in Windows), but you also see some specific options that are useful in managing photos:

■ **Preview** This option opens the photo in Vista's new Photo Gallery Viewer, which is explored in the section "Use the Photo Gallery."

■ **Edit** This option opens the photo once again in Vista's new Photo Gallery Viewer where you can make some basic editing adjustments to the photo. Naturally, you can also open the photo in other photo editing software packages.

View Your Photos as a Slide Show

Windows Vista has a built-in slide show feature, so you can view the photos in a folder as a slide show. In the folder, click the Slide Show option that appears on the toolbar. Your photos come to life in a full-screen, automatically advancing slide show. However, if you move your mouse, you can see control options that let you manually advance or back up during the slide show. You can also stop the slide show with the manual controls or press the ESC key on your keyboard.

17

- ■ **Print**   This option opens a photo-printing wizard, which you can learn more about in the section "Print Your Photos."
- ■ **Rotate Clockwise/Counterclockwise**   Click these options to rotate the photo.
- ■ **Set as Desktop Background**   Use this option to quickly set the photo as your desktop background photo.

Use the Photo Gallery

Windows Vista includes a new feature called the Windows Photo Gallery. In the past, different photo management features were found in different places, such as in folder tasks or by right-clicking. Now, you can double-click, or right-click, any photo, and then click Preview or Edit, and you get Windows Photo Gallery. The *Windows Photo Gallery* option puts all your photo management features in one handy location, as you can see in Figure 17-3.

FIGURE 17-3   Photo Gallery Viewer

In Figure 17-3, you see the Gallery view where you can browse through all photos or videos on your computer. Just click one to see a full photo view of it. Notice you have several toolbar options that enable you to manage the photo and use it. The following sections explore these options.

File

The *File drop-down menu* enables you to delete the photo, rename it, duplicate it, copy it, or access the photo's properties. These items are all self-explanatory. You also see an Options feature, which opens a basic options window with General and Import tabs. On the *Import tab,* you can determine settings for different devices and media, such as your camera, CDs, DVDs, and such. You can determine where you want the photos imported, possible tags, and what should happen after you import (such as Open Windows Photo Gallery). Take a look at these settings and choose the options you want.

Fix

The *Fix option* opens a pane with some fixing tools, as you can see in the following illustration. You can click an option and adjust the photo as desired. You can use the Auto Adjust feature, which runs a filter over the photo to try to correct lighting and such. You can also manually adjust the exposure or color, crop the photo, or fix red eye. These tools are quick and easy, as well as helpful with minor photo problems.

Info

If you click the *Info option,* the pane opens with data about your photo. The good thing here is you can add tags to your photo. *Tags* are essentially category labels that can enable you to search for certain kinds of photos. For example, in the following illustration, I added the tag "nature" by clicking the Add Tags button and typing the word "nature." Now, if I search for "nature" in the Photo Gallery, this photo appears as a search result because it was tagged in that way. You can add multiple tags to a photo to make searching under different topics or categories easier.

Print

The *Print button drop-down menu* gives you two options: Print the Photo or Order Prints. You can find out more about printing photos in the section "Print Your Photos," but if you want to order photos online, you can use the feature here to connect to an online printing service, such as Shutterfly. Of course, you don't have to use this online ordering feature—you can also order prints from any online service directly through your Internet browser, such as Internet Explorer, by simply accessing the desired web site and following the instructions.

E-Mail

The *E-mail option* enables you to attach a photo or movie to an e-mail message. The good thing about attaching a photo or movie using the Windows Photo Gallery is the *Attach feature* gives you the option to resize your photo to get the photo to a reasonable size for e-mailing. As you see in the following illustration, you can choose a size from the drop-down menu and you can see an estimated file size before you attach it to your e-mail message.

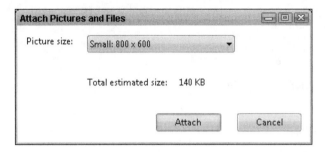

Burn

The *Burn option* enables you to create a Video DVD, or a Data Disc. If you choose the Video DVD option, your photo or movie is sent to Windows DVD Maker (see the color insert in this book for instructions). If you choose the *Data Disc option,* you can burn your photos or movies to a CD or DVD for data storage.

Make a Movie

This option imports your photos or movie clips to Windows Movie Maker, which is software that enables you to edit and assemble movies. The button here is simply a quick way to import photos and videos, and to access Movie Maker. You can learn more about Windows Movie Maker in Chapter 16.

Open

The *Open option* gives you a list of programs that can open photos, so you can open the photo in one of those programs. Simply click Open and a list of available programs on your computer appears. Click one to open the photo in that program.

Control Toolbar

Finally, Windows Photo Gallery gives you a control toolbar, found along the bottom of the interface. From left to right, you have the following button options:

- **Display Size**   Use the drop-down arrow to adjust the display size of the photo you're currently viewing.
- **Fit to Window**   If you zoomed in on the photo using the Display Size option, simply click the Fit to Window button to return to a size where the photos fit inside the window area in Windows Photo Gallery

17

- ■ **Previous and Next buttons**   You see a previous and a next button that enable you to click through a collection of photos and see each of them individually.
- ■ **Play Slide Show**   The larger center button enables you to see all the photos in the folder as a full screen slideshow.
- ■ **Rotate**   Two buttons here enable you to rotate a photo either counterclockwise or clockwise.
- ■ **Delete**   This quick delete button enables you to delete the photo.

Print Your Photos

In addition to ordering your photos online, you can also print them on your color printer. As a general rule, any inkjet printer can produce quality photos, even the inexpensive $99 inkjet printers you see at discount department stores. Now, maybe you have tried to print your photos and ended up with terrible results. That certainly isn't unusual, and there are two primary reasons why printed photos may not look great: paper and resolution.

The first reason your photos may not look great is this: you can't print quality photos on standard typing paper that you use to print text. This paper isn't designed to hold the ink, so individual dots of ink run together, giving you a smeared and dull-looking photo. If you want to print effective photos, you must use photo paper. Photo paper, which is sold in packs at any department store, is designed to hold the ink and give you the results you want. Photo paper isn't cheap, of course, but you'll need to use it to print photos. Most brands you'll find at any department store work well, so before you go any further with printing, make sure you have some photo paper on hand.

The second reason your photos may not look great is *resolution,* which refers to the number of pixels in a digital photo. Digital photos are made of tiny dots of color (pixels) that create images. The number of pixels you have in a photo determines the quality of the photo when it is printed. If not enough pixels are present, the pixels get stretched to make the size photo you want. For this reason, if you have a low-resolution photo, you can't print a quality 5 by 7 or 8 by 10 photo because there isn't enough resolution. Exploring resolution and your camera settings is beyond the scope of this book, so I suggest you study your camera's manual or a general digital photography book, so you understand resolution more fully. Overall, though, the important thing to remember is you need to shoot at a high resolution if you want to print larger photos, such as 8 by 10s.

In the past, printing photos could be a real chore because it was difficult both to control the size of the printed photo and to print several photos on the same page. The good news is Windows Vista fixes this problem with the Photo Printing Wizard, which you can access from the Windows Photo Gallery. The following steps show you how to use this wizard to print your photos:

1. In the folder containing the photos you want to print, double-click the desired photo to open the Windows Photo Gallery.
2. Click the Print button on the toolbar. This opens the Print Pictures window, as you can see in the following illustration.

3. From the drop-down menu, choose the desired printer you want to print to, the number of copies you want, and other such settings.

4. In the right pane, choose the desired size, such as a full-page photo, 8 by 10 photo, 5 by 7 photo, and so forth.

5. You can click the Options link to access additional settings, such as sharpening and color management, which may be helpful for your particular printer. When you're done, simply click the Print button.

Burn Your Photos to a CD

Like any file, you can burn photos to a CD to store them. You can use your CD-burning software as you would with any file, or you can click the Burn button found on the toolbar in the folder with your photos. Overall, burning photos to a CD works the same as burning any other file—Windows Vista just tries to simplify the process by giving you a direct link in the folder.

If you have a CD burner, you can also right-click any file, click Send To, and then choose your CD drive from the context menu that appears.

Use Windows Slideshow

The name Windows Slideshow is a bit misleading at first. When you read the name, you probably think of creating some kind of slideshow within Windows that you can show to other people, such as you might do with the PowerPoint application. In reality, though, Windows Slideshow is

17

something completely different and it's a rather cool feature if you have the hardware to support it. Windows Slideshow is a feature that enables you to connect a secondary device to your computer and use it to see your calendar, read e-mail messages, or even scan news stories, even if your computer isn't turned on.

Two basic kinds of devices are compatible with Windows Slideshow. The first are those integrated with your computer, such as small color displays that may be embedded in the lid of a laptop or a monochrome display embedded in a keyboard. The second are those that are separate from your computer, such as dedicated displays, wireless LCD panels, and even mobile photos and televisions with slideshow capabilities. Devices you purchase must be compatible with Windows Slideshow and you'll even see a Windows Slideshow logo on those devices. You can also check www.microsoft.com for more information.

Once you have the appropriate hardware installed, you can access Windows Slideshow in the Control Panel to configure the device (if necessary), and then determine what Gadgets are available for use. Naturally, this is a new feature and you should expect to see more compatible phones and other devices appear on the market soon.

Chapter 18

Take Care of Windows Vista

How to...

- Access disk properties
- Run disk tools
- Configure and manage scheduled tasks
- Automatically install Windows update

Windows Vista is an advanced operating system (OS) that, for the most part, can take care of itself. Hardware management, and even error correction, can be done automatically. Unlike with computer systems of the past, you don't have to spend much of your time thinking about care and maintenance. However, Windows Vista provides you with tools that can help keep the Vista system running at its peak. In this chapter, we explore those tools, how you can use them, and how they help your system run better. Most of the tools you learn about in this chapter have to do with hard disk maintenance. After you review the information in this chapter, be sure you also read Chapter 19, which covers more advanced disk management features in Windows Vista.

Hard Disk Basics

Before we explore hard disk maintenance, let's first take a quick look at hard disk basics. After all, maintaining and caring for a part of your computer is much easier if you have some basic understanding of it. Every Windows Vista computer has at least one hard disk. A *hard disk* is made up of a platter (or multiple platters) that holds magnetic material. This platter is hard, not flexible like other types of storage media, such as magnetic tape. When the OS needs either to read from or write information to the disk, the platter spins—often faster than 100 mph—and data is read from or written to the disk in small chunks called *bytes*. This is why you hear a churning noise from within your computer when you open or save files, open programs, or perform other memory-related actions on your computer. The churning noise is the disk drive arm moving back and forth, reading that data.

You can think of the hard disk as the computer's storage area. All applications, files, folders—practically everything that is installed or exists on your computer—resides on the hard disk, including the Windows Vista OS itself. Because the hard disk is one giant storage area, keeping the disk in tip-top running shape is important. The tools found in Windows Vista can easily help you optimize the hard disk.

File System Basics

As you now know, a hard disk is a storage area where all files, applications, and other types of system information are stored. When you want to view a file or even open a program, Windows Vista accesses the hard disk to retrieve the information. However, hard disks are basically blank slates, and Windows Vista cannot store information on a hard disk until it is partitioned and formatted. *Partitioning* is a process that logically divides the disk into different segments, which can be managed independently. *Formatting* is a process that logically divides the disk into sections, so information can be stored on the disk in an organized way. Think of the hard disk as a filing cabinet, and the file system as the folders placed in the filing cabinet. Windows Vista uses a file system to organize data, so it can be easily recorded and retrieved. Without a file system, Windows Vista would have no way to keep track of the information stored on the hard drive.

Windows Vista supports two different kinds of file systems: FAT32 and NTFS. FAT32 was used by Windows 95 SE and Windows 98, as well as Windows Me (and also supported by Windows 2000), and NTFS was used by Windows NT, Windows 2000, and Windows XP. In truth, Windows Vista works just like Windows XP, because it can read either FAT32 or NTFS. Without getting into too many gory details, the following two sections tell you about each type of file system.

FAT32

FAT32 (the acronym FAT stands for file allocation table) is a basic file system that has been around for quite some time. FAT12 was the original FAT file system, and it was used to organize and manage small disks, such as floppy disks. FAT16 was used for computer hard disks. Then, FAT32 came onto the scene when large (more than 1GB) hard drives became popular a few years back. FAT32 is a simple file system Windows Vista can use to manage your computer's hard disks. FAT32 supports basic folder security.

NTFS

NTFS, a much more complex file system than FAT32, is a file system first introduced with Windows NT. NTFS supports both folder and file security. This means you can place security restrictions on folders, as well as finely control access to resources with users and groups. NTFS is also supported in Windows Vista and is considered a much more powerful file system than FAT32.

 You can format your computer's hard drive with either FAT32 or NTFS—Chapter 19 explores this issue in more detail.

Set Hard Disk Properties

As you've learned throughout this book, almost everything in Windows Vista has properties pages—a place where you can get more information about a feature or component. Your hard disks, removable disks, and CD/DVD-ROM drives are no exception. If you open Computer from your Start menu, you see an icon for each drive available on your computer. You can see your C drive; a floppy drive; a CD/DVD-ROM drive; possibly other drives, such as a Zip or Jaz drive; and even portable devices if they're attached to your computer, as Figure 18-1 shows.

As you can see in Figure 18-1, my own computer has two hard drives (*C* and *D*), a CD-ROM drive, and several removable drives. You can also inspect your computer's disk drives using the Computer Management console found in Administrative Tools in the Control Panel, as Figure 18-2 shows. The Computer Management console is a powerful tool, which we explore in more detail in Chapter 19.

18

FIGURE 18-1   Computer contents

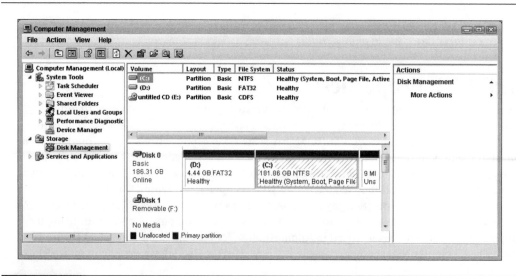

FIGURE 18-2   Computer Management console

If you right-click any of the hard disks and choose Properties, you can see a standard properties sheet with seven basic tabs. Each tab contains some maintenance and management features, and the following sections examine each of them individually. Also, note, you can right-click any removable storage media, such as floppy drives and CD-ROM drives, and choose Properties to view their properties sheets.

The tools and options presented in the following sections apply only to writable disks— they do not apply to read-only CD-ROM or DVD-ROM disks.

General Tab

One of the best things about the *General tab* is the pie graph, shown in Figure 18-3. You can access your drive's General tab at any time and see exactly how much disk space is used and how much disk space is free (available for use). You get this usage information for any writable disk, including your floppy drive.

In addition to getting information quickly, you can do only two other things on the General tab. First, you can enter a label for the disk. The label isn't anything usable to you, so most people don't put anything here. The other option on the General tab is the Disk Cleanup option, which you will occasionally find useful.

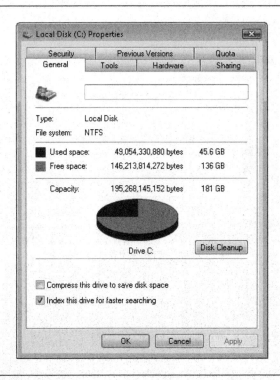

FIGURE 18-3   General tab

18

Disk Cleanup is a utility that inspects your hard disk and looks for files that can be safety deleted. By deleting unused or unneeded files, you free up disk space that can be used for other purposes.

To run the Disk Cleanup utility, follow these steps:

1. On the General tab, click the Disk Cleanup button.

2. Disk Cleanup scans your disk, and then provides you with a window, shown in Figure 18-4, that has two tabs—Disk Cleanup and More Options. The Disk Cleanup tab lists categories of potential "delete" items and the amount of disk space you can gain by emptying each one.

3. To inspect a category, select it and click the View Files button. This feature enables you to specify which items within a category you want to delete.

4. When you're sure what items/categories you want to delete, select the check boxes next to those categories, and then click OK.

Remember, Disk Cleanup examines only certain areas of your computer, such as temporary files and downloaded Internet items. Disk Cleanup doesn't inspect every possible category of items that can be deleted—much of that work is left to you. So, how often should you use Disk Cleanup? A typical user should run this utility once every three months to see if any unused files can be deleted to free up disk space.

FIGURE 18-4   Disk Cleanup utility

Tools

The *Tools tab* gives you three important tools you can use to keep your computer disks happy and working efficiently, shown in Figure 18-5. The following sections tell you all about these tools.

Error Checking

Error Checking is the first tool option you see. If you click the Check Now button, the Error Checking tool is opened, as Figure 18-6 shows, so you can check your disk for errors. The small dialog box gives you the options to fix errors found automatically, and to scan for and attempt recovery of bad sectors.

NOTE *If you don't have the Automatically Fix File System Errors check box enabled, Error Checking prompts you to OK its fix for every error it finds (which can get annoying).*

The Scan For and Attempt Recovery of Bad Sectors option allows Error Checking to check the file system of the disk and attempt to resolve any problems that exist with sectors on the physical disk. As a general rule, you should also enable this option when using Error Checking, so you can get a more thorough disk examination.

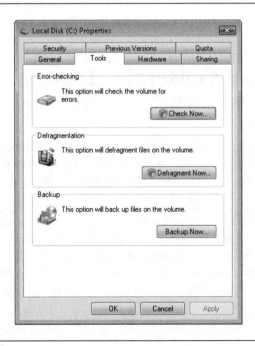

FIGURE 18-5   Tools tab

18

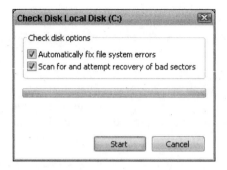

FIGURE 18-6   Error Checking tool

So, now that you know what the options are, what should you do? First, let me note that Error Checking is automatically run during reboot after an improper system shutdown. Let's say your computer locks up, and you have to turn the power off, and then turn it back on. During reboot, Error Checking checks your file and folder structure. If you use your computer a lot, it doesn't hurt to run the Error Checking test every few weeks, just to make sure your files and folders are up to par.

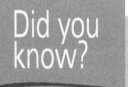

About Conserving Disk Space

If you have a newer computer, conserving disk space probably isn't a big concern to you—after all, it isn't uncommon for a typical computer to ship with a 80GB or larger hard drive. That's a lot of storage space; but if you use Windows Movie Maker and Windows Media Player a lot, and if you hang onto all your video and multimedia files, you need a lot of disk space. Here are some quick and helpful tips to conserve disk space on your computer:

- Uninstall games and programs you don't use. Programs take up a lot of space. If you aren't playing all ten of those games you installed, get rid of them. You can always reinstall one if you need it later but, in the meantime, free up that disk space!

- Old personal files can easily be saved to floppies or CDs for storage.

- Check Programs in Control Panel occasionally. If you download a lot of utilities from the Internet, you may need to remove the unneeded or unwanted ones.

- Use folder compression (see Chapter 4). Compression helps save disk space and doesn't interfere with your work.

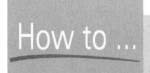

Avoid Disk Errors

Disk errors are part of life and nothing to be too concerned about, as long as you allow Error Checking to fix them from time to time. Although a number of different actions and problems can cause disk errors, here are some operation tips to help you avoid them:

■ Always turn off your computer from the Start menu. This enables Windows to shut down in a proper manner. Avoid shutting down your computer by turning off the power button.

■ Uninstall programs by using the program's uninstall feature or Add/Remove Programs in the Control Panel. Don't delete a program's folder to uninstall it unless no other way works.

■ If you experience a lockup or some other problem that forces a hard reboot, allow Error Checking to run at reboot to catch any new errors.

TIP *Error Checking may take half an hour or longer to run, depending on the size of the disk being scanned.*

Disk Defragmenter

Windows Vista includes a *Disk Defragmenter utility,* which you can access from the Tools tab. Before you use Disk Defragmenter, you need to know a little bit about fragmentation, so you understand the process.

Fragmentation, a normal part of disk usage, occurs at the file system level. Windows Vista is unable to use a disk of any kind unless the disk is formatted. Formatting logically divides the disk into sectors and clusters—basically making a grid out of the disk, so blocks of data can be stored on it. The grid allows Windows Vista to keep up with which block of data is stored where; otherwise, the disk would become a big confusing mess. To create this grid, Windows Vista uses a file system (FAT32 or NTFS), as previously discussed. Once the file system is in place, Windows Vista can write and read data to and from the hard disk.

In Windows Vista, data generally is stored on the disk in a contiguous manner. *Contiguous* means data is stored in order. For example, let's say you're working again on that Great American Novel. When you save the document, it's divided into pieces—or blocks of data—and stored in a row on the disk. Later, when you make changes to the document, those changes are stored at the end of the row. Over time, as you save, edit, and delete different files, changes to those files are moved to available, but noncontiguous, storage blocks on the disk, so files become *fragmented*—in other words, they aren't stored in a contiguous manner. When you want to open

18

a file, Windows Vista must gather the fragmented pieces together from your hard disk. Because the pieces are in different places, this can take longer than it should. The short of it is simply that heavily fragmented drives can cause Windows Vista to run slower than it should.

The Disk Defragmenter utility takes all the data on your hard disk and reorganizes it, so the data is stored in a contiguous format—or at least close to it. The Disk Defragmenter utility enables you to create a schedule for the tool to run, or you can run the tool manually by clicking the Defragment Now button, as shown in Figure 18-7, if defragmentation is needed.

You can watch the display change as the Disk Defragmenter utility reorganizes information. Note, the utility won't get 100 percent of your files reorganized—this is normal and nothing to be concerned about because the files that are running Windows at the moment cannot be moved and reorganized. Defragmentation may take some time to complete, especially for large hard drives, so be patient.

Once defragmentation is complete, you can click the View Report button to find out more information about the condition of the disk. The report gives you overall information about the number of fragments, the disk size, free space, used space, and other related information.

So, how often should you defragment your drives? The simple rule of thumb is based on how often you use your computer. If you're a typical home user, you should run the Disk Defragmenter utility about once every two or three months. If you use your PC every day (all day) as I do, and you use a lot of files, you should defragment your drives once a month. Doing this helps keep your file system in peak operating condition. The good news about Windows Vista is the disk defragmenter is set up to run weekly be default. So, if you leave the configuration as it stands, disk defragmentation runs on its own.

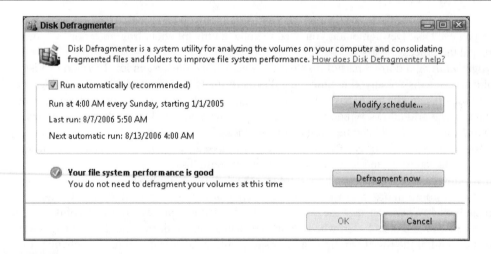

FIGURE 18-7   Disk Defragmenter

Backup

Windows Vista Professional includes a *Backup utility* that enables you to back up entire disks or individual folders to a backup storage location. See Chapter 19 to learn more about Windows Backup.

Hardware

The *Hardware tab* lists the disk drives on your computer and gives you information about each one (including whether the disk is working properly), as Figure 18-8 shows. You can also click the Troubleshoot button to get help if you're having drive problems. And, you can click the Properties button, which opens the standard Device Manager properties sheets for the hard disk.

Sharing

Just as with folders, you can share any drive on your computer, so others on a network can access it. The Sharing tab you see is just like all other Sharing tabs in Windows Vista (you can learn more about network shares in Chapter 11). Under most circumstances, you wouldn't want to give someone else full access to your entire hard drive, but you may want to give someone access to a CD-ROM or Zip drive.

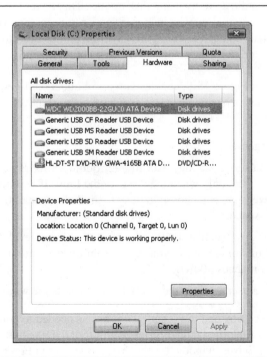

FIGURE 18-8   Hardware tab

18

Security

The *Security tab* you see here is like all Security tabs that are available for different files and folders in Windows Vista. Here, you can configure advanced security options for the drive. See Chapter 13 to learn more about security features in Windows Vista.

Previous Versions

The Previous Versions tab is like all other Previous Versions tabs found on properties pages within Windows Vista. The *Previous Versions tab* enables you to move back to a previous version of the folder, so it functions like a backup feature. For the Computer folder, however, this tab doesn't serve much purpose.

Quota

If your drives are formatted with NTFS, you also see a Quota tab. Windows Vista supports a Disk Quotas feature, which first appeared in the Windows 2000 OS. *Disk quotas* are designed for network computers where a computer's hard drive is shared with other network users. For example, say your Windows Vista computer is shared on a network. Your computer has two hard drives, one of which is shared. Network users can store documents in various folders on this drive and, essentially, your computer acts like a file server. You can configure how much disk space users may consume on the drive by using disk quotas. This feature prevents a user from storing information on the drive that may be inappropriate or unnecessary. If you aren't sharing drives on a network, you have no need to configure anything on this tab. However, if you're using your Windows Vista computer as a storage/file server on a network, read on to learn about disk quota configuration.

The *Quota tab,* shown in Figure 18-9, enables you to set quota configurations for the particular hard disk you're using. As you can see, you have some standard configuration options that let you do the following:

- Enable quota management.
- Deny disk space to users once they exceed their quota limits. By default, quota management warns users only when they're over the limit. If you need to impose strict quota limits, however, you can choose to deny them disk space until they remove files to free up usable disk space.
- Set a limit based on size (such as 1MB), as well as a warning level. For example, if you set a limit of 1MB of storage space, you might want to configure the warning level to appear when a user reaches 800KB.
- Log an event when a user exceeds the quota limit or meets the warning level.

Simply select these check box and radio button options as needed to configure quota behavior. Next, you need to click the Quota Entries button found at the bottom of the Quota tab. Doing this opens the Quota Entries window for the drive, as shown in Figure 19-10.

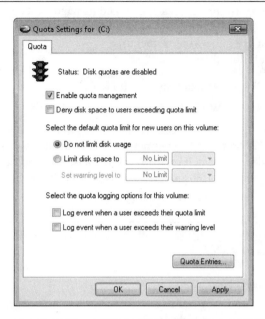

FIGURE 18-9 Quota tab

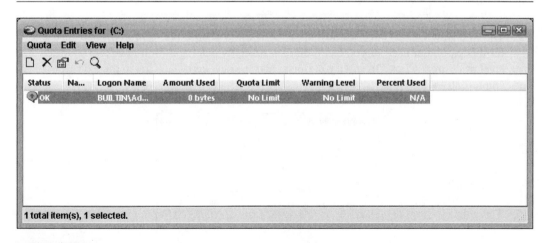

FIGURE 18-10 Quota Entries

18

You use the *Quote Entries window* to create, edit, and manage quota entries. You can also make editorial changes to any quota entries you configure, and you can delete entries by selecting the entry, and then using the window menus.

To create a quota entry, follow these steps:

1. On the Quota tab, click the Quota Entries button.

2. In the Quota Entries window, choose Quota | New Quota Entry.

3. The Select Users window appears. Use the Object Types button and Locations button to select the desired user or group on your network. You can also use the Advanced button to perform a more detailed search of the Windows network directory (Active Directory). Once you select the desired user/group, the entry appears in the Select Users window, as shown here. Click OK.

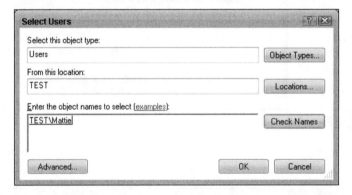

4. The Add New Quota Entry window appears. You can choose not to limit disk space usage for that particular user, or you can limit disk space by placing a limit level and warning level as desired. Click OK after you finish, and the new entry appears in the Add Bew Quota Entry window.

Schedule Tasks

Remember I said you should run Error Checking and Disk Cleanup at regular intervals? What if you don't want to remember and keep up with these housekeeping tasks? The good news is you don't have to. You can use a Windows Vista feature called *Task Scheduler,* so you can schedule these utilities to run automatically on your computer at certain times and on certain days.

You can find Task Scheduler in Control Panel | Administrative Tools, as Figure 18-11 shows. Here, you find preconfigured tasks that Windows Vista needs to use to run properly, so you should leave the current tasks configured as they are. However, you can also create your own.

Create a Task

You can easily create a task to run when you need it to run. Just follow these steps:

1. In the Task Schedule, click the Create Task option.

2. On the General tab, give the task a name and a description, if you like, and then choose a desired security setting. The default option to run the task only when the user is logged on is typically the best.

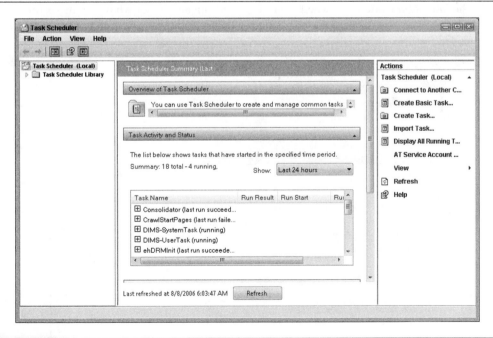

FIGURE 18-11   Task Scheduler

18

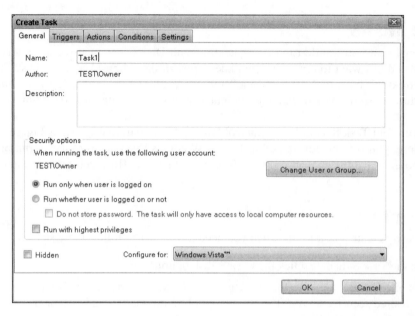

3. On the Triggers, Actions, and Conditions tabs, you can choose triggers, actions, or conditions for the task to run. For example, you can use the Triggers tab to create a schedule of how often and when the task should run and under what conditions the task should expire. Click through the options you see on these tabs and choose any needed features.

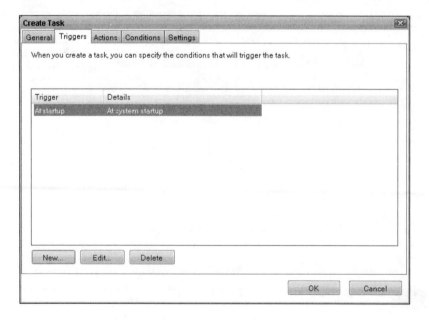

4. On the Settings tab, you can choose some basic settings for Vista to use if the task is missed, if it fails, or what Vista should do if the task doesn't end by the requested time. Choose the desired options and click OK.

NOTE

You can configure as many scheduled tasks as you like, however, each task should be configured to run at a different time. In other words, some programs, such as Error Checking and Disk Defragmenter, cannot run at the same time. Also, use as many scheduled tasks as you need, but don't overschedule them. Having too many tasks running at close intervals sometimes causes more confusion than necessary and may degrade Windows Vista performance.

Use Windows Update

Windows Update is a great feature of Windows Vista that enables you to update Windows Vista automatically as fixes and software updates are released from Microsoft (see Figure 18-12).

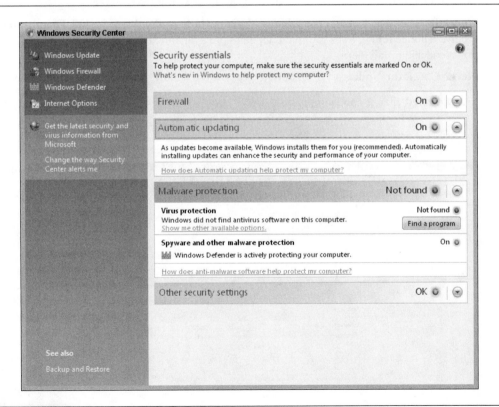

FIGURE 18-12   Windows Update is turned on

Updates from Microsoft are often several megabytes in size. If you're using a dial-up Internet connection, you can expect the update process to take considerable time to download.

By default, Windows Update is turned on and working, as you can see by accessing the Security Center in the Control Panel.

If you want to adjust Windows Update settings, click the Windows Update link in the left pane of the Security Center. In the Windows Update window, click the Change Settings link in the left pane. You can see options to:

- **Install Updates Automatically** This is the default setting. Automatic Updates checks for updates automatically, downloads them, and installs them without any intervention from you. Note, you can choose the download time you want. If your computer has an always-connected broadband connection, every day during the middle of the night works great, but your computer must be turned on for the process to work.

- **Download Updates for Me, But Let Me Choose Whether to Install Them** This option downloads the updates, but it doesn't install them until you're ready.

- **Check for Updates, But Let Me Choose Whether to Download and Install Them** You receive a notice telling you Automatic Updates are available, but you choose when to download and install them.

- **Never Check for Updates** This option turns off the feature, which isn't recommended.

Make any desired changes and simply click OK.

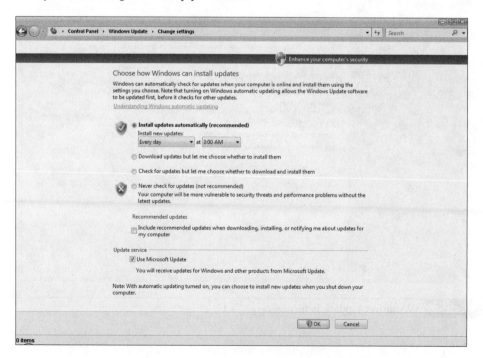

Part IV

Optimize, Troubleshoot, and Fix Windows Vista

Chapter 19 Manage Disks

How to...

- ■ Configure Windows Vista disk volumes
- ■ Use Vista Backup and Restore features
- ■ Use BitLocker Drive Encryption

Windows Vista includes a number of features that make disk management easy. As you work with Windows, the importance of effective disk management cannot be overstated—after all, it is the hard disk(s) on your computer that must store all your information, including the Windows Vista operating system (OS). The more you know about effective disk management and how to administer and maintain hard disks on your system, the more likely you are to have a computer that runs in peak condition and never to lose data from your hard disk. In this chapter, we explore several disk management features in Windows Vista.

Manage Disks

The Computer Management console, found in the Administrative Tools folder in the Control Panel, provides a section called Storage. If you click the plus (+) sign next to Storage, you see three categories available one of which is Disk Management, as Figure 19-1 shows. Click Disk Management and the Disk Management console, by default, provides you with an interface to manage the drives on your computer.

If you spend a few moments clicking around in the Disk Management console, you can see that both the list and graphical portions tell the same things about your disks—the layout, type, file system, status, capacity, and so on. Disk Management in Windows Vista and the available options will be new to you if you haven't used Windows 2000 or Windows XP in the past. The following sections explore these management concepts and tasks, so you can see how to manage the hard disks on your computer.

Understanding Dynamic Disks

Dynamic disks, which first came onto the scene with Windows 2000, give you more management and configuration options than basic disks. First, I need to define these two terms. A *basic disk* in Windows Vista refers to standard disk configurations in earlier versions of Windows, such as 9*x* and NT. With a basic disk, you can configure different drives by segmenting the disk into different partitions, and you can perform basic disk-management tasks. *Dynamic disks,* on the other hand, give you more flexibility, enable you to make changes without rebooting, and use volumes instead of partitions. Essentially, from your perspective, a partition and a volume are the same thing—both logically segment the disk—but dynamic disks don't have volume number limits, and you can change drive letters and paths on the fly. In short, dynamic disks give you the full range of disk features available in Windows Vista, while basic disks are supported for backward compatibility.

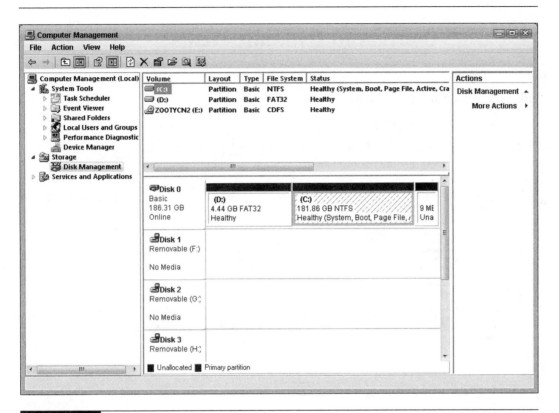

FIGURE 19-1   Disk Management console

Now, if all this seems like alien gibberish to you, don't worry. If you're a home user or even an office user, you probably don't need to worry about the differences between basic disks and dynamic disks, and you probably won't need to make any disk changes at all. But, dynamic disks will be an important feature if your computer has several hard disks or if you're an intermediate-level user who wants to take full advantage of all Windows Vista Disk Management has to offer.

 If you're using a dual-boot system where multiple operating systems are available on your computer, don't convert any disks that house a "down-level" OS, such as Windows 9x or Me.

If you want to convert a disk to a dynamic disk, at least 1MB of free disk space must be available on the disk for the conversion to take place. Once the upgrade is complete, you cannot reverse it unless you delete all the volumes (and, hence, all the information) from the disk. You must also be logged on as the computer's administrator to complete any disk conversion actions.

To begin, you must first convert any basic disks on your computer to dynamic disks. This process is easy and safe, and the following How To box gives you the steps.

19

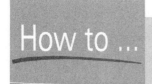

Convert to Dynamic Disks

To convert a basic disk to a dynamic disk, follow these steps:

1. In the Computer Management console, expand Storage and select Disk Management.

2. In the Disk Management console's right pane, right-click the disk number (such as Disk 0 or Disk 1), and choose Convert to Dynamic Disk, as shown.

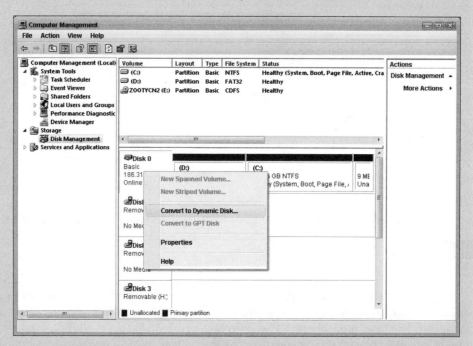

3. In the Convert to Dynamic Disk window, select all the drives you want to convert. If only one drive needs converting, that's all you see here. If more than one needs converting, you have the option of selecting them and converting them all at the same time. This process is safe, so feel free to convert more than one disk at a time if needed. Make your selections and click OK.

4. A window appears listing the disk(s) that will be converted. Click the Convert button to continue.

5. A message appears stating you won't be able to start another OS from any volume on these disks. Click Yes to continue.

The disk is converted and now appears as a dynamic disk in the console.

You cannot upgrade removable media, such as CD-ROMs or Zip disks, to dynamic disks. Dynamic disks are supported only for fixed disks. You cannot use dynamic disks on portable computers.

Understanding Disk Status

Dynamic disks provide status information to you in the Disk Management console (see the How To "Convert to Dynamic Disks"). A number of possible status indications can be displayed, and these enable you to determine what might be wrong with a disk.

The actual disk state is shown in the graphical portion of the window under the disk number (Disk 0, Disk 1, and so on). Disks may display the following states:

- **Online**   The disk is functioning properly.

- **Online (Errors)**   The disk is functioning, but input/output errors have been detected. Run the Error Checking tool by right-clicking the desired disk, and then choosing Properties | Tools to try to correct the problems.

- **Off line/Missing**   The disk is not functioning or is not accessible. Possible hardware problems may be causing this state. Right-click the disk number in the console and choose the Reactivate Disk option.

- **Foreign**   A new disk from another Windows Vista computer has been installed on your computer, but it has not been set up for use on your computer. Right-click the disk and choose Import Foreign Disk to set it up for use on your computer.

- **Unreadable**   The disk is not accessible because of failure or corruption. You can try to reactivate the disk by right-clicking the disk number in the console and choosing Reactivate Disk.

- **Unrecognized**   The disk is formatted with a file system that is not recognized. This error occurs when you install a new disk into the computer that came from another OS. You can reformat the disk, so Windows can use it, but any existing data on the disk will be lost.

In addition to these disk states, each volume found on each disk also displays a status, which is shown in the Disk Management console. The following status readings may be seen:

- **Healthy**   The volume is functioning properly.

- **Healthy (At Risk)**   The volume is functioning, but errors have been detected. Run the Error Checking tool to attempt to fix the problems.

- **Initializing**   You have created a new volume, and Windows Vista is preparing it for use. This status will change to Healthy once the initialization is complete.

- **Failed**   The volume cannot be automatically started and has failed.

Formatting a Disk

In some circumstances, you may need to reformat a hard disk. When you format a disk, all information on that disk is erased and a new file system is created. Obviously, you will lose any data stored on the disk, so a format operation should not be taken lightly and should be performed only if absolutely necessary. The Windows Vista system doesn't let you reformat a disk that holds the OS software, because this action would delete the software from your computer. However, if your computer has other hard drives, you are free to reformat those. To reformat a disk, right-click the drive (such as *D, E,* and so on) and choose Format. The Format dialog box appears, as shown in Figure 19-2. Use the File System drop-down menu to select the desired file system, and give the volume a label. You may want to use the Quick Format option, which essentially erases the information from the disk and creates a new file system for you. Click Start to continue.

NTFS is the file system of choice for Windows Vista. So, what do you do if you upgraded to Windows Vista and your disks are still formatted with FAT32? How can you get NTFS without losing data on the drives? The answer is simple—you can use a `convert` command at the command prompt. The process converts the disk volume to NTFS and retains all of your information. However, once you convert, you cannot revert to FAT32 without reformatting the disk, and you cannot convert a compressed Windows 98 volume—it must be uncompressed first. Otherwise, the process is quick and painless, and the following How To box shows you how.

Creating a New Volume

A *volume* is simply a portion of a hard disk that acts like a separate disk. Volumes give you a way of organizing hard drives for storage purposes. Depending on your storage needs, you may want to divide one or more of your computer's hard drives into logical volumes.

Windows Vista makes volume creation easy. At any time, you can create a new volume on any hard disk on your computer, provided enough free disk space is currently available to create

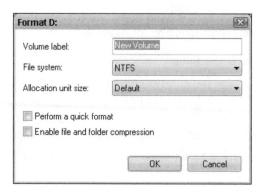

FIGURE 19-2   Format dialog box

Convert a Drive to NTFS

To convert a drive to NTFS, follow these steps:

1. Choose Start | Run, type **CMD**, and then click OK.

2. At the command prompt, type **Convert** *driveletter*: **/FS:NTFS** where *driveletter* represents the volume you want to format. For example, if I want to convert a volume labeled *E,* I would type **Convert E: /FS:NTFS**. Press ENTER.

3. The conversion takes place. When you reopen the Disk Management console, you can see the desired drive is now formatted with NTFS.

the volume. Note, creating a new volume doesn't damage any existing information on your drive, so no danger exists to current data.

To create a new volume, follow these steps:

1. On the disk where you want to create the new volume, right-click the Disk number (Disk 0, Disk 1, and so on) and choose New Volume.

2. The New Volume Wizard appears. Click Next on the Welcome screen.

3. In the Select Volume Type window, select Simple Volume and click Next.

4. In the Select Disks window, the maximum amount of free disk space that can be used is displayed in the right window. You can choose to use this amount of free disk space by clicking Next, or you can adjust it in the Select the Amount of Space in MB field. Make your selection and click Next.

5. In the Assign Drive Letter or Path window, use the drop-down menu to assign a drive letter. You can also mount the volume to an empty NTFS folder. This feature allows the drive to act like a folder on your hard disk and have a friendly name. You can also choose not to assign a drive or path, but this option is not typically recommended. Make your selection and click Next.

6. The Format Volume window appears. Choose the file system you want to use on the volume (preferably NTFS) and click Next.

7. Click Finish. The new volume is created and now appears in the Disk Management console.

Assigning a Different Drive Letter and Path to a Volume

You may need to reorganize volume labels or paths at different times, and the Disk Management console makes these changes easy. For example, let's say I have a volume labeled drive *H,* and

19

I want to assign that volume to an empty NTFS folder and give it the friendly name Company Documents. Then, I plan to store all kinds of company documents on that volume and share the volume on the network. I can easily make this change by right-clicking the volume and choosing Change Drive Letter and Path. I select the volume I want to change and click the Change button, which opens a dialog box where I can make the desired changes.

Extending or Shrinking a Volume

What happens if you are storing information on a particular volume and the volume begins to run short of disk space or is too large, so storage space is wasted? If additional free disk space is available on the actual disk to which the volume belongs, you can easily make the volume larger by extending it, or you can choose to shrink it, so some of the storage space is free for other use. This action doesn't damage any of the current data stored on the volume and is perfectly safe. To extend or shrink a volume, right-click it and choose Extend Volume or Shrink Volume. This action opens a simple wizard that guides you through the steps of making the volume size larger.

Other Volume Solutions

Windows Vista Ultimate provides some additional management features, and we look at those in the rest of this chapter. In addition to simple volumes, Windows Vista also supports other volume solutions, namely the spanned volume and the striped volume. You use the same New Volume Wizard to create these types of volumes, and the process is self-explanatory. To determine whether a spanned or striped volume is right for you, consider the following features of each.

Spanned Volume

A *spanned volume* combines various pieces of unformatted free space on several different hard disks to create one logical volume. For example, say your computer has four hard drives. On each of three drives, you have 20MB of free space, and on the last drive, you have 50MB of free space. Alone, none of these pieces of free space amounts to much storage room, but the spanned volume enables you to combine all these free spaces into one logical volume, which would be 110MB in size—a useful amount of space. To you, it appears as another volume to which you can save data. Windows Vista handles all the management tasks of writing and reading data to and from various disks for you. The result is this: you get more storage space by combining bits and pieces of storage on various drives might not otherwise be useful.

To create a spanned volume, you must have unformatted free space on at least 2 physical disks (up to 32 physical disks). The space you combine can vary—no rules exist except the two-disk minimum. However, once you create the spanned volume, you cannot reclaim a portion of it without deleting the entire spanned volume. This means you would have to move any data to other volumes before deleting the spanned volume. Also, this solution offers no *fault tolerance,* which means if one of the hard disks fails, the entire volume is lost, even though the other disks may still be functioning with no problems.

Striped Volume

The striped volume is a lot like the spanned volume. You combine free pieces of disk space on from 2 to 32 physical disks for storage purposes, but the *striped volume* writes data across the disk evenly and in blocks. This feature makes the read/write time faster, but it requires the pieces of free space be of equal size when creating the striped volume. The only reason for using a striped volume over a spanned volume is performance. The striped volume also provides no fault tolerance—if one disk fails, all data on the volume is lost.

To create a spanned volume or a striped volume, use the Disk Management console to select an area of free space on one of the disks, right-click it, and choose Create Volume. Follow the New Volume Wizard steps to create the desired volume type and combine the desired areas of free space.

Use Windows Vista Backup and Restore

I cannot overstate the importance of backing up your data. When you save a file to a computer's hard drive, it is safely held there until the next time you need it—unless something happens and the computer crashes. If you have used computers for any length of time, you know that sinking feeling in the pit of your stomach when you fear you have just lost an important file.

Backing up your data makes certain that the prospect of losing information never becomes reality. If something happens to your computer, the data is safely backed up somewhere safe, and you can retrieve it once the computer is up and running again. Fortunately, Windows Vista provides built-in backup and restore features that are easier to use and more flexible than ever before. In the following sections, you learn all about backing up and restoring data on your computer.

Backing Up Data

You can back up data in a number of ways: You can save data to a CD, a DVD, a removable disk drive, an external disk drive, or even another computer on a local network. You can manually save the files you want. If a problem ever occurs, you still have your data. However, backing up important information this way is time-consuming and heavily dependent on you. Why not let Windows Vista automatically handle this task for you? To help you accomplish your backup goals, Windows Vista gives you the Backup and Restore Center, which provides a number of different options. The following steps walk you through this feature and explain the available options to you:

1. Choose Start | Control Panel | Backup and Restore Center.

2. The Backup and Restore Center appears, shown in Figure 19-3. You have two basic sections of this interface. First, you can create a back up of files and folders of your choice, or you can use CompletePC backup to copy the entire hard drive. This gives you an "image" you can use to restore your computer fully in the event of a hardware failure, such as a disk drive crash. Choose the File and Folder Backup Wizard to make copies of your files and folders by clicking the Set Up Backup button.

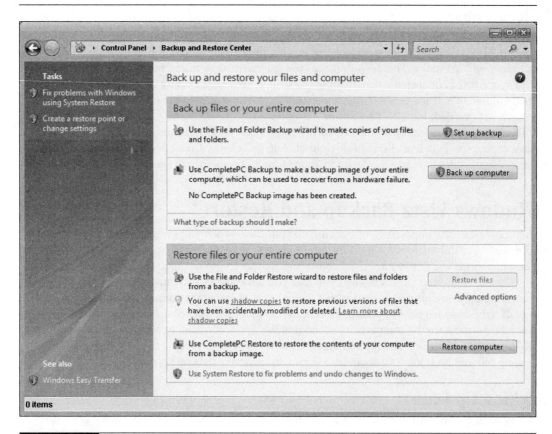

FIGURE 19-3 Backup and Restore Center

3. On the Backup or Restore window (see Figure 19-4), choose the location where you want to save your backup, such as your local computer, DVDs, or even on the network. Make your selection and click Next.

4. In the next window, you can choose the kind of files you want to backup, as shown in Figure 19-5. Simply select the kinds of files you want by clicking the check boxes or de-selecting them. Click Next.

5. In the next window, choose how often you want to back up these files by clicking the drop-down menu for each category. How often you back up data depends on your computer use. The more you create and edit files, the more often you should back up. For most home users, once weekly is typically a good choice. When you're done, click the Save Settings and Start backup button.

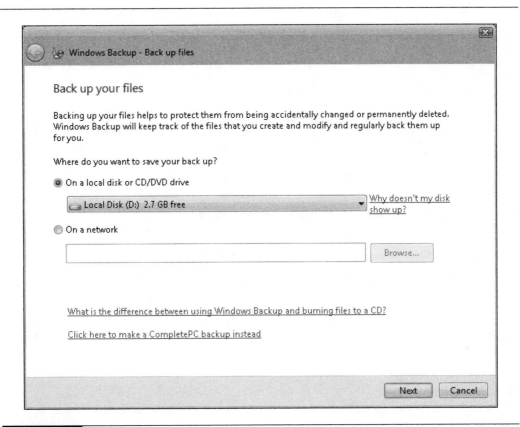

FIGURE 19-4   Choose a backup location

If you want to back up everything on your computer, so your OS and all data can be restored in case of hardware failure, use the CompletePC option. Follow these steps:

1. In the Backup and Restore Center, choose the Back Up Computer button.

2. In the next window, you can choose to back up the image to your computer or to one or more DVDs. If you choose the hard disk option, your disk must formatted with NTFS. Click Next.

3. Confirm your settings, and then click the Save Settings and Start Backup button.

Restoring Data

Just as you can back up your data, you can use the Backup and Restore Center to restore data to your computer. You can choose to use the File and Folder Restore Wizard to restore lost files

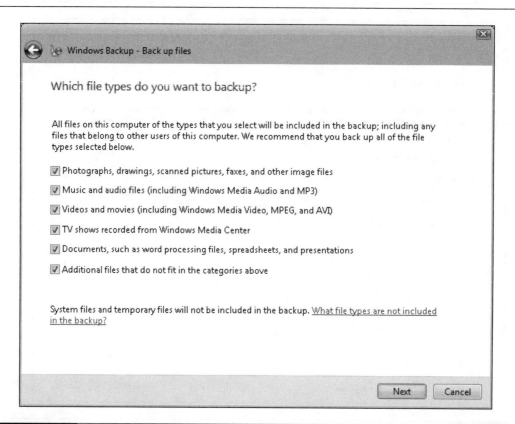

FIGURE 19-5 Choose the kinds of files you want to backup

and folders from a backup. You can also use Shadow Copies to restore previous versions of files that were accidentally deleted or modified. For example, let's say you're working on The Great American Novel, and you accidentally delete some sections. Windows Vista keeps previous versions of files and folders, which are saved as a "restore point." Any file or folder modified since the last restore point was made, which is typically 24 hours earlier, is saved and made available as a previous version. You can then restore the file from the previous saved version, called a *shadow copy*. You can perform this action, as well as restore lost files and folders, using the Restore Wizard. Follow these steps:

1. Choose Start | Control Panel | Backup and Restore.
2. Click the Restore Files button.
3. In the Restore Wizard, choose the Restore Files from the Latest Backup and click Next.

4. In the next window, you can choose to restore everything in the backup, or you can restore certain files or folders by simply browsing for them, as shown in Figure 19-6. If you made an accidental delete within a file or folder, use the browse feature to locate it. This is where Vista uses the shadow copy to restore the file or folder. Click Next.

5. You can choose to restore files and folders in the original locations, or you can specify a new location. Make your selection and click the Start Restore button.

In case your computer is greatly damaged and you want to do a complete restore—assuming you've backed up your computer using the CompletePC Backup—click the Restore Computer button. This process completely reformats your disks and overwrites all existing data on your computer, which means you only want to use this option when absolutely necessary. When you click the Restore Computer option, you see a warning message and instructions (see the following illustration) telling you to shut down the computer and restart it using the Windows

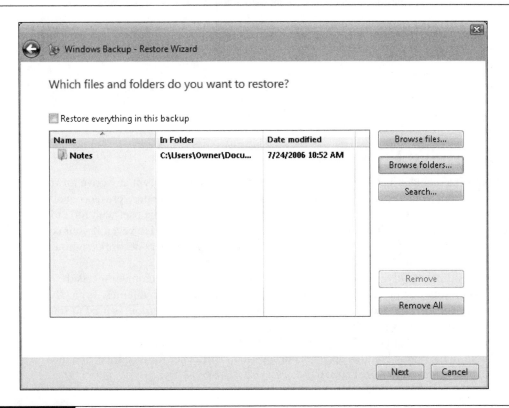

FIGURE 19-6   Choose what you want to restore

19

Recovery Environment by holding down the F8 key during startup. Once you access the Recovery Environment, choose the Windows CompletePC Backup and follow the instructions.

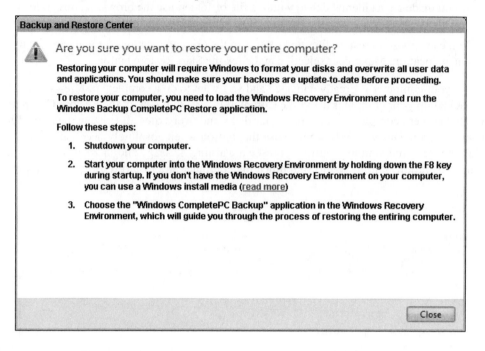

BitLocker Drive Encryption

Windows Vista includes a new security feature that enables you to encrypt any drive on your computer, which helps secure all data on that drive. This encryption feature prevents another user from gaining access to the data on your computer. If you're a home user with little to no security concerns, you don't need to use BitLocker Drive Encryption. However, if your computer contains sensitive data and, especially if it's used in a public or business network environment, the BitLocker Drive Encryption feature may be a great security option.

To use BitLocker Drive Encryption, you need to make sure your computer meets the requirements. Your computer is going to need at least two partitions or volumes. Typically, your C drive is encrypted and the other partition, called the *active partition,* is used to start the computer. Both partitions must be formatted with NTFS.

To turn on BitLocker Drive Encryption, click Start | Control Panel | Bit Locker Drive Encryption. In the dialog box that appears, click Turn on BitLocker for this drive, and then follow the basic instructions that appear.

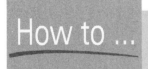

BitLocker Drive Encryption
Is a Hardware Security Feature

BitLocker Drive Encryption is a hardware-based security feature. It uses the Trusted Platform Module (TPM) to protect user data and ensure that a computer isn't tampered with, even if the computer is lost or stolen. A TPM is a microchip, typically placed on the motherboard of the computer. The microchip stores keys, passwords, and digital certificates. A TPM is more secure because it is a hardware solution rather than a software security solution. When you use BitLocker Drive Encryption, you encrypt the entire Windows volume and the encryption key is removed and stored on the TPM, allowing the whole partition to be encrypted, with the key safely tucked away in the TPM. When you boot the computer, the key is released from the TPM after OS integrity is established. However, your computer doesn't have to have TPM for BitLocker to work. In this case, you are required to create a startup key and provide it every time the computer is restarted to unlock the volume.

19

Chapter 20

Solve Problems with Windows Vista

How to...

- Use System Information
- Use the Performance Monitor
- Use problem-solving tools
- Troubleshoot your computer
- Use System Restore

Windows Vista is a complicated operating system (OS), full of features and functions, many of which go on behind the scenes. As with any complex OS, you may experience both occasional performance and functionality problems. I'm the first to say, however, that Windows Vista is as solid as a rock. In most cases, you can say goodbye to all those aggravating lockups and weird behavior problems you saw in the early days of Windows. If you use Windows XP, you can see the same stability and performance in Vista—with a friendlier attitude. In this chapter, we explore some tools and optimization features that can help you keep Vista in tiptop shape and, at times, even get out of jams.

Performance Information and Tools

Windows Vista includes a new feature called Performance Information and Tools, which you can access in the Control Panel. *Performance Information and Tools* essentially rates your computer's performance, tells you what's slowing it down, and gives you quick access to tools that might help correct the problem. When you open Performance Information and Tools, as shown in Figure 20-1, you see a listing of any performance issues. As you can see in the figure, I have some driver and startup problems on my PC. You can click each problem and view some details about it, with some suggestions for improvement.

The tool gives you a summary of the hardware on your computer and gives your computer a performance rating. The rating is based on your computer's hardware configuration. A higher rating means your computer will perform better and faster with advanced or resource-intensive tasks. A rating of 3 is sort of the mid-line rating for good performance. Notice the button option toward the bottom that says View Software Available for My Rating Online. The goal with performance rating is that software vendors will rate their software as well. This way, if you buy a game that requires a performance rating of 3, you know to check your PC's performance level within Performance Rating and Tools and see if your computer's hardware can handle the game. If this concept catches on, it certainly could help you know what software your computer can handle and what software it cannot.

Also notice you can access some common tools that may help your system's performance in the left pane. And, notice the Advanced Tools option. If you click this option, you see a window,

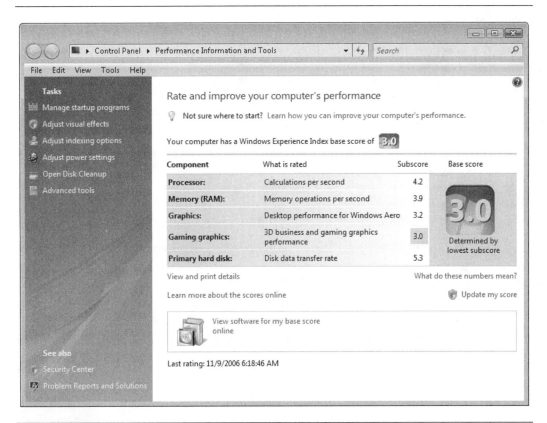

FIGURE 20-1 Performance Information and Tools

shown in Figure 20-2, that gives you access to some important tools. We explore some of these later in this chapter.

Use System Information

System Information is a powerful tool that provides all kinds of information about your computer system, and it includes some additional tools that can fix problems on your system, as you can see in Figure 20-3. You can access System Information by choosing Start | All Programs | Accessories | System Tools | System Information. System Information can be slow to start because it has to collect a lot of information, so be patient.

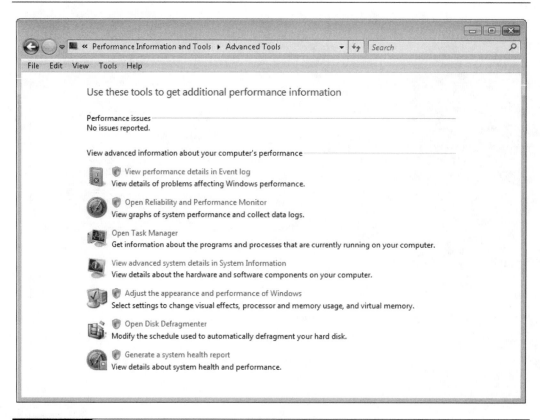

FIGURE 20-2   Advanced Tools

   *You can also reach System Information by choosing Start | All Programs | Accessories | Run, then typing **msinfo32**, and then clicking OK.*

If you look at the left pane, you see a list of information categories. Click the plus (+) sign next to each category, and you can select specific topics for which you want to gather information. Important to note here is you cannot configure or do anything with System Information, with the exception of the troubleshooting tools, but System Information is designed to give you . . . well, information. "Why?" you might ask. The answer is simple. The more information you can gather about your computer, the more likely you are to solve problems with your computer. On a more practical note, System Information is useful to telephone support personnel, who you may need to call in case of a problem you can't solve. Although having outside support is helpful, being able to solve your own PC problems is always best. The next

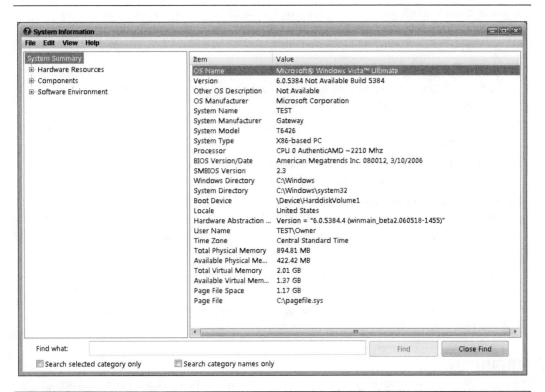

FIGURE 20-3 System Information

several sections tell you all about the information you can gain in each major category, and I point out some tips for you along the way.

System Summary

When you first open System Information, the default view is the *System Summary,* which provides an overview of your computer. You see everything from the OS to the total amount of RAM installed on your computer. This page is excellent to access if you want a quick report about the basics of your computer. You can print this page from the File menu.

Hardware Resources

The *Hardware Resources* category of System Information gives you a complete look at the hardware on your computer. This section is an excellent place to see exactly what's installed, what's working and what's not, and whether any conflicts exist.

If you encounter conflicts, you'll see warning messages in yellow, and conflict or error messages in red. This helps you quickly identify problems. By expanding Hardware Resources in the left pane, you see the following categories from which you can select and view:

- **Conflicts/Sharing**   This option tells whether any hardware conflicts are occurring between devices. In some cases, hardware devices share certain computer resources, and this section tells you about those as well.

- **DMA (direct memory access)**   This option tells you what devices have direct access to memory resources.

- **Forced Hardware**   If you have problems installing a device and it has been "forced" on to your system using manual settings, the device is listed here.

- **I/O (input/output system)**   This information gives a report about input/output operation. Technical support personnel may find this information useful.

- **IRQs (interrupt request lines)**   Each device uses an IRQ to access your computer's processor. This option tells you which device is using which IRQ.

- **Memory**   This option provides a list of memory resource assignments per device.

   *If you're having problems finding the information you need, try typing information into the Find What field that appears at the bottom of the System Information window.*

Components

The *Components category* provides a list of components installed and used on your system. Some of these also include additional submenus. System Information displays problems in yellow and red lettering, so you can easily identify them.

You gain information about the following:

- **Multimedia**   This option gives you information about your audio and video configurations.

- **CD-ROM**   Information is listed here about your CD-ROM drive.

- **Sound Device**   You can find information about your sound card here.

- **Display**   This option lists information about your display here.

- **Infrared**   If you're using any infrared ports, they are listed here.

- **Input**   Get information about your keyboard and mouse or other pointing device here.

- **Modem**   Modem information is listed here.

- **Network**   Network adapters, protocols, and WinSock information is provided here.

- **Ports**   Get information about ports on your computer (such as serial and parallel ports).

- **Storage**   Information about the drives on your computer is here.

- **Printing**   Find out about printers and print drivers here.

- **Problem Devices** If any devices aren't working correctly, they are listed here. This is a useful option to find troublesome devices.

- **USB (universal serial bus)** USB configuration and devices are listed here.

Software Environment

The *Software Environment* category provides information about the software configuration of Windows Vista. If any errors occur, you see them appear in red or yellow. This category can be useful to technical support personnel who are helping you solve a problem with Windows Vista.
You see the following information in this category:

- **System Drivers** This section lists the drivers that manage your computer's software environment.

- **Signed Drivers** This section provides a list of installed drivers that are certified by Microsoft, as well as any other drivers that aren't signed or whose status is unavailable.

- **Environment Variables** This section lists items such as your TEMP file, which is used for temporary files and other variables in the software environment.

- **Print Jobs** This option gives you the information found in your print queue.

- **Network Connections** This option lists all network connections currently held by your computer.

- **Running Tasks** This option lists all the tasks currently running on your computer.

- **Loaded Modules** This option lists all currently loaded software modules.

- **Services** This section lists the services, such as automatic updates, fax, and much more, which are currently installed on your computer.

- **Program Groups** This option lists all program groups currently configured on your computer.

- **Startup Programs** This option lists all programs configured to run automatically when your computer starts up.

- **OLE Registration (object linking and embedding)** Windows Vista uses OLE to allow the various system components and programs to communicate with each other. OLE information is listed here.

- **Windows Error Reporting** This section provides a listing of software errors reported by the system.

NOTE

The Windows Error Reporting *section is a great feature, because it lists all the application lockups and related service problems. If you're having trouble, this can be a great place to find the culprit!*

Use the Reliability and Performance Monitor

The Reliability and Performance Monitor is a new name and look for a basic tool that's been around in Windows for years: Performance Monitor. The good news is this tool was revamped and is much better at giving you understandable information. The *Reliability and Performance Monitor* enables you to gather real-time data about the performance of various system components and processes. You can examine this data and locate potential performance problems. Once you identify the source of performance problems, you can then take an appropriate course of action to solve those problems.

The Reliability and Performance Monitor may seem a little intimidating at first, and it can be a complex tool. Don't worry, though—if you study this section and spend a little time with the tool, you can, quickly and easily, learn a lot about the performance of your computer system.

Reliability and Performance Monitor Interface

The Reliability and Performance Monitor is available in Administrative Tools in the Control Panel. Before showing you how the tool works, I want to give you a brief overview of its interface, as shown in Figure 20-4. If you've never used the Performance Monitor, it's important

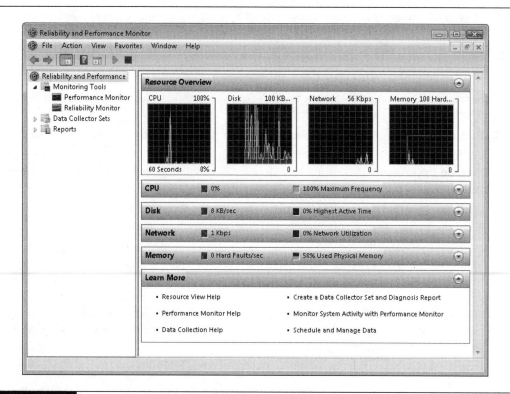

FIGURE 20-4   Reliability and Performance Monitor

for you to spend some time using it. Fortunately, the interface is rather easy and intuitive, and you can be a pro in no time after you begin working with it.

The *Reliability and Performance Monitor* is a standard interface with a selection pane on the left side. When you first open the tool, you see a Resource Overview, shown in Figure 20-4. You get quick information about the performance of your CPU, disk, network usage, and memory. If any of these seem exceptionally high for extended periods of time, this may be your first sign that Vista is having a problem. The good news is you can dig deeper and use the Monitoring tools, which consist of the Performance Monitor and the Reliability Monitor.

Using the Performance Monitor

The *Performance Monitor* works by creating charts, graphs, or reports for counters that you select. A *counter* is a particular Windows Vista component or service that can be monitored. By adding counters to the console, you can view information about the performance of a particular component or service. You can use as many or as few counters as you want to gain the information you need.

As you can see in Figure 20-5, the Performance Monitor interface is a basic Windows interface. You primarily interact with the Performance Monitor by using the right console pane, which is divided into three divisions (from the top):

- ■ **Toolbar**   The toolbar contains icons you'll use regularly to generate the types of charts and information you want. The toolbar contains the following button options, shown from left to right in the following illustration: View Current Activity, View Log Data, Line/Histogram/Report menu, Add, Delete, Highlight, Copy Properties, Paste Counter List, Properties, Zoom, Freeze Display, Update Data, and Help. You use the toolbar to manage the Performance Monitor as needed.

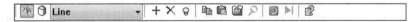

- ■ **Information area**   The information area contains the chart, histogram, or report you want to view. Click the desired button on the drop-down menu on the toolbar to view counter information in the desired format.

- ■ **Counter list**   The bottom portion of the window contains the counter list. All the counters displayed in this list are currently being reported in the information area. You can easily remove or add counters to the list using the toolbar. Each counter in the list is given a different color for charting and histogram purposes.

The primary functionality of the Performance Monitor is through the use of counters. Without counters, there is no way to break down performance information and view various components and services. As you might guess, a number of different counters can give you information on all kinds of system processes and services.

With an understanding of the counters available to you, you can use the Performance Monitor to gain valuable data for making decisions about performance and optimization in your environment. You can monitor activity for a period of time, and then save the data to a log file.

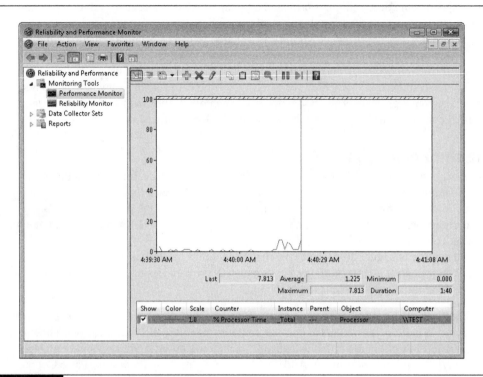

FIGURE 20-5   Performance Monitor

You can even set up logs and alerts, so data is gathered on a periodic basis automatically and you are alerted if certain values fall below a baseline you determine.

Your first action is to determine the manner in which you want to view information—in a chart, histogram, or report view. The type of counters you choose to view may also impact your choice, but once you make the decision, you can add the desired counters to the chart, histogram, or log. Adding counters is rather easy. Follow these steps:

1. In the Control Panel, open the Administrative Tools folder and double-click the Reliability and Performance Monitor. In the console, click Performance Monitor under Monitoring Tools in the left console pane.

2. On the Performance Monitor toolbar, select the type of view you want (graph, histogram, or report).

3. Click the Add button. The Add Counters window appears.

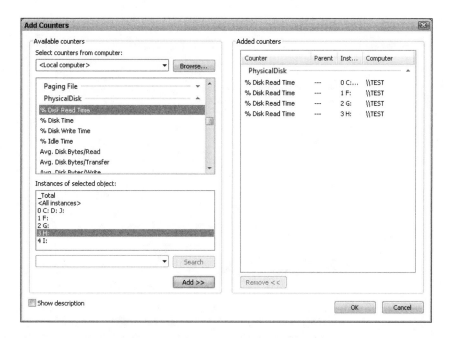

4. In the Available Counters section, select the object you want to monitor. For example, if your computer seems to have memory problems or is running slowly, you might want to choose the Memory or Processor object.

5. Click the Select Counters from the Instances of Selected Object box, and then select the desired counters in the list and click the Add button. If you want an explanation of the counter, select it, and then click the Show Description check box toward the bottom. Click the Add button to add selected counters

6. The counters you selected are now added to the Added Counters portion of the window and are charted (or reported, depending on your selection). Click OK. You can change charting or reporting views at any time, and you can remove counters from the console by selecting the counter and clicking DEL, or simply by clearing the check box next to them, as you can see in the following illustration.

Show	Color	Scale	Counter	Instance	Parent	Object	Computer
✓		1.0	% Processor Time	_Total	---	Processor	\\TEST
✓		1.0	% Disk Read Time	0 C: D: J:	---	PhysicalDisk	\\TEST
✓		1.0	% Disk Read Time	1 F:	---	PhysicalDisk	\\TEST
✓		1.0	% Disk Read Time	2 G:	---	PhysicalDisk	\\TEST
✓		1.0	% Disk Read Time	3 H:	---	PhysicalDisk	\\TEST

Reliability Monitor

Another new tool you can find in the Performance Diagnostic Console is the Reliability Monitor. The *Reliability Monitor* is a great tool because it shows you a System Stability Chart along with

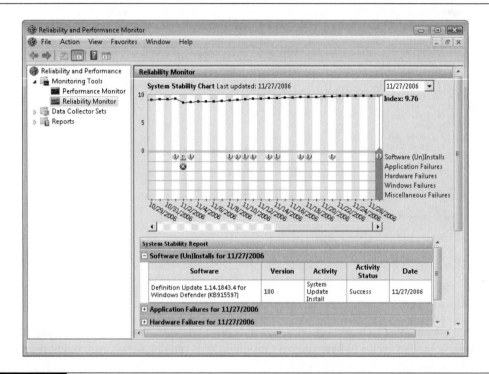

FIGURE 20-6 Reliability Monitor

categories for software uninstalls, application failures, hardware failures, Windows failures, and other miscellaneous failures. You can look at the chart, click on a failure date, and get more information. This chart won't help you fix any problems, but it can give you a more holistic look at what is going on with your computer. The sample you see in Figure 20-6 is from a test

Memory Diagnostic Tool

If you look in the Administrative Tools in Control Panel, you see a Memory Diagnostic Tool. If you click this tool, you are prompted to run the tool and restart your computer (the tool has to restart the computer to check the memory). You can close all your programs and run this tool. Your computer will boot into a DOS-based Memory Diagnostic program that tests your memory and tells you if errors exist.

computer and, as you can see, the stability chart shows a decline over time as I have tinkered with the computer and made changes. If your stability chart shows a decline, this tells you some problems might exist that need to be addressed concerning your computer.

Use System Properties to Optimize Windows Vista

You access System Properties in the Control Panel (or by right-clicking Computer on the Start menu and choosing Properties). When the System window opens, click the Advanced System Settings link in the left pane. When you access System Properties, you see an Advanced tab, among others, as shown in Figure 20-7.

A Performance section on the tab lets you deal with performance issues. You learn about your options in the following sections.

Performance Options

If you click the Settings button under Performance, you see a Performance Options window with a Visual Effects tab and an Advanced tab. The Visual Effects tab, shown in Figure 20-8, gives you another place to manage the way Windows handles the user interface in terms of icons,

FIGURE 20-7   System Properties

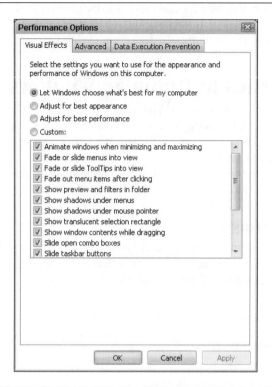

FIGURE 20-8 Visual Effects tab

animation, and other factors. The more visual effects in use, the more system resources are consumed. Under most circumstances, you don't need to do anything on the Visual Effects tab. But, if you want to disable a visual effects feature, just scroll through the list and clear the check box next to the option.

On the Advanced tab, shown in Figure 20-9, you see that, by default, the processor and memory usage are optimized for applications. This means processor cycles and memory usage are primarily configured to support applications over background or system process functions. For most users, these two settings should be left alone. If you're using your Windows Vista computer as a network server or a web server, though, you might consider changing this setting to Background Services. For most of us, these settings are fine as they are.

The final portion of the tab concerns virtual memory. Windows Vista, like other Windows operating systems, is configured to use virtual memory. Your computer has a certain amount of memory installed (256MB, 512MB, and so forth). When you use your word processor, open applications, surf the Internet, and perform other tasks on your PC, memory is used to hold programming information your computer needs to run the programs. When you have too many open programs, RAM begins to run low. In such cases, Windows can use a portion of your hard

Virtual Memory Is *Not* a Replacement for More RAM

Many people who learn a few things about virtual memory think they can configure their own settings to make Windows use more hard disk space—a replacement for physical RAM. This simply is not the case. Windows Vista can handle these settings, and overriding Windows Vista's settings is normally a bad idea. Virtual memory is used for overflow information—it's not designed to be a replacement for physical RAM chips. If you need a RAM upgrade, tinkering with virtual memory won't solve the problem. In fact, doing so may create more problems. My advice: Leave this setting alone! If your system needs more RAM, your best bet is to part with a few hard-earned dollars and install more RAM on your computer.

You can click Change and configure the Virtual Memory settings yourself, but this action is *not* recommended. Your best performance option is to allow Windows to continue using its own Virtual Memory settings—believe me, they are the best!

FIGURE 20-9 Advanced tab

disk to store information temporarily. This is called *virtual* memory because it isn't *real* RAM but, rather, a storage room borrowed from the hard drive. Windows Vista is programmed to set its own virtual memory settings, as you see in Figure 20-9.

Troubleshooting Tips

When you experience a problem in Windows, you can take some positive actions, or you can take some panic-driven actions that usually aren't very wise. Without getting into the murky details of troubleshooting, here's my list of troubleshooting tips you should always follow:

- *Relax*. If Windows Vista experiences a problem, don't get in a hurry. Your systems won't self-destruct to leak poisonous gas into the room and kill you. In other words, a problem with your system doesn't mean it needs to go to the computer ER—don't hurry.

- *Think*. What were you doing when the problem occurred? Consider grabbing a piece of scratch paper and writing down exactly what you were doing—what applications were open when the problem occurred? If serious problems exist with Windows Vista, you may need this information later. If you see an error message, write it down. If you have to talk with a help technician or another help resource, having this information could help.

- *Act*. Try one thing at a time to resolve the problem. With each action you take, write down what you did. Do *not* randomly press keys—do one thing at a time in an organized manner.

Now, you may think, "But that's just it—what action should I try?" The rest of this chapter answers that question.

Using CTRL-ALT-DEL

Although you won't experience the system lockup problems you did in previous versions of Windows, you may encounter an application that occasionally stops responding. In earlier versions of Windows, this would often bring your entire system to a standstill, but that typically isn't the case in Windows Vista. A system lockup occurs when an application is naughty and doesn't behave the way it should. The application can interfere with Windows Vista functionality, causing the application itself to lock. This means you can't do anything with the application by clicking buttons or doing anything else. In some cases, two open applications can interfere with each other, causing them both to lock.

In the case of a system lock, you should use your keyboard and press CTRL-ALT-DEL one time. This action takes you to a Vista selection screen where you can choose to Lock the computer, switch user, log off, change a password, or start Task Manager. Choose the Start Task Manager option. This action opens the Windows Task Manager dialog box, shown in Figure 20-10, where you can select the name of the program and click End Task on the Applications tab. This action forces the task to end, so you can get control of your computer. If you have any unsaved data in your application at the time it locked up, you'll probably lose that data (save data frequently when working to avoid such a loss). While you're looking at

FIGURE 20-10   Task Manager

the Task Manager, you can also explore the Processes, Performance, Networking, and Users tabs to find out current system information.

NOTE   *If you press CTRL-ALT-DEL twice, your computer will restart.*

In some cases, pressing CTRL-ALT-DEL will *not* give you control of the computer. This problem happens when errors occur within Windows Vista, possibly associated with an application, that causes the OS to "hard lock." In this situation, pressing CTRL-ALT-DEL doesn't do anything. Nothing happens when you press keys on your keyboard, and your mouse pointer is useless. In such cases, the only way to get control of Windows Vista is to turn off the computer using your computer's power switch. Just crawl under your desk, turn off the switch, wait at least ten seconds, and then turn the switch back on, so your computer can begin rebooting.

Use Windows Help

Windows Vista has a lean and responsive help file system, much better than the bulky help files that came with Windows XP. This system is easier to use, more attractive, and contains a wealth of information, both locally on your machine and on the Internet. You can easily access Windows Help by choosing Start | Help and Support. The Windows Help interface appears.

The Windows Help program has several major parts. The *Help screen* shows a number of topics and tasks from which you can select, as well as a Search option and a place for getting outside assistance. When you access Windows Help and Support, shown in Figure 20-11, you can find an answer to your question or problem by accessing one of the default categories in the middle of the page, or you can simply click in the search box and type your search.

Once you search for an item or click on a category, you see a page of possible answers to your query. Most Windows help files contain explanatory text, as well as links to other text or even links to open system components, a helpful feature. If you want to print something, notice you have a Print button at the top right of every page. Simply click this button to have the help page sent directly to your computer. As you're using Windows Help and Support, also notice a Windows Online Help icon is on the Home page. This new Windows Online help web site features community support and tools that enable you to get expert advice. Check out this site!

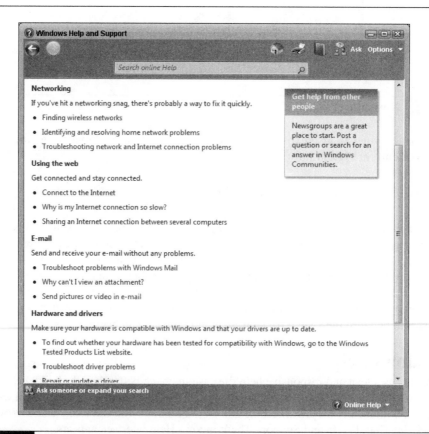

FIGURE 20-11 Windows Help and Support

Use Safe Mode

Safe Mode is a Windows Vista feature that enables you to start Windows with a minimal number of drivers. Safe Mode is used in instances when you cannot start Windows normally. Safe Mode is used to fix problems with your system—it essentially gets Windows up and running, but that's about it. Most major Vista features do not work in Safe Mode.

So, why would you use Safe Mode? Let's consider an example. Say you installed Fly-By-Night's Most Excellent Video Card (okay, it's just an example). You install the card and the driver for the card. When you restart Windows Vista, it boots, but then you get a "fatal exception" blue screen just before your Desktop appears. You try this over and over with the same result. More than likely, the video card's driver isn't working correctly with Windows Vista. You can boot the computer into Safe Mode, and Windows will load a basic VGA driver to use with the card. Once booted, you can use Device Manager to remove or update the bad driver.

A number of other repair tools require you to boot your computer into Safe Mode to work. Before showing you how to boot into Safe Mode, let me mention that you can choose some other boot options along with Safe Mode. You can access all these options by using the Windows Startup menu, which you see if you hold down the CTRL key on your keyboard when you turn on your computer. (If CTRL doesn't seem to work, press the F8 key on the keyboard when you start the computer.) You'll see a Startup menu that lets you choose Safe Mode, Safe Mode with Networking, and some other options. When your computer boots in Safe Mode, you can access the tools and Help you need to try to solve the problem. When you finish, just reboot the computer and it will boot into Normal Mode.

Use System Restore

In the process of learning to use Windows Vista, you no doubt have found several of its new features helpful and fun, and maybe others less so. However, there's one great feature that I hope you will never use: System Restore. What if your computer won't start? What if you install a bad application that wrecks your computer? No problem—just use System Restore and put your computer back exactly as it was before the problem, tragedy, or accident happened . . . with only a few mouse clicks. I've used System Restore numerous times after fouling up Windows Vista with my experiments, and I must say it has worked flawlessly for me without fail.

Are you intrigued? I know you are if you've ever worked with Windows, because bad configuration problems can be a serious troubleshooting problem. System Restore leaves that legacy behind, because you can easily restore your computer to a previous state. The following sections show you how to use System Restore.

Creating Restore Points

System Restore functions by creating restore points. A *restore point* is a "snapshot" of your computer's configuration stored on your hard disk. If System Restore needs to be used, it accesses a restore point to reconfigure your computer. This process brings your computer back to a stable state—a place where it was when the system was stable. Restore points enable your computer to "travel back in time" and be configured as it was when it was stable.

Important to note here is that System Restore restores your OS and applications only. It does not save and restore any files. For example, say you accidentally delete The Great American Novel you are working on. System Restore cannot be used to get your novel back. Incidentally, System Restore does not affect other files, such as e-mail and web pages. Performing a System Restore does not make you lose new e-mail or files—it only configures your system settings and application settings.

System Restore automatically creates restore points for you, so, in general, there is no need to create a restore point manually. However, what if you're about to try some configuration option or configure some software you know may be risky or that has caused you problems in the past? Before trying the configuration or software, you can manually create a restore point, so you can later restore your system to its present state. To create a restore point, follow these easy steps:

1. Choose Start | Control Panel | System. Click the System Protection link.

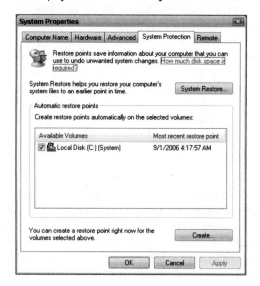

2. Click the Create button.

3. Type a name for the restore point and click Create.

4. The restore point is created.

What to Do If You Selected the Wrong Restoration Point

Let's say you run a restoration to solve a problem, but the point from which you chose to restore the data was not early enough. In other words, Windows Vista created a restore point while the current problem existed. What then? No problem. Simply run System Restore again, but select an earlier restore point to fix the problem.

Running System Restore

The eventful day finally arrives and you (or someone else) has done something bad to your computer. Now it either doesn't boot or it acts erratically. Whatever the problem, you can use System Restore to restore your computer settings as they were at an earlier time when it was functioning appropriately. The following two sections show you how to use System Restore.

If You Can Boot Windows...

If you can boot into Windows, follow these steps:

1. Choose Start | All Programs | Accessories | System Tools | System Restore.

2. Choose either the recommended restore or a different restore point. Make your selection and click Next.

3. If you decide to choose a restore point, you see a restore point selection screen, shown in the following illustration. Make your selection and click Next.

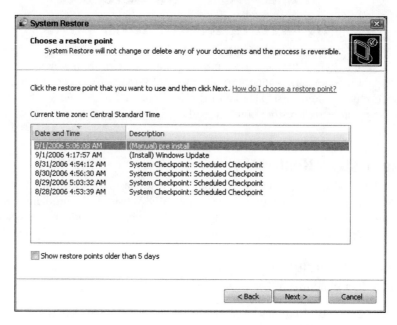

4. You see a confirmation window. Review this window and click the Finish button. System Restore automatically restarts your computer to apply the restore point.

If You Cannot Boot Windows...

If you cannot boot Windows, follow these steps to run System Restore:

1. Turn on your computer and hold down CTRL or the F8 key until you see the Startup menu options.

2. Choose Safe Mode, and then press ENTER.

3. Once Windows boots, you can then access System Restore as described in the previous steps.

Current documents, files, e-mail, and similar items are not *affected during a restoration. However, if you installed an application after the last restore point was made, you need to reinstall that application.*

Appendix

Install Windows Vista

How to...

- Prepare for a Windows Vista upgrade
- Upgrade to Windows Vista
- Get a computer with no operating system ready for installation
- Clean install Windows Vista
- Activate Windows Vista

If you're like me, you would almost rather have a root canal than install a new operating system (OS). Why? The answer is simple. Any time you install an OS, whether it be an upgrade or a clean install on a computer with no OS, you stand the risk of experiencing problems. But, you can relax—Windows Vista is rather easy to install, and as long as you're sure your computer's hardware is ready for Windows Vista, you're unlikely to experience any problems. This appendix is designed to help you plan and perform the installation. If you purchased your computer with Windows Vista preinstalled and, for some reason you need to reinstall it, you should also check the manufacturer's instructions for installations because they may be different than the information presented in this appendix.

Upgrade to Windows Vista

Most home or office users who purchase Windows Vista do so to upgrade their existing PC. This means you're likely to have a computer that runs Windows XP and now you want the latest and greatest. Unless you're buying a new PC with Windows Vista already preinstalled from the factory, you have purchased a Windows Vista upgrade CD-ROM and now you're ready to get started.

In a perfect world, upgrading your home or office PC would be a piece of cake. You pop the installation CD into your CD-ROM drive, answer a few questions from the setup program, and setup installs Windows Vista without any problem whatsoever. When you find that perfect world, let me know, so I can move there, too. The reality is that any number of problems can happen when upgrading to Windows Vista. However, if you upgrade smartly, the likelihood of encountering installation failure or problems is low. The trick is to do a bit of homework before installing Windows Vista to make sure your existing PC and OS are ready. Starting the installation and simply hoping for the best is all too tempting, but to upgrade smartly, you need to play detective for a few minutes and make certain all is well in your computer's environment before you start the upgrade. Upgrading smartly can help prevent a number of potential problems and it can help you find issues affecting the installation before you ever begin.

So, how do you upgrade smartly? The following sections explore the tasks you should perform before attempting an upgrade to Windows Vista.

Check the System Requirements

One big mistake computer users often make when attempting an upgrade or install is not checking the system requirements. Every piece of software, whether it is an OS or an application, has certain requirements that must be met before the software will function properly or before it can even be installed. Your computer must have hardware that can handle the Windows Vista software, so before you attempt the installation, check out your computer to see whether any potential problems exist. Windows Vista is demanding. One of the main causes of upgrade problems is the lack of proper system resources—so be careful! When you install Windows Vista, it checks your system before the installation begins, but even before you purchase Windows Vista, check out the system requirements. Review the information in the following sections to make sure your computer is ready for Windows Vista.

Processor

A computer's *processor* can be thought of as the computer's brain. The processor processes information that the OS or an application needs. For example, if you want your computer to multiply 467×345, that request is sent to the processor for completion. Once the processor performs the computation, it's returned to the requesting application (such as your system's calculator). In the past, processors weren't fast, because operating systems and applications weren't terribly complicated. However, with today's operating systems and applications, your computer's processor must be fast enough to handle Windows Vista and the many tasks it can perform.

For a Windows Vista installation, you need a processor that is at least an 800 megahertz (MHz)—the *megahertz* number is the speed at which the processor can run. Common manufacturers are Intel, AMD, and Via. For the best results, Microsoft recommends a 1 GHz 32-bit or 64-bit processor. In reality, you always want the fastest processor you can afford, because you'll see the best performance with a fast processor.

TIP

If your processor is too slow for Windows Vista, the odds are good that other components are too old as well. In most cases, upgrading your processor usually means you'll have to upgrade other components, such as RAM. This is why buying a new computer is often the best option.

Random Access Memory

You've probably heard the term "random access memory" or "RAM" plenty of times, even if you don't have your head stuck in the computer world. *RAM* is the amount of memory your computer contains to run current applications and processes. RAM enables you to work with a Microsoft Word document while also surfing the Internet. RAM lets you draw pictures and run programs—anything you do on your computer requires RAM. Simply put, the more RAM you have, the faster and better your computer will run, and the happier you'll be. For a Windows Vista installation, you need at least 512 megabytes (MB) of RAM. As with your processor speed requirement, 512MB is a bare minimum, and Microsoft recommends you have 1GB of RAM or more. As with the processor, think carefully before upgrading your RAM. Check your other system components and make certain they don't also need to be upgraded. The odds are good they do, and you may be able to buy a new computer with the same money you would spend on upgrades.

Hard Disk Space

Windows Vista needs some of your hard disk space for storage during and after the installation. Your computer's hard disk stores any data you choose to save, as well as your OS itself. To upgrade to Windows Vista, you must have 40GB hard drive with 15GB of free hard disk space. This means you must have that much spare room on your hard disk, so Windows Vista can store its files and operate (this will take up 15GB of the 40GB). To check your computer's hard disk space, double-click My Computer. You see your *C* drive in the window. Right-click the *C* drive icon, and then choose Properties. The General tab of the properties sheet shows you the amount of used and free space your disk contains.

What if you don't have enough free disk space? Then you need to free up some disk space by removing data from your hard disk. Removed items can include files, Internet pages, and even applications you no longer use. You need to make some decisions about what you want to remove, but you must free up enough disk space for the installation to be successful.

Other Requirements

Your processor, RAM, and disk space requirements are of utmost importance, but some other system requirements should be met to make the most of Windows Vista, so just take a minute to make sure you have these:

- Graphics Processing Unit (GPU)—Direct X 9 Capable. For the best result, you need a Direct X 9-capable GPU that supports a WDDM driver, Pixel Shader 2.0 in the hardware, and 32 bits per pixel capability
- DVD-ROM drive
- A mouse or other similar pointing device
- A keyboard

I told you those were easy. Now, you may also want to check a few other items. These aren't required for a Windows Vista installation, but they may impact how well your system works with Windows Vista and how happy you'll be with its functionality.

- If you plan to access the Internet (which I hope you do), you need at least a 56 Kbps modem. While the standard dial-up speed is only up to 56 Kbps, with an Ethernet or wireless adapters you now have a number of broadband options available to you, including DSL, cable, wireless, or satellite. Other than wireless, some of these enable you to connect through your USB adapter, but your performance may be slower than through your Ethernet adapter. None of these is required, of course, but while you're upgrading your system, this is an excellent time to look at your Internet connectivity speed and consider upgrading to a faster service, if necessary. If you plan on using DSL, cable, wireless, or satellite, be sure to contact your Internet service provider (ISP) to find out if your computer needs to meet any specific hardware needs.

■ To make use of all Windows Vista has to offer, you should have a good sound card, speakers (or headphones), and a good video card. A plethora of video and sound card products are compatible with Windows, so check your local computer store for information and pricing.

■ If you want to connect to a local area network (LAN), you need some kind of network adapter card. See Chapter 11 for more information.

Back Up Your Data

From painful past experience, I have learned always to back up any data that I don't want to lose before ever tinkering with my OS—and that includes an upgrade. If everything goes well during your upgrade, the computer will preserve all your data and settings, and you won't need any data you backed up because it will still reside on your computer. However, if things don't go so well, you will desperately need a backup of your critical data—the data you cannot afford to lose. This includes documents, spreadsheets, Internet information—you name it. Spend some time on your computer finding everything you can't live without, and then back up that data.

You can back up your data in a number of ways. First, Windows XP includes a Backup utility found in Accessories. You can use the Backup utility to create a backup file. You must then save this backup file to another location, such as a tape drive or even the hard drive of another computer. You may also have other backup programs and backup media you purchased. If not, backing up your data doesn't have to be difficult. Simply copy any files you don't want to lose to a CD/DVD.

Check Out Your Device Drivers

Every piece of hardware in your computer, including your printer, scanner, or modem, has a driver. A *driver* is a piece of software code that enables Windows to interact with the hardware device. Think of a driver as a car's steering wheel. To interact with your car and make it do what you want, you use a steering wheel to communicate with it, along with other controls such as the brake and gas pedal. For your computer to communicate and control a device, a driver must be installed. When you install a device, you usually use a CD-ROM that comes from the factory with your device. This installation media installs a driver Windows can use. Windows also has its own driver database, and in many cases, Windows can install and use one of its drivers to manage a device.

Drivers are always changing. When a new device is released—for example, a printer—the driver ships with it. However, as operating systems change, new drivers are developed, so your printer can work with the new operating systems. Before upgrading to Windows Vista, you should visit manufacturers' web sites for your computer's devices. Look for new drivers for your particular models and see if you can download any. Download the drivers and keep them. You may need these new drivers when you install Windows Vista, to ensure your hardware works well with your new OS. Check your device manufacturer's documentation for more information about downloading updated drivers. Even if you don't need to update drivers, you do need to round up your CD-ROMs, so you have access to your existing drivers in case you need them during installation.

Check for Viruses and Disable Antivirus Software

Before upgrading to Windows Vista, you should run a full virus check on your computer system using an antivirus program, such as one from McAfee, Symantec, or AVG. You may currently have one of these programs, or you may need to buy one. If you use the Internet, you should certainly have virus-detection software to make sure you can both detect and disinfect your computer in case of a virus. Antivirus software is normally under $50 and well worth your investment. If you don't have antivirus software, you can purchase it on the Internet, at any computer store, and in many department stores.

Refer to your owner's instructions and run a complete virus scan of your system. Make sure your software has current virus definitions, so it can detect the presence of a newer virus. Current definitions can be downloaded from the manufacturer's web site. Once the virus scan is complete and you have removed any viruses, you need to disable your antivirus software before running setup. Antivirus software will interfere with Windows Vista installation, so make certain you check the antivirus documentation and disable the software accordingly.

Shut Down All Programs

Before running Windows Vista setup, make certain you shut down all programs that are running and disconnect from the Internet. Also, if you have any programs that protect your Master Boot Record (MBR) by encrypting it, you need to uninstall that application. Some applications on the market today help protect your computer against sabotage or data theft by encrypting certain portions of your OS, so they cannot be read by unauthorized persons. This software is not normally installed as a part of a purchase package, but do check your original documentation and make certain you don't have any applications like this installed. If you do, uninstall them before attempting to run setup. These applications cause the Windows Vista upgrade to fail if they are running.

Upgrade to Windows Vista

Finally, after doing your detective work, you're ready to begin the upgrade to Windows Vista. Before you start, make sure you have everything gathered that you'll need. First, you need the Windows Vista CD-ROM and the product key. You can find the product key on a sticker on the back of your CD-ROM jewel case. You should also have any disks or CD-ROMs containing drivers for your hardware, in case Windows Vista cannot install one of the devices.

Now that you have your materials handy and you've checked out your computer to make certain it's ready for the upgrade, you're ready to begin. The following steps show you how to start the upgrade:

> **NOTE**
>
> *Windows Vista doesn't support Serial Key devices. If you're upgrading and you currently use Serial Keys with an alternative input device, you must turn off Serial Keys and install another input option before the upgrade. To turn off Serial Keys in Windows XP, open **Accessibility Options** in the **Control Panel**. On the **General** tab, under **Serial Key devices**, clear the **Use Serial Keys** check box.*

1. Insert the Windows installation disc into your computer's DVD or CD drive.

2. To see if your computer can run Windows Vista, open Windows Vista Upgrade Advisor by clicking Check Compatibility Online. (This step is optional.)

3. On the **Install Windows** page, click **Install Now**.

4. On the **Get Important Updates for Installation** page, choose to get the updates from Microsoft.com. The recommendation is that you get the latest updates to help ensure a successful installation and to help protect your computer against security threats. You need an Internet connection to get these updates.

5. On the **Type Your Product Key for Activation** page, type your 25-character product key, so installation can continue and your software can be activated once the installation is complete.

6. On the **Please Read the License Terms** page, if you accept the license terms, click **I Accept the License Terms**.

7. On the **Which Type of Installation Do You Want?** page, click **Upgrade**.

8. Continue to follow the instructions. Vista will now install files and upgrade your computer. You are prompted for information along the way and you can expect your computer to reboot a few times on its own.

> **TIP**
>
> *If installation doesn't go so well and you have problems starting Windows XP, see Chapter 20 for helpful troubleshooting tips.*

Install Windows Vista as a New Installation

You may need to install Windows Vista on a computer that doesn't have an OS or you may want a clean installation on a computer that does. A *clean installation* deletes everything on the computer and installs Vista as a new installation, rather than as an upgrade. For example, let's say you purchase a computer from a direct supplier or even over the Internet. These machines are often sold "unformatted" and without an OS. Or, perhaps your Windows XP computer has too many goofy system problems you don't want to contend with and you want to clean install Windows Vista, so it doesn't use and keep all those older OS files. No matter what your reason, you can clean install Windows Vista on a computer that has an OS, as well as on systems that do not.

This discussion brings up an important question. Should you format an existing hard drive and blow away your old OS so you can clean install Windows Vista? Not usually. Upgrading your existing OS to Windows Vista to preserve your system and hardware settings is best. In some cases, though, you may want to clean install to get away from problems in your older OS. This is, of course, fine. But, as a rule of thumb, always choose an upgrade over a clean install for Windows XP.

Prepare for a Clean Installation

Just like an upgrade, you need to spend a little time preparing for the clean installation. This means you need to examine your computer's hardware and make certain the computer meets at least the minimum hardware requirements. You also need to locate floppy disks and CD-ROMs that contain drivers for your computer's hardware. The Windows Vista DVD is bootable. This means if you place the DVD in the CD/DVD-ROM drive and turn on the computer, the installation DVD can start the computer for you and begin installation automatically. For a clean install, you can access an installation document on your Vista DVD, which can help you determine how to choose a partition for the Vista installation if you need additional help. Once you start the installation, simply follow the instructions as prompted.

Activate Windows Vista

Windows Vista includes a feature called activation. In a nutshell, Windows *activation* is a feature Microsoft uses to protect the licensing of software. The activation feature prevents someone from installing Windows on a bunch of computers using the same software key. Essentially, activation is just a step in the key and licensing agreement portion of setup.

Once you install Windows Vista, you have 30 days to activate the OS with Microsoft if you don't complete this step during installation. The activation doesn't need any information from you—so don't worry, this isn't like Big Brother or anything. The activation process records a serial number from your computer's hardware and couples it with your CD-ROM installation code. This way, if someone tries to install Windows Vista on a bunch of computers with a single CD-ROM, activation recognizes the key has already been used and it won't allow the activation to continue. Once the 30-day period expires, Windows Vista lets you use the Internet for an hour at a time, but that's it. Otherwise, it simply logs you out.

You can activate your Windows Vista computer in two ways: you can do it over the Internet or by manually calling the Microsoft product activation call center. Either way, the process is rather easy and straightforward. To activate your computer using a modem, just follow the onscreen prompts. If you need to call Microsoft to activate Windows, refer to the Windows Vista documentation that came with your installation DVD. That's all there is to it!

Index

A

Accessibility button, Internet
Options, 148
Accessibility Options, 21–22
accessories, 79–89
Calculator, 80
Command Prompt, 80
Connect to Network Projector, 81
Ease of Access, 89
Notepad, 81–82
Remote Desktop, 84
Run Dialog Box, 84
Snipping tool, 84–85
Sound Recorder, 85
Sync Center, 85–86
System Tools menu, 89
Tablet PC, 89
Welcome Center, 86–87
Windows Explorer, 87–88
Windows Paint, 83–84
Windows Sidebar, 88
WordPad, 89
access points, 183
activation, 350
Active Directory feature, Windows
Vista Ultimate, 184
active partition, 318
activity reports, 218
Add a Printer Wizard option,
Printers folder, 106–109
Add button, Phone and Modem
Options, 127–128
Add Device option, Control
Panel, 117
Add Hardware applet, Control
Panel window, 18
Add Hardware Wizard, Control
Panel, 95–96
Additional Drivers button, Printers
folder, 110–111
Add Port button, Windows Firewall
dialog box, 207

Add Program button, Windows
Firewall dialog box, 207
Adjust Date/Time option, Notification
Area, 10
Administrative tab, 32
Administrative Tools folder, 18
administrator account, 190
Advanced button, Display Properties,
48–49
Advanced Start Menu, 44
Advanced tab
Internet Options, 155
modem configuration, 134
Phone and Modem Options,
129, 134
Printers folder, 112–114
Windows Firewall dialog
box, 208
Windows Mail window, 172
Allowed Items, Windows Defender
program, 212–213
Allow or Block Specific Programs
option, Parental Controls, 218
antivirus software, 348
Appearance category, Internet
Options, 146–148
applets
Add Hardware, 18
Autoplay, 18
Color Management, 19
Indexing Options, 23–24
Internet Options, 24
iSCSI Initiator Control
Panel, 24
Pen and Input Devices, 30
Sound, 32
Tablet PC Settings, 34
Approved Sites tab, Internet
Options, 152
Area Code Rules tab, New Location
window, 132
Attach button, Windows Mail
window, 164–165

Attach feature, Pictures menu,
280–281
attachments, e-mail, 164, 166
audio, adding to movies,
268–269
Audio/Music section, Windows
Movie Maker, 268–269
Auto Adjust feature, Pictures
menu, 279
AutoComplete section, Internet
Options, 151, 153
Auto-Hide the Taskbar option,
Taskbar Appearance, 45
Automatically Fix File System Errors
check box, Local Disk
Properties, 291
AutoPlay applet, 18–19
Availability option, Printers folder,
112–113

B

Backup and Restore Center, 295,
313–318
backing up data, 313–315
overview, 18
restoring data, 315–318
BitLocker Drive Encryption, 18,
318–319
Block all programs check box,
Windows Security Center, 205
blocking senders, 169–170
broadband Internet connection,
125–126
Browse Folders option, Folder
Options, 56
Browsing History section, Internet
Options, 146–147
burning
with Photo Gallery, 281
with Windows Media Player,
251–252
with Windows Slideshow, 283

Buttons tab, Mouse properties, 26–27
bytes, 286

C

cable Internet access, 125–126
Calculator, 80–81
Calibrate button, Games option, 238
Calling Card tab, New Location
    window, 133–134
cameras, 32
    installing, 117–118
    managing properties, 119
Cancel option, Document menu, 115
Cancel Print Documents option,
    Printer menu, 115
CardSpace, Windows, 35
categories, 15
CD-ROM, 67–68, 326
Certificates section, Internet Options,
    151, 153
Change an Account option, User
    Accounts window, 194–196
Change button, Programs option,
    68–69
Change Home Page dialog box, 144
Change Picture feature, Welcome
    screen, 193
Change/Remove button, Programs
    option, 68–69
Change Scope button, Windows
    Firewall dialog box, 207
Chess Titans game, 236
Choose Program Options, Customize
    Start Menu window, 42
Classic Start Menu, 44
Classic View link, 16–17
clean installation, 349–350
Click Items as Follows option, Folder
    Options, 57
ClickLock option, Mouse
    Properties, 27
client computer configuration, and
    Remote Desktop, 223–224
clips
    combining, 263
    splitting, 262–263
    trimming, 265–266
clock, Notification Area, 10
Close option, Organize menu, 75
codecs, 256
Color Management applet, 19
Colors button, Internet Options, 148
Colors drop-down menu, 48
command prompt, 80
Compatibility Mode, 70–72

component management, 72–73
    turning off Windows
      feature, 73
    turning on Windows feature,
      72–73
Components category, 326
Compose tab, Windows Mail
    window, 171
compressed folders, 76–77
    adding items to, 76
    creating, 76
    removing items from, 76
    using extraction option with,
      76–77
compressing files, 69–70, 165, 292
computer
    See also computer
      personalization
    logging off, 10–11
    restarting, 12
    starting, 4
    turning off, 12
Computer Management console, 18,
    197–199, 287–288, 306
Computer option, Start menu, 41
computer personalization, 37–64
    configuring display, 46–53
      Desktop Background
        option, 49–50
      Display Settings tab, 47–49
      mouse pointers, 52
      Mouse Properties dialog
        box, 52
      Screen Saver option, 50–52
      themes, 53
      Theme Settings dialog
        box, 53
      Window Color and
        Appearance option, 49
      Windows Sounds dialog
        box, 52
    configuring folder views, 54–59
      General tab, 55–57
      Search tab, 58
      View tab, 57
    customizing Start menu, 41–44
      classic Start menu, 44
      Vista Start menu, 42–43
    customizing Taskbar, 45–46
    using Start menu, 38–41
    Windows Sidebar, 59–64
      Gadgets, 63–64
      starting and configuring,
        60–63

configuring
    display, 46–53
      Desktop Background
        option, 49–50
      Display Settings tab, 47–49
      mouse pointers, 52
      Screen Saver option, 50–52
      themes, 53
      Window Color and
        Appearance option, 49
      Windows Sounds dialog
        box, 52
    folder views, 54–59
      General tab, 55–57
      Search tab, 58
      View tab, 57
    Internet Explorer, 146–155
    modem, 126–134
      installing modem, 127
      properties, 127–134
    printer, 109–114
      Advanced tab, 112–114
      device settings, 114
      General tab, 109–110
      Ports tab, 112
      Security tab, 114
      Sharing tab, 110–112
Conflicts/Sharing option, Hardware
    Resources, 326
connections
    broadband, 125–126
    dial-up, 124–125
    Remote Desktop, 84
Connections tab, Internet Options,
    153–154
Connection tab, Windows Mail
    window, 172
Connect to a Network Projector
    feature, Accessories option, 81–82
Connect to a Network Wizard, 175
Connect to Network Projector
    feature, 81
Connect To option, Start menu, 41
Connect to the Internet Wizard,
    135–136, 140
Contacts button, Windows Mail
    window, 162
Content Advisor section, Internet
    Options, 151–152
Content tab, Internet Options,
    151–153
Control Panel, 13–36
    Add Hardware applet, 18
    Administrative Tools, 18
    Autoplay applet, 18

Backup and Restore Center, 18
BitLocker Drive Encryption, 18
Color Management applet, 19
Date and Time icon, 19–20
Default Programs icon, 20–21
Device Manager, 21
Ease of Access Center, 21–23
Folder options, 23
Fonts folder, 23
Game Controllers icon, 23
Indexing Options applet, 23–24
Internet Options applet, 24
iSCSI Initiator Control Panel
    applet, 24
Keyboard icon, 24–25
    Hardware tab, 25
    Speed tab, 25
Mail icon, 26
Mouse icon, 26–29
    Buttons tab, 26–27
    Hardware tab, 29
    Pointer Options, 28–29
    Pointers tab, 27–28
    Wheel tab, 29
Network and Sharing center, 29
Offline Files, 29
opening, 14–17
parental controls, 29
Pen and Input Devices
    applet, 30
People Near Me, 30
Performance Information and
    Tools, 30
Personalization option, 31
Phone and Modem icon, 31
Power options, 31
Printers folder, 31
Problem Reports
    and Solutions, 31
Programs and Features, 31
Regional and Language
    Options, 32
scanners and cameras, 32
Sound applet, 32
Speech Recognition icon, 32
Start Menu icon, 34
Sync Center, 32
System icon, 33
Tablet PC Settings applet, 34
Taskbar, 34
Text to Speech tab, 34
uninstalling programs, 68–69
User Accounts icon, 35
Welcome Center, 35

Windows CardSpace, 35
Windows Defender, 35
Windows Firewall, 35
Windows Slideshow, 35–36
Windows Update, 36
Windows Vista Security
    Center, 32
Windows Vista Sidebar, 35
Control Panel option, Start menu, 41
Control Panel window, 14–17
controls, parental. *See* Parental
    Controls
control toolbar, Photo Gallery, 281–282
Copy option, Organize menu, 75
Copy Protect Music check box,
    Windows Media Player, 249
counter, 329–331
Counter list, Performance
    Monitor, 329
Country/Region drop-down menu,
    New Location window, 131
Create a New Account option, User
    Accounts window, 192–194
Create Mail button, Windows Mail
    window, 162, 163
credits, adding to movies, 269–270
CTRL-ALT-DEL, 336–337
Cursor Blink Rate setting, Keyboard
    Properties, 25
Customize Start Menu window, 40
customizing
    Start menu, 41–44
        classic Start menu, 44
        Vista Start menu, 42–43
    Taskbar, 45–46
Cut option, Organize menu, 75

D

Data Disc option, Pictures menu, 281
Date and Time icon, 19–20
DDERR_ GENERIC error, 238
Default Programs icon, 20–21
Default Programs option,
    Start menu, 41
Defender, Windows. *See* Windows
    Defender
Delete Browsing History option,
    Tools menu, 145
Delete button
    Windows Mail window, 162
    Windows Photo Gallery, 282
Deleted Items folder, Windows Mail
    window, 165
Delete option, Organize menu, 75
deleting folders, 74

desktop, 3–12
    exploring Start menu, 10
    logging off computer, 10–11
    managing Taskbar, 10
    Recycle Bin, 6–9
        changing properties to suit
            needs, 8–9
        using as way station, 6–8
    restarting computer, 12
Desktop Background option, 49–50
Details option
    Pictures menu, 277
    Views menu, 7, 58–59
device drivers, 347–348
Device Manager, 97–102
    device properties, 97–102
        Driver tab, 99–102
        General tab, 98
    overview, 21
devices
    non-plug-and-play, installing,
        95–96
    plug-and-play
        installing, 94–95
        removing, 95
Device Settings tab, Printers
    folder, 114
Devices tab, Windows
    Media Player, 255
Diagnose Connection Problems
    option, Tools menu, 145
Diagnose Internet Connection option,
    Control Panel, 137
Diagnostics tab, Phone and Modem
    Options, 129
dialing rules options, New Location
    window, 131–132
Dialing Rules tab, Phone and Modem
    options, 130–134
dial-up Internet connections, 124–125
digital cameras and scanners,
    117–119
    installing, 117–118
    managing properties of, 119
digital data, importing to Windows
    Movie Maker, 260–262
    from DV camera, 261
    existing video or pictures on
        computer, 261–262
digitally signed driver, 99
Digital Subscriber Line (DSL)
    Internet access, 125–126
direct memory access (DMA) option,
    Hardware Resources, 326
DirectX problems, 238

Disk Cleanup utility, 290
Disk Defragmenter utility, 293–294
disk management, 305–319
    assigning different drive letter
        and path to volume, 311–312
    BitLocker Drive Encryption,
        318–319
    creating new volume, 310–311
    disk status, 309
    dynamic disks, 306–309
    extending or shrinking
        volume, 312
    formatting disk, 310
    other volume solutions, 312–313
        spanned volume, 312
        striped volume, 313
    Windows Vista Backup and
        Restore, 313–318
        backing up data, 313–315
        restoring data, 315–318
Disk Management console, 306–307
Display All Control Panel Options
    and All Folder Contents option, 58
display configuration, 46–53
    Desktop Background option,
        49–50
    Display Settings tab, 47–49
    mouse pointers, 52
    Screen Saver option, 50–52
        Power Options window, 52
        Screen Saver tab, 51–52
    themes, 53
    Window Color and Appearance
        option, 49
    Windows Sounds dialog box, 52
Display Delete Confirmation Dialog
    check box, Recycle Bin Properties
    window, 9
Display option, Components
    category, 326
Display Settings tab, 47–49
Display Size option, Windows Photo
    Gallery, 281
Display tab, Remote Desktop
    Connection dialog box, 225–226
DMA (direct memory access) option,
    Hardware Resources, 326
documents, problems printing, 116
Do Not Show Hidden Files and
    Folders; Hide Protected Operating
    System Files option, 58
Download Codecs Automatically
    check box, Windows Media
    Player, 256
downloading programs from Internet,
    69–70

Download Updates for Me, But Let
    Me Choose whether to Install
    Them option, Windows Update
    window, 302
Drive Encryption. *See* BitLocker
    Drive Encryption
Driver Details button, Device
    Manager option, 99–101
Driver option, Printers folder,
    112–113
Driver tab
    Device Manager option,
        99–102
    Phone and Modem Options, 129
DSL (Digital Subscriber Line)
    Internet access, 125–126
DV camera, 261
dynamic disks, 306–309

E

Ease of Access Center, 21–23, 89
Edit menu, Windows Mail
    window, 162
Edit option, Pictures menu, 277
Effects, Windows Movie Maker,
    267–268
e-mail
    attaching files to, 164–165
    attaching photos or movies to,
        280–281
    attachments, 164, 166
    receiving, 165–166
    sending, 163–164
Empty Recycle Bin option, 7, 8
Enable Advanced Printing Features
    option, Printers folder, 114
encryption. *See* BitLocker Drive
    Encryption
Enhancements option, Now Playing
    menu, 246
Environment Variables section,
    Software Environment category,
    327
error checking, 291–293
Error Checking option, Local Disk
    Properties, 291–293
Error Correction feature, Windows
    Media Player, 255
Exceptions tab, Windows Firewall
    dialog box, 205–206
expansion slots, 175
Experience tab, Remote Desktop,
    224–225
Extract Compressed Folders option,
    76–77
Extra Large Icons option

Pictures menu, 276
Views menu, 7, 58–59

F

Failed reading, Disk Management
    console, 309
FAT (file allocation table), 287
FAT32 file system, 287
Favorites Center, Internet Explorer,
    141–142
Fax and Scan application, 117
fax support, 117
feeds, 145, 151, 153
file allocation table (FAT), 287
File drop-down menu, Photo Gallery,
    279
File menu, Windows Mail
    window, 161
files
    attaching to e-mail, 164–165
    compressing, 69–70, 165, 292
    overview, 77
file sharing, 188
file system basics, 286–287
File Types tab, Windows Media
    Player, 256
Find button, Windows Mail
    window, 162
firewalls. *See* Windows Firewall
FireWire card, 261
Fit to Window option, Windows
    Photo Gallery, 281
Fix option, Photo Gallery, 279
Flicks tab, Pen and Input Devices
    applet, 30
Folder and Search Options, Organize
    menu, 75
folder compression, 76–77
    adding items to compressed
        folder, 76
    creating compressed folder, 76
    extraction option, 76–77
    removing items from
        compressed folder, 76
Folder List button, Windows Mail
    window, 162
folder management, 73–76
    creating, 74
    deleting, 74
    renaming, 74
    using folder menu options,
        74–75
    viewing menus, 76
Folder options, 23, 58, 73
Folders pane, Windows Mail
    window, 162

folder view configuration, 54–59
   General tab, 55–57
   Search tab, 58
   View tab, 57
Fonts button, Internet Options, 148
Fonts folder, Control Panel, 23
Forced Hardware category, Hardware
   Resources, 326
Foreign state, Disk Management
   console, 309
formatting disk, 310
Forward button, Windows Mail
   window, 162
fragmentation, 293
Freecell game, 236
Full Screen option, Tools
   menu, 145

G

gadgets, 63–64
Game Controllers icon, Control
   Panel, 23, 234–235
games, 233–241
   installing and playing own
     games, 237
   managing game controllers,
     234–236
   and Parental Controls, 217
   playing with Windows XP,
     236–237
   sound recorder, 240–241
   troubleshooting problems,
     237–238
     DDERR_ GENERIC, 238
     DirectX problems, 238
     game controller does not
       work, 237–238
     game lockup, 238
   volume controls, 238–240
Games button, Parental Controls,
   217–219
garbled printed text, 116
General tab
   Device Manager option, 98
   folder views, 55–57
   Internet Options, 146–148
   Local Disk Properties, 289
   New Location window, 131
   Printers folder, 109–110
   Recycle Bin Properties
     window, 8
   and setting hard disk properties,
     289–290
   Windows Mail window, 171

glass style display, 49
Global Settings button, Recycle Bin
   Properties window, 9
Group Policy feature, Windows Vista
   Ultimate, 184
groups, 197–199
Groups container, Computer
   Management console, 199
Group Similar Taskbar Buttons
   option, Taskbar Appearance, 45
guest account, 190

H

hard disk
   basics, 286
   setting properties, 287–298
     General tab, 289–290
     Hardware tab, 295
     Previous Versions tab, 296
     Quota tab, 296–298
     Security tab, 296
     Sharing tab, 295
     Tools tab, 291–295
   space, 346
hardware management, 91–104
   non-plug-and-play devices,
     installing, 95–96
   overview, 92–93
   plug-and-play devices
     installing, 94–95
     removing, 95
   troubleshooting tips, 103–104
   using Device Manager, 97–102
   Windows Update driver settings,
     102–103
   Windows XP, 93–94
Hardware Resources category,
   System Information, 325–326
Hardware tab
   hard disk properties, 295
   Keyboard properties, 25
   Local Disk Properties, 295
   Mouse properties, 29
Hardware Troubleshooter, 104
Hardware Update Wizard, 99–101,
   112–113
Healthy reading, Disk Management
   console, 309
Hearts game, 236
Help and Support feature, Start
   menu, 41
Help menu, Windows Mail
   window, 162
Help screen, 338

Help with Playback feature, Now
   Playing menu, 246
Hide Extensions for Known File
   Types option, 58
High Contrast option, Ease of Access
   Center, 23
Hold Mismatched Documents option,
   Printers folder, 114
Home button, Internet Explorer, 144
Home Networking Wizard, 179
home networks, 173–188
   basics, 174–175
   file sharing, 188
   Internet Connection Sharing
     (ICS), 176, 182–183
   planning, 175–176
   printer sharing, 188
   Setup Network Wizard, 177–182
   using Windows Vista on large
     networks, 184–185
   Virtual Private Networking
     (VPN), 185–187
   wireless networks set up,
     183–184
Home Page category, Internet
   Options, 146–147
hosts, 176
HTML (Hypertext Markup
   Language), 140
HTTP (Hypertext Transfer
   Protocol), 140
Hypertext Markup Language
   (HTML), 140
Hypertext Transfer Protocol
   (HTTP), 140

I

ICS (Internet Connection Sharing),
   176, 182–183, 204
Identities, Windows Mail, 170
Import From Digital Video Camera
   button, Windows Movie
   Maker, 261
Import Media Items dialog box,
   Windows Movie Maker, 261–262
Import tab, Pictures menu, 279
Indexing Options applet, Control
   Panel, 23–24
Info option, Photo Gallery, 280
Information area, Performance
   Monitor, 329
Infrared section, Components
   category, 326
Initializing reading, Disk
   Management console, 309

InkBall game, 236
input/output system (I/O) category,
    Hardware Resources, 326
Input section, Components
    category, 326
installing
    cameras, 117–118
    modem, 127
    new printer, 106–109
    new programs, 67–68
    own games, 237
    scanners, 117–118
Install Updates Automatically option,
    Windows Update window, 302
internal modem, 125–127
Internet
    downloading programs from,
        69–70
    playing games over, 237
    terms and technology, 140
Internet Connection Firewall, 35–36
Internet connections, 123–137
    configuring modem, 126–134
        installing modem, 127
        properties, 127–134
    creating, 134–137
    defined, 124–126
        broadband connections,
            125–126
        dial-up connections,
            124–125
Internet Connection Sharing (ICS),
    176, 182–183, 204
Internet Explorer
    configuring through Internet
        Options, 146–155
        Advanced tab, 155
        Connections tab, 153–154
        Content tab, 151–153
        General tab, 146–148
        Privacy tab, 150–151
        Programs tab, 154–155
        Security tab, 148–149
    Favorites Center, 141–142
    feeds, 145
    Home button, 144
    and Internet Connection Sharing
        (ICS), 183
    Page button, 145
    tabs, 142–144
    Tools drop-down menu, 145
Internet Explorer icon, Start menu, 140
Internet Options, Tools menu,
    145–146

Internet Options applet, Control
    Panel, 24
Internet service provider (ISP),
    124, 159
Internet time tab, Date and Time
    Properties, 20
interrupt request lines (IRQs), 101
I/O (input/output system) category,
    Hardware Resources, 326
IRQs (interrupt request lines), 101, 326
IRQs (interrupt request lines)
    category, Hardware Resources, 326
iSCSI Initiator Control Panel applet, 24
ISP (Internet service provider),
    124, 159

K

Keep Printed Documents option,
    Printers folder, 114
Keep the Taskbar on Top of Other
    Windows option, Taskbar
    Appearance, 45
Keyboard category, Remote Desktop,
    225–227
Keyboard icon, Control Panel, 24–25
Keyboard option, Remote Desktop, 225

L

L2TP (Layer 2 Tunneling
    Protocol), 185
Language options, 32
Languages button, Internet
    Options, 148
Languages tab, 32
Large Icons option
    Pictures menu, 276
    Views menu, 7, 58–59
Layer 2 Tunneling Protocol
    (L2TP), 185
Layout option, Organize menu, 75
Layout tab
    Printers folder, 110
    Windows Mail window,
        166–167
Library, Windows Media Player,
    247–250, 255
Loaded Modules option, Software
    Environment category, 327
Local Area Connection button, Tasks
    pane, 179–180
local printer, 107
Local Resources tab, Remote
    Desktop Connection dialog box,
    225–227

Lock button, Start menu, 41
Lock the Taskbar option, Taskbar
    Appearance, 45
lockups, 238
logging off computer, 10–11
Log off option, Start menu, 11
Log Off/Shut Down options, Start
    menu, 41

M

Magnifier option, Ease of Access
    Center, 22
Mail icon, 26
maintenance, 285–302
    file system basics, 286–287
        FAT32, 287
        NTFS, 287
    hard disk basics, 286
    scheduling tasks, 299–301
    setting hard disk properties,
        287–298
        General tab, 289–290
        Hardware tab, 295
        Previous Versions tab, 296
        Quota tab, 296–298
        Security tab, 296
        Sharing tab, 295
        Tools tab, 291–295
    Windows Update, 301–302
Make Movie option, Photo
    Gallery, 281
Manage Add-ons option, Tools
    menu, 145
Manage Network Connections, Tasks
    pane, 179
Master Boot Record (MBR), 348
MBR (Master Boot Record), 348
Media Player. *See* Windows Media
    Player
Medium Icons option
    Pictures menu, 276
    Views menu, 7, 58–59
megahertz (MHz), 345
Memory Diagnostic Tool, 332
Memory option, Hardware
    Resources, 326
menus
    See also names of specific menus
    organizing, 75
    viewing, 76
Message menu, Windows Mail
    window, 162
message rules, 167–170
    blocking senders, 169–170

creating new rule, 168
  managing, 168–169
MHz (megahertz), 345
Microsoft Spynet program, 211
Minesweeper games, 236
modems, 126–134
  installing, 127
  properties, 127–134
    Advanced tab, 134
    Dialing Rules tab,
      130–134
    Modems tab, 127–129
Modem section, Components
  category, 326
Modems tab, Phone and Modem
  Options, 127–128
Monitor Area, Windows Movie
  Maker, 259–260
More Options feature, Now Playing
  menu, 246
Motion option, Mouse Properties, 28
mouse, 26
Mouse Properties dialog box, 52
  overview, 52
  properties, 26–29
    Buttons tab, 26–27
    Hardware tab, 29
    Pointer Options, 28–29
    Pointers tab, 27–28
    Wheel tab, 29
movies. *See* Windows Movie Maker
Multimedia option, Components
  category, 326

N

Narrate Timeline option, Windows
  Movie Maker, 269
Narrator option, Ease of Access
  Center, 22
network adapter card, 174
Network and Sharing Center, 29, 179,
  181, 188
Network Connections section,
  Software Environment
  category, 327
Network Folder, Start menu, 41
Network Map, Network and Sharing
  Center, 181–182
network projectors, connecting to, 81
Network section, Components
  category, 326
Network tab
  Recycle Bin Properties window, 9
  Windows Media Player, 256

Never check for updates option,
  Windows Update window, 302
New Area Code Rule window, New
  Location window, 132–133
New Driver button, Printers folder,
  112–113
New Location window, Phone and
  Modem Options, 130–131
New Mail Rules, Windows Mail
  window, 167–168
New Message pane, Windows Mail
  window, 163
New Modem Wizard, 127
non-plug-and-play devices, installing,
  95–96
Notepad, 81–82
Notification Area, 5, 10, 46, 60
Now Playing area, Windows Media
  Player, 244–247
NTFS, 287, 311–312

O

object linking and embedding
  (OLE Registration), Software
  Environment category, 327
offline files, 29
Off line/Missing state, Disk
  Management console, 309
OLE Registration (object linking
  and embedding), Software
  Environment category, 327
on button, 4
Online (Errors) state, Disk
  Management console, 309
Online state, Disk Management
  console, 309
On Resume, Password Protect check
  box option, 52
On-Screen Keyboard option, Ease of
  Access Center, 23
Open option, Photo Gallery, 281
Options button, Windows Defender
  program, 210–211
Organize menu, 7, 75

P

Page button, Internet Explorer, 145
panes, Windows Mail, 161
Paper/Quality tab, Printers folder, 110
parental controls, 29, 151, 213–218
  overview, 29
  setting up, 214–218
    activity reports, 218

allowing or blocking
  specific programs, 218
configuring Web
  restrictions, 215–217
games, 217
setting time limits, 217
partitioning, 287
passwords, 4, 191
Paste option, Organize menu, 75
Pause option, Document menu, 115
Pause Printing option, Printer
  menu, 115
Pen and Input Devices applet, 30
Pen Options tab, Pen and Input
  Devices applet, 30
People Near Me feature, 30
Performance Diagnostic console, 18
Performance Information and Tools,
  30, 322–323
performance management, 224–227
Performance Options window,
  System Properties, 333–336
Performance settings, Windows
  Media Player, 255
personalizing computer, 31, 37–64
  configuring display, 46–53
    Desktop Background
      option, 49–50
    Display Settings tab, 47–49
    mouse pointers, 52
    Mouse Properties dialog
      box, 52
    Screen Saver option,
      50–52
    themes, 53
    Theme Settings dialog
      box, 53
    Window Color and
      Appearance option, 49
    Windows Sounds dialog
      box, 52
  configuring folder views, 54–59
    General tab, 55–57
    Search tab, 58
    View tab, 57
  customizing Start menu, 41–44
    classic Start menu, 44
    Vista Start menu, 42–43
  customizing Taskbar, 45–46
  using Start menu, 38–41
  Windows Sidebar, 59–64
    gadgets, 63–64
    starting and configuring,
      60–63

phishing, 145
Phone and Modem icon, Control Panel, 31
Phone and Modem Options icon, Control Panel, 127
Photo Gallery, 278–282
    Burn option, 281
    control toolbar, 281–282
    E-mail option, 280–281
    File drop-down menu, 279
    Fix option, 279
    Info option, 280
    Make Movie option, 281
    Open option, 281
    Print drop-down menu, 280
Photo Gallery Viewer, 277
Photo Printing Wizard, 282
Photoshop Elements files (PSD), 68
Pin to Start Menu, 39
Player tab, Windows Media Player, 254
playlist, creating in Windows Media Player, 250
Playlists option, Windows Media Player, 250
Play Slide Show button, Windows Photo Gallery, 282
plug-and-play devices
    installing, 94–95
    removing, 95
Plug and Play technology, 92–95, 117–118, 274
Plug-ins option, Now Playing menu, 246
Plug-Ins tab, Windows Media Player, 255
Pointer Options tab
    Mouse Properties, 28
    Pen and Input Devices applet, 30
pointers, mouse, 27–29, 52
Point-to-Point Tunneling Protocol (PPTP), 185
POP3 (Post Office Protocol 3), 159–160
Pop-up Blocker option
    Internet Options, 151
    Tools menu, 145
Ports section, Components category, 326
Ports tab, Printers folder, 112
Post Office Protocol 3 (POP3), 159–160
power options, 31, 52
Power Options window, 52–53
PPTP (Point-to-Point Tunneling Protocol), 185

Preview button, Screen Saver Settings, 51
Preview option, Pictures menu, 277
Preview pane, Windows Mail window, 163, 165
Previous and Next buttons, Windows Photo Gallery, 282
Previous Versions tab, Local Disk Properties, 296
Print button
    Internet Explorer, 145
    Windows Mail window, 162
Print button drop-down menu, Pictures menu, 280
Print Directly to Printer option, Printers folder, 113
Print drop-down menu, Photo Gallery, 280
printer pools, 115
Printers folder, 31, 106–117
    configuring printers, 109–114
        Advanced tab, 112–114
        device settings, 114
        General tab, 109–110
        Ports tab, 112
        Security tab, 114
        Sharing tab, 110–112
    installing new printer, 106–109
    managing print jobs, 114–115
    troubleshooting printer problems, 116–117
        certain document will not print, 116
        printed text garbled, 116
        printer does not work, 116
        printing very slow, 116
        print quality poor, 117
    using fax support, 117
printing photos, 282–283
Printing Preferences button, Printers folder, 110
printing problems, troubleshooting, 116–117
    certain document will not print, 116
    garbled text, 116
    poor quality, 117
    printer not working, 116
    slow printing, 116
Printing section, Components category, 326
Print Jobs option, Software Environment category, 327
Print option, Pictures menu, 278
print queue, 114

Print Spooled Documents First option, Printers folder, 114
Print Test Page button, Printers folder, 109–110
Priority button, Windows Mail window, 163
Priority option, Printers folder, 112–113
Privacy settings, Windows Media Player, 256
Privacy tab, Internet Options, 150–151
Problem Devices option, Components category, 327
Problem Reports and Solutions option, Control Panel, 31
problems. See troubleshooting
processor, checking system requirements of, 345
Program Compatibility Wizard, 70–72
Program Groups option, Software Environment category, 327
programs, 66–72
    allowing or blocking specific, and Parental Controls, 219
    downloading from Internet, 69–70
    installing, 67–68
    uninstalling, 68–70
        downloading programs from Internet, 69–70
        using programs in control panel, 68–69
        using program's uninstall option, 68
Programs and Features, 31
Programs tab
    Internet Options, 154–155
    Remote Desktop Connection dialog box, 227
Properties button, Phone and Modem Options, 128
Properties option, Organize menu, 75
proxy servers, 36, 153
PSD (Photoshop Elements files), 68

Q

Quarantined Items, Windows Defender program, 211
Quick Launch, 45
Quick Tabs button, web browser, 143–144
Quota Entries window, Local Disk Properties, 298
Quota tab, hard disk properties, 296–298

R

RAM (Random Access Memory), 67, 345–346
Random Access Memory (RAM), 67, 345–346
Read tab, Windows Mail window, 171
Receipts tab, Windows Mail window, 171
Recent Items folder, Start menu, 40, 41
Recovery Environment, Backup and Restore Center, 318
Recycle Bin, 5–8
    changing properties, 8–9
    using as way station, 6–8
Recycle Bin Properties window, 8
Regional and Language Options, Control Panel, 32
Regional options, 32
Regional Options tab, 32
Reliability and Performance Monitor, 328–330
Reliability Monitor, 331–332
Remember Each Folder's View Settings option, 58
Remote Assistance, 227–230
Remote Computer Sound option, Remote Desktop, 225
remote connections
    Remote Assistance, 227–230
        requesting, 229–230
        turning on, 228
    Remote Desktop, 219–227
        configuring client computer, 223–224
        enabling, 221–223
        making connection, 224
        managing performance, 224–227
Remove button
    Phone and Modem Options, 127–128
    Programs option, 68–69
Remove Properties, Organize menu, 75
Rename option, Organize menu, 75
renaming folders, 74
Repeat Delay slider bar, Keyboard Properties, 25
Repeat Rate slider bar, Keyboard Properties, 25
Reply All button, Windows Mail window, 162
Reply button, Windows Mail window, 162
reports, activity, 218

resolution, 282
Resources tab, 101–102
restarting computer, 12
Restore All Items button, Recycle Bin Tasks window, 8
restore points, 339–341
restoring data, 315–318
Rip feature, Windows Media Player, 250–251
Rip Music tab, Windows Media Player, 249, 255
Rip Music to This Location option, Windows Media Player, 249
Rip Settings option, Windows Media Player, 249
RJ-45 plug, 174
Roll Back Driver button, Device Manager option, 99–101
Rotate button, Windows Photo Gallery, 282
Rotate Clockwise/Counterclockwise option, Pictures menu, 278
routers, 176
Run dialog box, 41, 84
Running Tasks option, Software Environment category, 327

S

Safe Mode, 339
satellite Internet access, 125–126
Save Movie File, Windows Movie Maker, 270
Scan button, Windows Security Center, 209
Scan For and Attempt Recovery of Bad Sectors option, Local Disk Properties, 291
scanners, 32
    installing, 117–118
    managing properties, 119
scans, running, 209–210
scheduling tasks, 299–301
Screen Resolution slider bar, Display Settings, 47
Screen Saver option, 50–52
    Power Options window, 52
    Screen Saver Settings, 50–51
    Screen Saver tab, 51–52
Search category, Internet Options, 146–148
Search feature, Start menu, 40
Search tab, Folder Options, 58
security, 201–230
    See also parental controls
    and hard disk properties, 296

Windows Defender, 208–212
    running scans, 209–210
    using tools, 210–212
Windows Firewall, 202–208
    checking, 204
    configuring settings, 205–208
    issues with, 203–204
Security Center, 32
Security feature, Windows Vista Ultimate, 185
Security Report feature, web browser, 145
Security settings, Windows Media Player, 256
Security tab
    Internet Options, 148–149
    Local Disk Properties, 296
    Printers folder, 114
    Windows Mail window, 172
Select All option, Organize menu, 75
senders, blocking, 169–170
Send/Receive button, Windows Mail window, 162
Send tab, Windows Mail window, 171
Services section, Software Environment category, 327
Set as Desktop Background option, Pictures menu, 278
Set Programs button, Internet Options, 154
Settings button, Screen Saver Settings, 51
Setup a Network Wizard, 177–178
Setup icon, 67
Setup Network Wizard, 177–182
shadow copy, 316–317
Share Name button, Printers folder, 110–111
sharing files/printers, 188
Sharing tab
    hard disk properties, 295
    Printers folder, 110–112
shortcuts, 6
Show List Pane, Now Playing menu, 246
Show on Start Menu, Customize Start Menu window, 43
Show Quick Launch option, Taskbar Appearance, 45
Shut Down option, Start menu, 12
Sidebar. *See* Windows Sidebar
Signatures tab, Windows Mail window, 171
Signed Drivers section, Software Environment category, 327

Sign In to Microsoft Communities button, Windows Mail window, 162
Simple Mail Transfer Protocol (SMTP), 158
Skin Chooser feature, Windows Media Player, 252–254
skin mode, 246
Slideshow. *See* Windows Slideshow
Slide Show Gadget, 64
Slide Show option, Pictures menu, 277
slow printing, 116
Small Icons option
  Pictures menu, 276
  Views menu, 7, 58–59
SMTP (Simple Mail Transfer Protocol), 158
SnapTo option, Mouse Properties, 29
Snipping tool, 84–85
Software Environment category, System Information, 327
Software Explorer, Windows Defender program, 212–213
Solitaire game, 236
sound (volume), 10, 238–240
Sound applet, 32
Sound Device, Components category, 326
Sound Recorder, 85, 238–241
Sounds dialog box, 52–54
Space Available option, 9
spam, 167
spanned volumes, 312
Speech Recognition icon, Control Panel, 32–33
Speed tab, Keyboard properties, 25
Spelling tab, Windows Mail window, 163, 171
Split Clip button, Windows Movie Maker, 263
Spooling option, Printers folder, 112–113
Spool Print Documents so Program Finishes Printing Faster option, Printers folder, 113
Spynet program, 211
spyware, 208–209
Starband website, 126
Start button, 5
starting computer, 4
Start menu, 10–11, 34, 38–39, 66
  customizing, 41–44
    classic, 44
    Vista, 42–43
  exploring, 10
  using, 38–41

Start menu properties, 66
Start menu size, Customize Start Menu window, 43
Start Printing after Last Page Is Spooled option, Printers folder, 113
Start Printing Immediately option, Printers folder, 113
Start Recording button, Sound Recorder, 85
Startup Programs option, Software Environment category, 327
stateful firewall, 203
Stop Recording button, Sound Recorder, 85
Storage section, Components category, 326
storyboard, creating, 264–265
Storyboard/Timeline views, Windows Movie Maker, 259–265
striped volumes, 313
switches, 174
Switch Primary and Secondary Buttons box, Mouse Properties, 27
Sync Center, 32–33, 85–86
Sync interface, Windows Media Player, 252
System Drivers section, Software Environment category, 327
System icon, 33
System Information, 323–327
  Components category, 326–327
  Hardware Resources category, 325–326
  Software Environment category, 327
  System Summary category, 325
system properties, 333–336
System Protection link, System Properties, 340
system requirements, 345–347
  hard disk space, 346
  other requirements, 346–347
  processor, 345
  random access memory, 345–346
System Restore, 339–342
  creating restore points, 339–341
  running if Windows can be booted, 341–342
  running if Windows cannot be booted, 342
System Stability Chart, Performance Monitor, 331–332
System Summary, 325
System Tools menu, 89

T

Tablet PC Settings applet, 34, 89
Tabs, Internet Explorer, 142–144
Tabs category, Internet Options, 146–148
Tags button, Pictures menu, 280
Take No Action option, 18
Take Speech Tutorial option, 32–33
Taskbar, 5, 34
  customizing, 45–46
  managing, 10
Taskbar Appearance tab, 45–46
Task Manager option, 336–337
tasks, scheduling, 299–301
Task Scheduler, Local Disk Properties, 299
Tasks option, Folder Options, 55–56
Tasks pane, Windows Movie Maker, 259–260
TCP/IP (Transmission Control Protocol/Internet Protocol), 140, 178
Text to Speech tab, Speech Properties, 34
themes, 53
Theme Settings dialog box, 53–55
Tiles option
  Pictures menu, 277
  Views menu, 7, 58–59
time limits, setting, 217
Time Limits option, Parental Controls, 217–218
titles, adding to movies, 269–270
Titles and Credits, Windows Movie Maker, 269–270
Toolbar
  Performance Monitor, 329
  Windows Movie Maker, 259–260
Toolbars option, Tools menu, 145
Tools drop-down menu, Internet Explorer, 145
Tools menu, Windows Mail window, 162
Tools option, Windows Defender, 210–212
  Allowed Items option, 212
  Microsoft Spynet option, 211
  Options button, 210
  quarantined items, 211
  Software Explorer, 212
  Windows Defender web site, 212
Tools tab, setting hard disk properties, 291–295
  Backup, 295

Disk Defragmenter, 293–294
Error Checking, 291–293
TPM (Trusted Platform Module), 319
transitions, Windows Movie Maker, 266–268
Transmission Control Protocol/Internet Protocol (TCP/IP), 140, 178
trim feature, Windows Movie Maker, 265
troubleshooting, 336
    CTRL-ALT-DEL, 336–337
    game problems, 237–238
        DDERR_ GENERIC, 238
        DirectX problems, 238
        game controllers do not work, 237–238
        game lockup, 238
    hardware, 103–104
    printer problems, 116–117
        certain document will not print, 116
        garbled text, 116
        poor quality, 117
        printer does not work, 116
        slow printing, 116
    Safe Mode, 339
    System Restore, 339–342
        creating restore points, 339–341
        running if Windows can be booted, 341–342
        running if Windows cannot be booted, 342
    Windows Help, 337–338
Trusted Platform Module (TPM), 319
Trusted Sites and Restricted Sites options, Internet Options, 149
turning off computer, 12

U

UAC (User Account Control), 198
UNC (Universal Naming Convention), 75
Undo/Redo option, Organize menu, 75
Uninstall button, Device Manager option, 99–101
uninstalling programs, 68–70
    downloading programs from Internet, 69–70
    using programs in control panel, 68–69
    using program's uninstall option, 68

Universal Naming Convention (UNC), 75
universal serial bus (USB) section, Components category, 327
Unreadable state, Disk Management console, 309
Unrecognized state, Disk Management console, 309
Update, Windows. *See* Windows Update
Update Driver button, Device Manager option, 99–101
updates button, Start menu, 41
upgrading to Windows Vista, 344–349
    backing up data, 347
    checking device drivers, 347–348
    checking for viruses, 348
    checking system requirements, 345–347
        hard disk space, 346
        other requirements, 346–347
        processor, 345
        random access memory, 345–346
    disabling antivirus software, 348
    shutting down all programs, 348
    starting upgrade, 348–349
Urge button, Windows Media Player, 246, 248
USB (universal serial bus) section, Components category, 327
User Account Control (UAC), 198
user accounts
    defined, 190–191
    managing, 191–197
        changing accounts, 194–197
        creating new accounts, 192–194
    overview, 35
user names, 4, 40

V

viewing and managing photos, Windows Slideshow, 274–278
View menu, Windows Mail window, 162
views, changing in Windows Mail, 166–167
Views menu, 7, 58–59, 76
View Source feature, web browser, 145
View tab, Folder Options, 57–58
virtual memory, 335–336
Virtual Private Networking (VPN), 185–187

viruses, 166, 348
Visibility option, Mouse Properties, 29
Visual Effects tab, Performance Monitor, 333–334
Visualizations option, Now Playing menu, 246–247
volume (sound), 10, 238–240
Volume Controls, Windows Sounds, 238–239
volumes
    assigning different drive letter and path to, 311–312
    creating new, 310–311
    extending, 312
    shrinking, 312
    spanned, 312
    striped, 313
VPN (Virtual Private Networking), 185–187

W

Wait for Dial Tone Before Dialing check box, Phone and Modem Options, 128
Wait scroll box, Screen Saver Settings, 52
Web Page Privacy Report features, web browser, 145
Web restrictions. *See* parental controls
Welcome Center, 35, 86–87
Wheel tab, Mouse properties, 29
Window Color and Appearance option, 49
Window Color and Appearance option, Display Settings, 49
Windows Calendar button, Windows Mail window, 162
Windows CardSpace, 35
Windows Defender, 35, 208–212
    running scans, 209–210
    using tools, 210–212
        allowed items, 212
        Microsoft Spynet, 211
        options, 210
        quarantined items, 211
        Software Explorer, 212
        Windows Defender web site, 212
Windows Defender program, 35, 71, 208–210
Windows Error Reporting, Software Environment category, 327
Windows Explorer, 87–88

Windows Features, 72–73
Windows Firewall, 35–36, 202–208, 222–223
    checking, 204
    configuring settings, 205–208
    issues with, 203–204
    overview, 35
Windows Help, 337–338
Windows Mail, 157–172
    attaching files to e-mail, 164–165
    changing views, 166–167
    customizing, 171–172
    defined, 158
    Identities, 170
    interface, 161–163
    managing accounts, 171
    message rules, 167–170
        blocking senders, 169–170
        creating new rule, 168
        managing, 168–169
    receiving attachments, 166
    receiving e-mail, 165–166
    sending e-mail, 163–164
    setting up, 159–160
Windows Media Player, 243–256
    Burn feature, 251–252
    configuration options, 254–256
    Library, 247–250
        adding item to, 250
        creating playlist, 250
    Now Playing area, 244–247
    Rip feature, 250–251
    Skin Chooser, 252–254
    Sync feature, 252
Windows Media Video (WMV), 261
Windows Messenger, 145, 153
Windows Movie Maker, 257–271, 281
    adding audio, 268–269
    adding titles and credits, 269–270
    benefits to using, 258–259
    importing digital data, 260–262
        from DV camera, 261

        existing video or pictures on computer, 261–262
    making movies, 262–268
        combining clips, 263
        creating transitions, 266–268
        splitting clips, 262–263
        trimming clips, 265–266
        workspace, 264–265
    opening, 259–260
    publishing movies, 271
    saving movies, 270
Windows Paint, 83–84
Windows Paint program, Accessories option, 83–84
Windows Photo Gallery, 278–279
Windows Sidebar, 5, 59–64, 88
    gadgets, 63–64
    overview, 35
    starting and configuring, 60–63
Windows Slideshow, 273–284
    burning photos to cod, 283
    connecting to PC, 274
    overview, 35–36
    Photo Gallery, 278–282
        Burn option, 281
        control toolbar, 281–282
        E-mail option, 280–281
        File drop-down menu, 279
        Fix option, 279
        Info option, 280
        Make Movie option, 281
        Open option, 281
        Print drop-down menu, 280
    printing photos, 282–283
    using, 283–284
    viewing and managing photos, 274–278
Windows Sounds, 52, 240
Windows Troubleshooter, 98, 116
Windows Update, 36, 102–103, 145, 301–302

Windows Vista
    activating, 350
    installing, 349–350
    optimizing, 321–342
        See also troubleshooting
        Performance Information and Tools, 322–323
        Reliability and Performance Monitor, 328–333
        System Information, 323–327
        System Properties, 333–336
    upgrading to, 344–349
        backing up data, 347
        checking device drivers, 347–348
        checking for viruses, 348
        checking system requirements, 345–347
        disabling antivirus software, 348
        shutting down all programs, 348
        starting upgrade, 348–349
Windows Vista Ultimate, 184
Windows XP
    hardware, 93–94
    playing games with, 236–237
        games installed with Windows Vista, 236
        games on Internet, 237
    website, 94
wireless networks, 183–184
WMV (Windows Media Video), 261
WordPad, 89
Work Offline option, Tools menu, 145
Workspace, Windows Movie Maker, 264–265

Z

Zoom and Text Size feature, web browser, 145